50 STATES
of
MURDER

AN ATLAS OF AMERICAN CRIME

HAROLD SCHECHTER

WORKMAN PUBLISHING | NEW YORK

For John Meils

Text Copyright © 2025 by Harold Schechter

Hachette Book Group supports the right to free expression and the value of copyright. The purpose of copyright is to encourage writers and artists to produce the creative works that enrich our culture.

The scanning, uploading, and distribution of this book without permission is a theft of the author's intellectual property. If you would like permission to use material from the book (other than for review purposes), please contact permissions@hbgusa.com. Thank you for your support of the author's rights.

Workman
Workman Publishing
Hachette Book Group, Inc.
1290 Avenue of the Americas
New York, NY 10104
workman.com

Workman is an imprint of Workman Publishing, a division of Hachette Book Group, Inc. The Workman name and logo are registered trademarks of Hachette Book Group, Inc.

Design and cover by Jack Dunnington

Cover photos: Michigan State Police (left); Washington State Archives—Digital Archives (right)
Additional photo credit information is on page 280.

The publisher is not responsible for websites (or their content) that are not owned by the publisher.

Workman books may be purchased in bulk for business, educational, or promotional use. For information, please contact your local bookseller or the Hachette Book Group Special Markets Department at special.markets@hbgusa.com.

Library of Congress Cataloging-in-Publication Data is available.

Print ISBN: 978-1-5235-2414-3
Ebook ISBN: 978-1-5235-2416-7

First Edition September 2025

Printed in the United States of America on responsibly sourced paper.

Printing 1, 2025

50 STATES
of
MURDER

AN ATLAS OF AMERICAN CRIME

CONTENTS

INTRODUCTION | 8

ALABAMA | 10
The Original Sin City · A Recidivist Runs Rampant · The Code Blue Junkie

ALASKA | 14
The Mad Trapper · Hunting Humans · Mountain Man Murderer · Portrait of a Serial Killer: Israel Keyes

ARIZONA | 20
Mobile Home Invasion · The Beauty School Barbarian · The Namesake: Ernesto Miranda · Not-So-Heroic Hogan · The Sleepwalking Defense

ARKANSAS | 26
The Gallows Trio · The Villainous Vet · A Hilltop Hell

CALIFORNIA | 30
The Chicken Coop Murders · A Kidnapping Comeuppance · Lethal and Lightning · Femme Fatale: Louise Peete · A Boat Bombing in Newport · The Jesus of Chatsworth · Baby Crazy in Los Angeles · A Very Bad Monday in San Diego · The Covina Massacre

COLORADO | 40
A Beer Scion Disappears in Morrison · Shock Jock Shot in Denver · The Broomfield Teen Who Put a Hit on Herself

CONNECTICUT | 44
A Twelve-Year-Old Goes to the Gallows · The Windsor Murder Factory · A Wood-Chipping in Newton · Carnage in Cheshire · The Connecticut Cannibal

DELAWARE | 50
A Fiery Execution in New Castle · The Jilted Paramour · A Sibling Slaughter

FLORIDA | 54
The Vampire Rapist · A Bully Slayed in Weston · A Child Snatched in Sarasota · The Hammer Boy Strikes · The Miami Zombie

GEORGIA | 60
Atlanta's Jack the Ripper · Downfall of a "King" · The Crippler of Fayetteville

HAWAI'I | 64
The Waialua Monster · A Honolulu Serial Killer · Oyako-Shinju in Honolulu · The Xerox Massacre

IDAHO | 70

An Explosive Episode in Caldwell · Flypaper Lyda · Idaho's Jack the Ripper · Claude Dallas: Idaho Outlaw

ILLINOIS | 76

The Last Train to Wayne · A Chi-town Love Quadrangle · Chicago's Most Beautiful Murderess · A Pedophile Strikes in Chicago · Carnage in a Cave · A Last Ride in Urbana-Champaign

INDIANA | 84

A Klansmen Killer · A Butcher Dies in Yorktown · Principal Redden Goes on a Rampage

IOWA | 88

A Boy Murderer in Clayton County · The Unsolved Axe Murders of Villisca · Cornfield Killer · The Cain and Abel Murders

KANSAS | 94

A Kid Killer in Johnson County · A Husky Horror · The Wichita Hotel Sniper · A Bombing in Olathe

KENTUCKY | 100

A Brother's Vengeance · The Six-Year-Old Slayer · The Last Legal Hanging in Kentucky

LOUISIANA | 104

A Phenomenally Depraved Scoundrel · Toni Jo Goes to the Electric Chair · "Lucky" Willie and "Gruesome Gertie"

MAINE | 108

The Purrington Family Massacre · Brutality in Brunswick · A Murderous Madwoman · A Cook Rampages in Newry

MARYLAND | 114

The Not-Quite-Perfect Crime · The Unsolved Murder of Sister Cathy · Life Imitates Art in St. Michaels

MASSACHUSETTS | 118

The Boston Belfry Slayer · A Miscreant in Yarmouth · Jolly Jane Lays Waste · The Boston Giggler · Another Monster in the Mystic · "Killer Nanny" Goes Free

MICHIGAN | 126

The St. Aubin Avenue Massacre · The Ypsilanti Ripper · Master Bob in Grosse Pointe

MINNESOTA | 130

The Minneapolis Svengali · A Hitman Hired in St. Paul · The Wannabe Vampire of St. Cloud · Versace Killer Starts His Spree

MISSISSIPPI | 136

"Were murdered December 17, 1880" · The Legs Murder · Socialite Killed by Same · The Devil Himself Did It?

MISSOURI | 140

Stack Lee Becomes Legend · The Original Frankie and Johnny · The Union Station Massacre · The Hitchhiking Killer · Gypsy-Rose Gets Her Revenge

MONTANA | 146

A Loner Killer in Gallatin · The Missoula Mauler · A Marriage Gone Bad in Glacier

NEBRASKA | 150

The Nebraska Fiend · A Guilty Killer Confesses · A Judge Gunned Down in Lincoln · The Maniac Sniper of Omaha

NEVADA | 156

Murder of "The Comstock Queen" · A Forensic First · Loveless in Elko

NEW HAMPSHIRE | 160

A Grim Memorial in Pembroke · An Obsession Turns Deadly · The Bear Brook Murders · Student Killers in Etna

NEW JERSEY | 166

A Tell-Tale Heart in New Brunswick · The Torch Slayer Strikes · A Murderous Minister · The Tragedy Behind Megan's Law · A Killer Nurse in New Jersey

NEW MEXICO | 172

The Headless Man of Taos · Alien Killers in Albuquerque? · An Abused Teen Snaps in Roswell

NEW YORK | 176

"The Female Jack the Ripper" · A Historic Execution · A Child Jekyll and Hyde in Troy · The First Woman in the Electric Chair · The Phantom Murderer · A Parrot Drops a Dime in New York City · A New York Post Headline Says It All

NORTH CAROLINA | 184

A Reverend in Name Only · A Family Annihilator in Winston-Salem · The Lynch Killings · A Superstar's Father Is Killed · A Wide Receiver Takes a Bad Route

NORTH DAKOTA | 190

A Murdering "Eccentric" in Niagara · A Cattle Dispute Turns Murderous in Turtle Lake · A Clown, a Hunter, and a Lion Walk into a Bar

OHIO | 194

The Tanyard Murder · The Olympian Killer · The Inwood Park Horror · A Notorious Killer and His First Victim · A Butcher in Brookfield

OKLAHOMA | 200

A Shootout in Sapulpa · "French Fries!" in McAlester · The Oklahoma Girl Scout Murders · Sirloin Stockade Massacre · Going Postal in Edmond

OREGON | 206

The Violent Life of Michele Dee Gates · A Monster Mom in Springfield · A Mystery Writer Doesn't Get Away with Murder

PENNSYLVANIA | 210

The "Girl Torturer" of York · The York Witchcraft Murder · The Poison Ring · The "Babes in the Woods" Tragedy · An Amish Man Unhinged

RHODE ISLAND | 216

A Minister Goes Free in Tiverton · A Murder Fantasy Made Real · The Warwick Slasher · A Sex Worker Serial Killer in Woonsocket

---

SOUTH CAROLINA | 220

The Last Hanging in Charleston · Last Wills and Testaments · The Eyedrop Killer

---

SOUTH DAKOTA | 224

A Union Disintegrates in Sioux Falls · The Human Monster · A Recidivist Meets His End in Spearfish · The Duct Tape Killer of Sioux Falls

---

TENNESSEE | 230

The Night Marauder · Stringbean Shot Dead in Goodlettsville · The Soul Sucker

---

TEXAS | 234

Alligator Joe of Elmendorf · The Texarkana Moonlight Murders · The Not-Beatnik Killers · The Candy Man of Deer Park · A Misogynist Turns Murderous in Killeen · The Eyeball Killer

---

UTAH | 242

A Crack Shot in Bingham · A Soldier Snaps in Salina · A Killer's Last Laugh · The Ogden Horror · A Forger-Turned-Bomber in Salt Lake

---

VERMONT | 248

Mother-in-Law Murdered in Williston · The Monster from Duxbury · The Meanest Man in a Pretty Town · An Innocent Man Goes Free in West Dover

---

VIRGINIA | 254

A Wife Killer from Richmond · The Virginia Court Massacre · Life Imitates Art in Norfolk · The Hampton Roads Killer

---

WASHINGTON | 260

The Fasting Fiend of Starvation Heights · A Midlife Obsession Ends Badly in Puyallup · The Wah Mee Massacre · The Bellevue Thrill Killers

---

WEST VIRGINIA | 266

Testimony from the Beyond · An Unexplained Familicide · A folie à deux in Star City

---

WISCONSIN | 270

An Infamous Hanging in Kenosha · Massacre at the "Bungalow of Love" · The Wisconsin Ghoul · A Congregant Snaps in Brookfield

---

WYOMING | 274

Governor Skin Shoes? · Wyoming's Death Rider · Tarzan of the Tetons · A Comeuppance in Cheyenne

---

PHOTO CREDITS | 280

INDEX | 282

INTRODUCTION

In the spring of 2021, the satiric news website *The Onion* ran a piece titled "The Most Infamous Crimes in Every State."

"On January 18, 1982, the unsuccessful hijacking of a syrup truck left 2 dead and 16 sticky," read the entry for Vermont. For Alaska: "In 1989, serial killer Ernest Underwood attempted a murdering spree, driving over two hundred miles without encountering a single victim." And—in the cheerfully tasteless fashion typical of America's self-described "Finest News Source"—Ohio's read: "On one hand, the Kent State Massacre was one of the worst acts committed by the US against its own citizens, but on the plus side, it did inspire a pretty great song by Crosby, Stills, Nash & Young."

These parodies were meant, of course, to do nothing more than provoke a few chuckles. For a student of American crime like me, however, they raised an interesting question: Is there such a thing as a crime that reflects the typical (or stereotypical) traits associated with the state where it took place? Certain crimes do in fact seem so inextricably linked to their locales that it's impossible to imagine them happening anywhere else. Only the sex-and-drug-fueled, drop-out culture of hippie-era Southern California—with its occult dabblings and nothing-is-forbidden philosophy—could have produced the Manson murders. As both Terrence Malick and Bruce Springsteen have recognized, the barren landscape of Nebraska was not just the historical setting for the 1950s killing spree of the young outlaw-lovers Charlie Starkweather and Caril Ann Fugate, but the outward projection of their harsh, empty lives. And in his brilliant evocation of the remote, tightly knit world of Holcomb, Kansas—site of the Clutter family massacre—Truman Capote explores the complex relationship between the environment and the tragedy that transpired there.

These crimes are among the most notorious in US history. There's no particular geographical significance, however, to most of the murders committed every day. Apart from the identities of the principals—news accounts of young women slain by violent ex-boyfriends, to offer just one all-too-common example—are more or less the same everywhere in the country. Even when a crime is unique enough to shock, it rarely says much, if anything, about its locale. In June 1948, for instance, fourteen-year-old

Roy Adams of Chicago suffocated an eight-year-old girl after getting into an argument with her over a comic book. The tragedy was treated in the press not as symptomatic of Windy City lawlessness, but as a case study in the nefarious influence of comics on unstable young minds, a hot-button issue at the time. Horrific as it was, moreover, the case of the "Comic Book Slayer" (as the tabloids dubbed Adams) quickly faded into utter obscurity, marking a prime example of what the British call "fish-and-chip news": front-page sensation one day, discarded lunch wrapper the next.

On the other hand, for various reasons, certain crimes become an integral part of regional lore. Unlike, say, the Lizzie Borden axe slayings or the kidnap-murder of the Lindbergh baby, they have not entered into the national mythology. Though unknown to the wider public, they do occupy a prominent place in the criminal annals of their states. The 1840 murder of New Jersey banker Abraham Suydam that inspired Edgar Allan Poe's horror classic "The Tell-Tale Heart." The 1912 "Villisca Axe Murders" that claimed the lives of eight victims, including all six members of a single family, in a small town in Iowa. The "Inwood Park Horror" of 1937, when the mutilated corpse of a twenty-eight-year-old woman was found in a Cincinnati dance hall. The brutal 1953 abduction-murder of six-year-old Bobby Greenlease Jr., son of a multimillionaire car dealer, in Kansas City, Missouri.

For the most part, cases like these form the subject of this book. When I do deal with killers who have become notorious household names, I focus on their lesser-known homicides (e.g., Andrew Cunanan's slaying not of Gianni Versace in Miami, but of two intimate friends in Minnesota). In a book about each state's most infamous murders, readers may wonder why attention isn't paid to, say, the Jeffrey Dahmer atrocities in Milwaukee or the "Son of Sam" serial shootings in New York. The reason is simply that these and others of equally sensational stature have been covered to death (so to speak) in books, movies, television documentaries, and podcasts. Rather than repeat the details of such overly familiar horrors, I have tried to excavate and bring to light several hundred lesser-known, darkly fascinating cases that, taken together, form a unique criminal history of the United States.

ALABAMA

PHENIX CITY
THE ORIGINAL SIN CITY
11

BIRMINGHAM
THE CODE BLUE JUNKIE
13

MONTGOMERY
A RECIDIVIST RUNS RAMPANT
12

THE ORIGINAL SIN CITY

PHENIX CITY, ALABAMA • JUNE 18, 1954

In the decades before Las Vegas claimed the title, Phenix City—the county seat of Russell County, Alabama—gained a well-earned reputation as the nation's preeminent "Sin City." One journalist described it as an "unending series of night clubs, honky-tonks, clip joints, B-girl bars, whorehouses, and gambling casinos." Corruption was so deeply entrenched in the local government and police force that periodic campaigns by reformers invariably came to nothing.

It wasn't until the early 1950s that the Phenix City rackets came under threat from a formidable foe. His name was Albert Patterson. A onetime high school principal who, after switching careers to law, became a crusading politician, he ran for state attorney general in the spring of 1954, pledging to "purge Phenix City of corruption and stamp out organized crime wherever it exists." Though elected by a narrow margin, he never got a

Anti-vice crusader Albert Patterson

chance to take office. On the evening of Friday, June 18, 1954, Patterson left his law office and headed for his car, parked in an alleyway around the corner. Before he could get behind the wheel, a man wielding a .38-caliber pistol stepped up to him and shot him three times, once directly in the mouth. Staggering out of the alley, he collapsed onto the sidewalk and was dead before an ambulance arrived.

ALABAMA • 11

Raymond Eugene Brown's attorneys petitioned the court to have him tried as a juvenile, but he was ruled fit to stand trial as an adult.

Responding to public outrage over the assassination, Governor Gordon Persons sent hundreds of National Guardsmen to Phenix City. Martial law was imposed and, within months, every gambling den and brothel had been raided and shut down, scores of arrests had been made, and the political machine had been dismantled. Within a year, the reformation of Phenix City would be so complete that it was honored with a coveted All-American City Award by the National Civic League.

On the testimony of various eyewitnesses, three men were indicted for the murder of Albert Patterson: a corrupt deputy sheriff named Albert Fuller, who reportedly "took in as much as six thousand dollars weekly from gambling and prostitution protection," and two bitter political foes of the victim, Circuit Solicitor Arch Ferrell and Silas Garrett, attorney general at the time of the assassination. Only Fuller was convicted. Sentenced to life imprisonment, he was paroled after ten years. Ferrell was acquitted, but Garrett—consigned to a Texas mental hospital after suffering a nervous collapse—was never brought to trial.

A RECIDIVIST RUNS RAMPANT

MONTGOMERY, ALABAMA
OCTOBER 1, 1960, AND
AUGUST 10, 1987

Fourteen-year-old Raymond Eugene Brown, a high schooler who played on the junior varsity football team, needed money for a new pair of cleats, so on the night of October 1, 1960, he snuck into the nearby home occupied by his great-grandmother, grandmother, and aunt. When the latter heard him rummaging through a bedroom dresser and went to investigate, he attacked her with a six-inch kitchen knife, stabbing and slashing her 123 times. He then butchered his grandmother and great-grandmother in their beds. Promptly arrested, he was sentenced to three life terms but, proving to be a model prisoner, was paroled after twelve years.

Brown was back behind bars a short time later after attempting to rape his landlady and strangling her nearly to death when she put up a fight. He won parole again in June 1986. The following

12 • 50 STATES OF MURDER

year, on August 10, 1987, he murdered his live-in girlfriend, Linda LeMonte, cutting her open from throat to pelvis and mutilating her breasts, vagina, and rectum. He also raped and stabbed to death her ten-year-old daughter, Sheila Smoke, leaving the knife protruding from her navel. Arrested two days later, he was condemned to the electric chair but died in 2008, before the sentence could be carried out.

THE CODE BLUE JUNKIE

BIRMINGHAM, ALABAMA
MARCH 27, 1991

In hospital parlance, a "code blue" refers to an announcement that an adult patient is having a sudden cardiac or respiratory emergency that requires immediate intervention. On the afternoon of March 27, 1991, nurse Joseph Dewey Akin was spotted emerging from the room of quadriplegic Robert J. Price moments before the latter—whose heart rate had tested normal earlier in the day—went into coronary arrest. A code blue was immediately issued.

Among the team of doctors and nurses responding to the alert was Akin, who, as a fellow nurse later testified, always seemed weirdly "hyped up" by such crises. When a doctor called out for a shot of the adrenaline drug epinephrine to be administered to Price, Akin injected him instead with a fatal overdose of the anesthetic lidocaine—a tragic accident, so Akin claimed, committed in the heat of the moment. It soon came to light that whenever Akin was employed at a hospital, the rate of code blues rose alarmingly.

Some of his co-workers believed that he got a perverse thrill from such emergencies—so much so that he deliberately induced heart failure in patients so he could sprint to their rescue and seem like a hero. He got such a rush from these frantic efforts at resuscitation that they called him a "code blue junkie." One woman came forward who had barely survived Akin's ministrations. Suffering shortness of breath from an allergic reaction, she had gone to the emergency room, where she was prescribed a shot of antihistamine. Instead, Akin surreptitiously injected her with a near-fatal dose of adrenaline. Further investigation revealed that there had been at least seventeen suspicious deaths at Akin's former workplaces. A search of his suburban home turned up vials of epinephrine that had been stolen from the hospital ICU.

Arrested for Price's murder, he was tried in 1992. The jury took just over an hour to find him guilty. Five years later, the conviction was overturned on appeal. His second trial ended with a hung jury. To avoid a third trial, he pleaded guilty to manslaughter and was sentenced to fifteen years, minus time already served. Two days after the plea, he was set free.

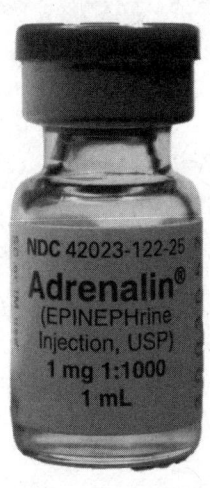

ALASKA

MANLEY HOT SPRINGS
MOUNTAIN MAN MURDERER
18

NUSHAGAK DISTRICT
THE MAD TRAPPER
15

KNIK RIVER
HUNTING HUMANS
16

ANCHORAGE
**PORTRAIT OF A SERIAL KILLER:
ISRAEL KEYES**
19

JUNEAU

THE MAD TRAPPER

Nushagak District, Alaska • ca. 1919–1931

A figure out of Alaskan lore, the man known as Klu-tuk—a member of the Indigenous Yup'ik people, closely related to the Inuit—conducted a reign of terror during the early decades of the twentieth century that left as many as twenty people dead. A fur trapper who regarded the upper watersheds of Bristol Bay as his personal territory, he hunted down anyone, Indigenous or white, he viewed as an interloper, dispatching them with his .30-30 Winchester rifle. Such was the fear he inspired that mining companies were reluctant to operate in the area. Under pressure from corporate interests, the territorial government devoted years to hunting down the "Mad Trapper" (as he came to be known), but search parties were no match for Klu-tuk's wilderness skills.

Klu-tuk, the "Mad Trapper" of Bristol Bay watersheds

In September 1927, he came close to being apprehended when two trappers, along with their guide, managed to take him captive. While two of the men hiked off to alert authorities, the third—a burly outdoorsman named Kelvig—remained behind in their tent to keep watch over their prisoner. When the pair returned to the tent hours later, they found Klu-tuk gone and Kelvig face down in a pool of blood, a bullet hole in his arm, and a fatal axe wound in the back of his head. Much to the relief of inhabitants of the region, Klu-tuk was found dead in his cabin, apparently of natural causes, in late August 1931. According to local superstition, his ghost still haunts the wild landscape he so jealously guarded in life.

HUNTING HUMANS

KNIK RIVER, ALASKA • 1973–1983

Robert Hansen, hunter of humans

Afflicted with a severe stutter in his childhood, a disabling shyness, and a case of acne so severe that he would later describe his adolescent face as "one big pimple," Iowa-born Robert Hansen grew up feeling shunned by the world and especially by women, for whom he developed a profound lifelong hatred. He was twenty-one in 1960 when, with the help of a teenage accomplice, he burned down a school bus garage in revenge for the mockery he had suffered in high school. Convicted of arson, Hansen was sentenced to three years in prison and served twenty-three months before being granted parole.

Relocating to Anchorage, Alaska, in 1967, he established himself as a successful entrepreneur and owner of a thriving bakery business. He also gained local renown as an expert hunter, bagging record-breaking game—caribou, grizzlies, mountain rams—with a rifle and bow and arrow. He was able to venture far into the wilderness with an airplane he purchased after collecting a $13,000 insurance payout for a household burglary that, as events would prove, he had staged himself. In 1971, Hansen was arrested a second time after forcing an eighteen-year-old girl into his car at gunpoint, binding her, driving her out of the city, and raping her. Hit with a five-year sentence, he was diagnosed as a "manic-depressive" by a court-ordered psychiatrist and, after demonstrating "sufficient improvement through therapy," paroled after only six months.

Five years later, he was arrested again, this time for stealing a chainsaw. Deemed potentially "dangerous during manic episodes," he was treated with the mood stabilizer lithium and paroled after serving a fraction of his five-year sentence. None of these crimes, not even the assault on the adolescent girl, however, could compare to the enormities that would earn Hansen the name the "Butcher Baker."

Beginning in 1973, when he was thirty-four years old, Hansen flew dozens of sex workers and topless dancers to his mountain retreat. Those who provided sex for free—"who came across with what I wanted," as he later put it—were taken back to Anchorage unharmed. The ones who resisted or demanded payment met a terrible fate. After keeping them tied up in his cabin for several days of rape and torture, he would release them naked into the wilderness. Then, after giving them a head start, he would stalk them with his hunting rifle.

At least seventeen women, ranging in age from sixteen to forty-one, were slain in this hideously depraved "sport"—the

Hansen's aviation map, indicating where his victims were buried

real-life version of Richard Connell's famous 1924 story, "The Most Dangerous Game." The end came for Hansen in 1983, when one of his intended victims managed to break free as he was attempting to force her into his plane. The police picked Hansen up for questioning and quickly punctured his alibi. Before long they had found incriminating evidence in his possession, including the murder weapon and a map marked with the burial sites of his prey. Sentenced to 461 years in prison without the possibility of parole, he died in captivity in 2014 at the age of seventy-five.

ALASKA • 17

MOUNTAIN MAN MURDERER

Manley Hot Springs, Alaska
May 17, 1984

A native of suburban Chicago with a lengthy arrest record for various weapons violations, twenty-five-year-old Michael Silka was a wilderness buff from early adolescence. He made his way to Alaska in the early spring of 1984, renting a shack on the outskirts of Fairbanks where he planned to live out his mountain man fantasies. Not long after his arrival, a local named Roger Culp, upset over Silka's erratic behavior, went to his shack to have a word with him and was never seen again. The following day, neighbors noticed a pool of blood behind the shack and notified the state troopers who, misunderstanding the call, believed that it was Silka who had gone missing. A pair of officers came to investigate but left after Silka stuck his head out the door and explained that the blood was from a freshly skinned moosehide.

Nine days passed before new information about Culp's disappearance reached law enforcement. After returning to the shack and determining that the blood was human, police suspected that Silka had killed Culp. By then, however, Silka was gone. Heading to Manley Hot Springs, a remote village with a population of seventy, he set up camp at a boat landing a few miles outside of town. Four days after his arrival, seven Manley residents, including a couple with a two-year-old son, visited the landing and vanished. So had Silka.

When authorities learned that the "Weirdo Drifter" (as townspeople had come to name him) was being sought for a murder in Fairbanks, police assumed—correctly, it turned out—that the missing people had been shot and dumped in the river. More than fifteen troopers in boats, two helicopters, and three small airplanes launched a search, eventually spotting the fugitive on a riverbank where he had beached his motorized getaway boat, stolen from one of his victims. As one of the choppers hovered overhead, Silka—who was rated an expert marksman during a stint in the army—opened fire with a rifle, killing a trooper before being shot to death himself by the man's partner. As for the motive behind Silka's rampage, none was ever established.

The motive of Michael Silka's spree killing is still unknown.

PORTRAIT OF A SERIAL KILLER:
ISRAEL KEYES

Anchorage, Alaska
February 1, 2012

On the night of February 1, 2012, eighteen-year-old barista Samantha Koenig disappeared from her workplace, a shack-like coffee stand across the road from a Home Depot parking lot. Security cameras revealed that she had been abducted by a large, muscular man, his features obscured by his hoodie, who had driven her away in a pickup truck.

Three weeks later, her kidnapper left a ziplock bag tacked to a trailhead bulletin board. Inside were a ransom note and a picture of Koenig sprawled naked on a mattress, her mouth duct-taped, her eyes squeezed shut, but apparently alive. The note demanded $30,000 for her safe return, the money to be deposited in Koenig's bank account. Monitoring the suspect's movements through the ATM withdrawals he made using his victim's bank card, lawmen finally tracked him to a small town in Texas where his rental car was spotted in a motel parking lot, and he was taken into custody. His name was Israel Keyes.

Raised in hardscrabble circumstances in a fanatically religious household, Keyes began manifesting the classic behavior of the budding serial killer—fire-starting, animal torture—as an adolescent. A student of serial murder who had read every book on the subject he could get his hands on, he identified closely with Ted Bundy and took perverse pride in the methodical way he had perpetrated his own atrocities. He admitted that he had taken Koenig to a shed behind his house, where he raped her twice and strangled her to death before leaving on a two-week family vacation. Upon his return, he had sex with her corpse, then wrote the ransom demand, and—after taping her mouth, sewing her eyelids shut, and applying makeup to her face to hide the evidence of her decomposition—took the photos to accompany the note. He then dismembered the body and disposed of the pieces in a frozen lake by cutting a hole through the ice.

Though Keyes confessed to only one other crime—the abduction-murder of a Vermont couple who had gone missing in June 2011—he hinted at more, possibly as many as eleven in various states, as well as a number of bank robberies. He died by suicide in his cell in December 2012, slitting his wrists with a razor he had somehow managed to acquire.

ARIZONA

NAVAJO COUNTY
MOBILE HOME INVASION
21

SCOTTSDALE
NOT-SO-HEROIC HOGAN
24

PHOENIX
THE NAMESAKE: ERNESTO MIRANDA
23

MESA
THE BEAUTY SCHOOL BARBARIAN
22

PHOENIX
THE SLEEPWALKING DEFENSE
25

MOBILE HOME INVASION

NAVAJO COUNTY, ARIZONA • DECEMBER 1, 1953

Towing a four-room mobile home behind their pickup, the Allen family—twenty-seven-year-old machine tool repairman Raymond Allen, his twenty-three-year-old wife, Betty Faye, and their ten-month-old infant—were on their way from Pennsylvania to California when Raymond pulled off the highway for the night not far from Holbrook, New Mexico. The three were sound asleep at 10:00 p.m. when a pistol-wielding man entered their unlocked trailer and announced, "This is a holdup. Tell me where your money is and everything will be all right."

Ordering the two adults onto their stomachs, he bound them by the ankles and wrists, their hands behind their backs, and shoved gags into their mouths. After dragging Raymond to the front of the trailer, he tore off Betty's clothes and spent the next few hours raping her, beating her, and holding lit matches to her flesh and hair. Struggling frantically against his bonds while listening to his tortured wife's screams, Raymond managed to free his legs and stagger out onto the highway, where he stopped a truck whose driver jumped out and cut his hands free.

Rushing to his pickup, Allen got the six-gun he carried in his glove compartment. Soon after, the stranger, having realized his captive was free, appeared at the trailer door. Allen fired six times. Hit in the stomach, the man managed to run about two hundred yards before dropping to the ground, gravely wounded but alive. Inside the trailer, Betty lay dead, strangled with a bedsheet. The baby was unharmed,

Carl J. Folk in custody

though—from the state of the mattresses, which the killer had soaked in kerosene—it was clear that he had intended to murder all three of the Allens before setting the trailer on fire.

Public outrage was inflamed when it turned out that the perpetrator—a fifty-five-year-old carnival concession operator named Carl J. Folk—had been convicted of raping a sixteen-year-old girl in July 1949. Sentenced to ten to fifteen years in prison, he was subsequently judged to be insane, sent to an asylum that November, and, after being deemed "completely recovered," paroled in 1950.

At his trial for the torture-murder of Betty in February 1954, medical experts for the defense testified that the defendant was afflicted with general paresis—"syphilis of the brain," as newspapers described it. The jury, however, agreed with the prosecution's psychiatric witnesses who asserted that Folk—who burst into frequent sobs throughout the proceedings—was only feigning madness. He died in the gas chamber on March 4, 1955. His last words were, "I still think I'm not guilty."

THE BEAUTY SCHOOL BARBARIAN

MESA, ARIZONA
NOVEMBER 12, 1966

In 1966, two of the most infamous mass murders in US history took place within a few weeks of each other: Richard Speck's slaughter of eight student nurses in mid-July and Charles Whitman's "Texas Tower Sniper" shootings on August 1. The crimes shocked and horrified the world. One person, however, had a different response. He yearned to achieve the same notoriety by emulating the killers. A sociopathic, eighteen-year-old high school senior named Robert Benjamin Smith began planning his massacre immediately after the Whitman and Speck atrocities made international headlines. He considered various sites, including a high school and bank, before settling on the Rose-Mar College of Beauty, a school for aspiring cosmetologists that was not far from his home.

During the week of November 7, 1966, Smith purchased two hunting knives and a box of ammunition for the .22-caliber six-gun his parents had gotten him for target shooting. Thinking it might be fun to tie up his victims and watch them slowly suffocate, he also bought two hundred feet of nylon cord and twenty-five plastic food-storage bags. Early Saturday morning, November 12, armed with his supplies, he walked a mile and a half to the beauty school. Hoping to "make a name for himself" by killing forty people, he was disappointed to find only seven inside: four teenaged beauticians in training and a twenty-seven-year-old customer, along with her two small children, a three-year-old girl and her infant sister.

Herding the woman and children into the back room, he had them lie face down in a circle like the spokes in a wheel, their heads in the center, their legs stretched behind them. When the plastic bags proved too small for their intended lethal purpose, he abandoned his plan to suffocate his captives and proceeded to shoot each in the head, killing three of the young trainees, the mother, and her three-year-old daughter. Playing dead, the other student survived, as did the three-month-old infant, who was wounded in the arm but saved when her dying mother rolled over and shielded the child with her body.

Sentenced to death in October 1967, Smith was granted a new trial on appeal—a decision that so outraged the public that newspapers called for the impeachment of the judges who made the decision. By the time Smith was convicted again, the US Supreme Court had placed a moratorium on the death penalty, and he was sentenced to life without parole.

Robert B. Smith, the first copycat mass shooter, escorted to his arraignment

La Amapola, the Phoenix dive bar where Ernesto Miranda was killed

THE NAMESAKE:
ERNESTO MIRANDA

Phoenix, Arizona
January 31, 1976

Born in Mesa, Arizona, to Mexican immigrants, Ernesto Miranda was in and out of trouble with the law from the time he hit adolescence. Between the ages of thirteen and twenty, he was arrested for crimes ranging from burglary and car theft to attempted rape and armed robbery. On March 3, 1963, then twenty-three years old, he waylaid an eighteen-year-old woman as she walked home at night from her job at a local movie theater, forced her into his car, took her out to the desert, and raped her before driving her back into the city and dropping her off.

A week later, the woman's brother-in-law spotted a car that matched the description of the rapist's vehicle; after the license plate number was traced, Miranda was picked up and brought in for questioning. Following a two-hour interrogation—during which, according to Miranda, his questioners threatened "to throw the book" at him—he confessed and signed a written statement introduced as evidence during his trial that June.

Convicted of rape and kidnapping, Miranda was sentenced to twenty to thirty years in prison. In a series of appeals that went all the way to the US Supreme Court, lawyers for Miranda argued that, because their client was never informed of his constitutional rights to remain silent and have an attorney present during questioning, his signed statement was invalid and could not be used as evidence against him.

In a landmark decision, the court agreed with the argument, and the Miranda rule, designed to protect a suspect in police custody from self-incrimination, became the law of the land. Though Miranda was granted a new trial, he was convicted again. Paroled in 1972, he fell back into a life of petty crime and did another year behind bars after an arrest for possession of a gun. On the last night of January 1976, he was playing cards in a seedy Phoenix bar when he got into a fight over money with two Mexicans and was stabbed to death. Newspapers around the nation never failed to mention that when Miranda's killer was caught, police promptly read him his Miranda rights.

NOT-SO-HEROIC HOGAN

Scottsdale, Arizona
June 29, 1978

With a gift for wisecracking patter, Bob Crane first made a name for himself as a radio personality in Los Angeles before setting his sights on an acting career. It wasn't long before he had landed guest spots on a number of popular television series, displaying a roguish charm that eventually earned him a regular supporting role in a hit sitcom. In 1965, he shot to stardom when he signed to play Col. Robert E. Hogan on *Hogan's Heroes*, a prime-time comedy about a motley collection of World War II POWs who, under the leadership of their crafty commander Hogan, scheme to make life miserable for their bumbling German captors.

Now a Hollywood celebrity, Crane was portrayed by his studio as a happy-go-lucky, all-American success story and a "confirmed family man." The description was an example of PR puffery at its most shameless. Coexisting with Crane's genuinely affable nature was an unbridled sex addiction that remained an open secret in the industry. Following the cancellation of *Hogan's Heroes* in 1971, Crane's career went into a steep decline until he was reduced to performing on the dinner theater circuit.

At the same time, his sexual behavior took an even darker turn. Equipped with a video camera supplied by his partner-in-sleaze, John Henry Carpenter, he recorded his countless sordid encounters, assembling a sizable collection of homemade porn. While on tour in the summer of 1978, the forty-nine-year-old Crane was found brutally murdered in the Scottsdale, Arizona, apartment where he was staying. His head had been so savagely bludgeoned with an unknown—and never identified—object that his face was hard to recognize, and an electrical cord was knotted around his neck.

The likeliest suspect was Carpenter, an unsavory character who'd recently had a falling out with Crane. Tried for the murder in 1994, Carpenter was acquitted and went to his death proclaiming his innocence. The case remains officially unsolved.

Bob Crane in his prime as Col. Robert Hogan

Scott Falater and his doomed wife, Yarmila

The backyard pool where Yarmila's body was found

THE SLEEPWALKING DEFENSE

Phoenix, Arizona
January 16, 1997

At about 7:00 p.m. on January 16, 1997, forty-one-year-old Scott Falater arrived home from his electrical engineering job and sat down to dinner with his family, which included his high school sweetheart wife of twenty years, Yarmila, and their two children, Megan and Michael, ages fifteen and twelve. Once the meal was done, he retreated to his upstairs workspace, where he prepared a quiz for the class on Mormon scripture he was scheduled to teach the following morning.

At roughly 9:00 p.m., after being informed by Yarmila that the backyard pool filter was malfunctioning, he went out to fix it, but, unable to do much in the dark, came back inside where his wife was dozing on the living room couch in front of the TV. Kissing her goodnight, he went upstairs to their bedroom and changed into his pajamas. About an hour later, his next-door neighbor Greg Koons heard strange moaning sounds coming from the Falaters' backyard, went onto his patio to investigate, and saw someone lying on the ground.

He assumed the person was drunk until he saw Scott emerge from the house, put on a pair of gloves, drag Yarmila's body—as Koons now realized—to the edge of the swimming pool, roll her in, and hold her head under water. When police, responding to Koons's frantic 911 call, arrived on the scene, they discovered that Yarmila had been stabbed forty-four times with a hunting knife, though an autopsy revealed that she was still alive when her husband drowned her. What made the case a nationwide media sensation was Falater's defense: He claimed to have been sleepwalking when he murdered his wife.

Because Scott's actions didn't conform to any known somnambulistic behavior—besides putting on his gloves, he hid the murder weapon, changed from his bloody clothes into clean pajamas, and calmed the family dog to keep it from barking—the jury sided with the prosecution. Falater was found guilty of first-degree murder and sentenced to life.

ARKANSAS

FAYETTEVILLE
THE GALLOWS TRIO
27

RANDOLPH COUNTY
THE VILLAINOUS VET
28

DOVER & RUSSELLVILLE
A HILLTOP HELL
29

★ LITTLE ROCK

THE GALLOWS TRIO

Fayetteville, Arkansas • August 12, 1845

Hangings were nothing new in 1845 Arkansas. In August 1836, for example, just two months after Arkansas was granted statehood, a Black man named Bunch, having gotten into an altercation with a white man, was strung up by a racist mob in the new state's first lynching. It wasn't until nine years later, however, that the first *legal* hangings took place in Arkansas, when an elderly couple, Crawford and Lavinia Burnett, died together on the gallows.

On August 12, 1845, Jonathan Selby, a reclusive bachelor living a few miles outside of Fayetteville, was murdered for the money he was reputed to keep stashed in his home. For reasons lost to history, suspicion immediately fell upon the two Burnetts, along with their thirty-four-year-old son, John. Their guilt was confirmed by another family member, fifteen-year-old daughter Minerva, who told authorities that her parents had planned the murder and that John had carried it out, shattering Selby's skull with a hatchet before ransacking his house.

Before the trio could be arrested, however, John fled to Missouri. Tried separately in October 1845, Crawford and Lavinia were convicted largely on Minerva's testimony. They were hanged less than thirty days later, an event attended, as the newspapers reported, "by an immense multitude of both sexes, old and young."

Before the hangman drew the cap over her face, Lavinia—described by one witness as "an old hag of the damnedest cast"—declared her belief that, as a devout Roman Catholic, "she would be saved." Crawford, meanwhile, went to his death with no trace of remorse, snarling that he "was as good as any man." Not long afterward, John was tracked down, arrested, brought back for trial, and convicted. On December 4, 1845, he was hanged on the same scaffold where his parents died less than two months before.

John R. Kizer fatally ingested strychnine poison before standing trial—he would die minutes after this photo was taken.

THE VILLAINOUS VET

RANDOLPH COUNTY, ARKANSAS
1925–1936

A respected livestock veterinarian, John R. Kizer nevertheless had no love for dogs, the result of being bitten by one as a child. So intense was his aversion that he was known to inject any obstreperous canine that crossed his path with poison. Like many other serial murderers, he eventually progressed from animal cruelty to homicide.

His first human victim was his wife of eight years, the former Birdie Brooks. Not long after he persuaded her to take out a life insurance policy, she fell ill and was treated by her husband, who injected her arm daily with his own specially prepared medication. Three weeks after the arm became so grotesquely swollen that it had to be amputated, she died. Not long afterward, having set his matrimonial sights on the happily married Mary Anderson, Kizer contrived to do away with her husband, who suffered an ostensible heart attack during a visit from him. Luckily for her, the newly widowed Mrs. Anderson declined his proposal.

A year later, Kizer moved into the home of his ailing niece, Mrs. Robert Riggs, who expired after her uncle began ministering to her with his hypodermic needle. Her husband followed soon afterward—though not before being finagled into leaving Kizer his farm and the $10,000 insurance money he had collected when his wife died. Next were two elderly, infirm women, his aunt Lizzie Robinson and her best friend Willa Brown, who offered to leave Kizer their property when they passed if he agreed to move in with and care for them. Both were dead within the year after receiving medical treatment from Kizer.

In early 1929, he wed again, this time to a widow, Rozena Anderson, who died after he cajoled her into taking out a large life insurance policy. Over the next few years, he did away with his wealthy in-laws and his stepson, Bonner. The sudden death of the popular sixteen-year-old provoked outrage among the townspeople, already suspicious of the number of Kizer's relations who had met similar ends. Arrested for the murder of Bonner, Kizer killed himself by swallowing strychnine before he could be tried.

A HILLTOP HELL

DOVER & RUSSELLVILLE, ARKANSAS
DECEMBER 22-28, 1987

A decorated veteran who spent a combined twenty-two years in the navy and air force and retired with the rank of master sergeant, Ronald Gene Simmons enforced a strict military discipline on his wife and seven children, brooking no dissent from his desires and demands. His daughter, Sheila Maria, was just seventeen when he began sexually abusing her. She gave birth to their child within a year.

Threatened with arrest after social services got wind of the incestuous relationship, Simmons moved his family from New Mexico to a thirteen-acre hilltop tract of land outside of Dover, Arkansas, where they lived in a converted mobile home without indoor plumbing and subsisted on the earnings from Simmons's string of low-paying jobs in the nearby town of Russellville. His tightly controlled world began to come apart when Sheila—his "little princess," the love of his life—got married and left the house, and his long-suffering wife, Becky, began openly speaking of divorce.

Sometime in November 1987, Simmons began planning the act of apocalyptic violence that would earn him a place in the annals of infamy as the perpetrator of the most appalling familicide in US history. Over the next several days, beginning on December 22, 1987, with his family assembled for the holidays, he shot, bludgeoned, strangled, or drowned his wife, children, infant grandchildren, sons- and daughter-in-law—fourteen victims in all. Some of the bodies were buried in a newly dug cesspit, some stashed in car trunks, others left in the trailer where they fell.

On December 28, Simmons drove into Russellville, where he shot and killed a former co-worker who had rebuffed his romantic advances and a fireman and part-time truck driver who had the bad luck of being in the way. Several of his other targets were shot but survived. Once his rampage was over, Simmons calmly surrendered to police. Refusing to appeal his death sentences for the sixteen homicides, he was executed by lethal injection in June 1990.

Ronald Gene Simmons, the nation's most infamous family annihilator (left); a map of Simmons's killing spree (right)

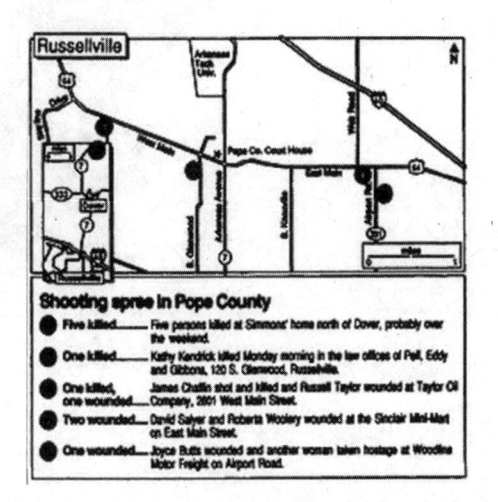

ARKANSAS • 29

CALIFORNIA

SACRAMENTO

SAN JOSE
A KIDNAPPING COMEUPPANCE
32

LOS ANGELES
LETHAL AND LIGHTNING
33

LOS ANGELES
BABY CRAZY IN LOS ANGELES
37

CHATSWORTH
THE JESUS OF CHATSWORTH
36

COVINA
THE COVINA MASSACRE
39

PACIFIC PALISADES
FEMME FATALE: LOUISE PEETE
34

NEWPORT HARBOR
A BOAT BOMBING IN NEWPORT
35

WINEVILLE
THE CHICKEN COOP MURDERS
31

SAN DIEGO
A VERY BAD MONDAY IN SAN DIEGO
38

Northcott Ranch, site of the Wineville Horrors

THE CHICKEN COOP MURDERS

Wineville, California
1926–1928

From his earliest years, Gordon Stewart Northcott manifested symptoms of mental disturbance. Even his pathologically doting mother, Louise, admitted, with considerable understatement, that her adored son's mind was "never just right." In 1924, the family migrated from their native Saskatchewan, Canada, to California, where then-eighteen-year-old Northcott, explaining that he wanted to become a chicken farmer, persuaded his subservient father to purchase three acres of land in the small community of Wineville.

Disinclined to perform all the hard labor his new enterprise required, he traveled back to Canada and—under the pretense of taking his thirteen-year-old nephew, Sanford Clark, on a sightseeing excursion—kidnapped the boy and brought him back to his ranch. Over the next two years, Northcott imprisoned Clark, regularly beat and sodomized him, and forced him to participate in the atrocities that would come to be known as the "Wineville Chicken Coop Murders."

Announcing that he was "going away for fresh meat," Northcott—a textbook sadistic pedophile—would abduct young boys, then drive them back his ranch, where they would be imprisoned in a chicken coop, repeatedly raped, and, in an unknown number of cases, bludgeoned to death with an axe before being buried in quicklime. On one barely credible occasion, his mother, evidently at the prompting of her darling boy, took part in the slaying.

The Wineville horrors finally came to light in the fall of 1928, when Clark's eighteen-year-old sister, Jessie, worried about her brother's well-being, traveled to the farm and learned of the gruesome goings-on. Taken into protective custody, Clark told authorities of the horrors he had suffered and been witness to. By then, Northcott and his mother had fled to Canada.

They were arrested two months later and brought back for trial. To avoid the death penalty, Louise pleaded guilty to one count of murder and was sentenced to life in San Quentin. Her son was convicted of three first-degree murders and hanged in October 1930. The following month, to distance itself from the notoriety generated by the case, Wineville was rechristened Mira Loma.

A lynch mob batters down the jailhouse doors to get at the accused killers of Brooke Hart.

A KIDNAPPING COMEUPPANCE

SAN JOSE, CALIFORNIA
NOVEMBER 1933

On the evening of Thursday, November 9, 1933, sixty-two-year-old department store owner Alexander Hart was scheduled to attend a dinner at his country club. His twenty-two-year-old son, Brooke, offered to drive his father and left the store around 6:00 p.m. to fetch his car from a nearby lot. He never returned.

Later that night, his father received a call from an unidentified male, informing him that his son had been kidnapped and demanding $40,000 in exchange for the young man's safe return. Over the next few days—while one of the largest manhunts in California history was underway—Mr. Hart received further communications from the caller. The case finally broke on Wednesday, November 15, when the kidnapper telephoned to work out the details for the ransom payment.

As instructed by detectives, Mr. Hart kept the man talking for as long as possible while the operator traced the call to a pay phone at a garage, where police promptly arrived and arrested a dull-witted filling station attendant in his twenties named Harold Thurman. It didn't take long for interrogators to wrest the truth from him. He and his accomplice, a sociopathic oil company salesman named Jack Holmes, had waylaid Brooke as he drove from the lot. Jumping into the passenger seat, Holmes forced him at gunpoint to drive to a deserted country road with Thurman following behind. There, the kidnappers slipped a pillowcase over the young man's head, transferred him into the other car, and drove him to the San Mateo Bridge, where they bludgeoned him with a brick, bound his arms with baling wire, and threw him into the water.

A pair of duck hunters found his decomposed remains floating in a creek on Saturday, November 25. The following day, a mob of somewhere between three and six thousand enraged citizens laid siege to the jailhouse, battering down the door with a large metal beam taken from a nearby construction site. Thurman and Holmes were dragged from their cells, beaten bloody, stripped naked, and strung up from a pair of elm trees in nearby St. James Park. Far from condemning the lynching, Governor Rolphe applauded the perpetrators. "It is a fine lesson for the whole country," he proclaimed to reporters.

LETHAL AND LIGHTNING

Los Angeles, California • August 5, 1935

Though the circumstances of his third wife's death were highly suspicious—she supposedly drowned in a bathtub while recuperating from a car accident that left her husband unscathed—barber Robert James was able to collect on the hefty life insurance policy he had taken out on her shortly after they were married. A few years later, he came into another windfall when he insured his nephew's life for $5,000, then loaned the young man his car, which drove off a cliff when the steering wheel knuckle came loose.

Purchasing a barbershop with the proceeds, James married his twenty-eight-year-old manicurist, Mary Busch—wife number six—taking out three insurance policies on her life with double indemnity clauses. Three months later, he decided to cash in. Enlisting an accomplice, James purchased a pair of diamondback rattlesnakes named Lethal and Lightning from a Pasadena reptile dealer.

By then, Mary was pregnant and agreed to have an abortion to be performed at home. As she lay on the kitchen table, sedated with "whiskey and bromides," her eyes taped shut—supposedly to protect the identity of the doctor performing the illegal procedure—James stuck her foot into the box containing the rattlers, which bit her three times. After hours of waiting for the poison to do its work, he grew impatient. At around 1:00 a.m. that night—August 5, 1935—he finished her

Robert James (real name Major Lisenba), aka "Rattlesnake James"

off by drowning her in the bathtub. He and his confederate then carried her outside to the backyard fishpond, arranging the body to make it seem as if she had suffered one of her frequent fainting spells and drowned in the pond. When an investigator discovered that a previous, heavily insured wife had also drowned, authorities became suspicious and "Rattlesnake James" (as he would become known in the press) was soon under arrest. He went to the gallows on May 1, 1942, the last man to be executed by hanging in California.

FEMME FATALE: LOUISE PEETE

PACIFIC PALISADES, CALIFORNIA • MAY 29, 1944

By the time she was in her early thirties, the woman born Lofie Louise Preslar had been married and widowed twice, the result of both her husbands having died by suicide after discovering her affairs with other men. In 1914, at the age of thirty-four, she married her third husband, Denver door-to-door salesman Richard Peete, taking the name that would enter the annals of American serial murder: Louise Peete. Five years later, she abandoned him and their toddler daughter and took off for Los Angeles. No sooner had she arrived than she became involved with a wealthy oilman, Jacob Denton, who disappeared just two weeks after she moved into his fourteen-room mansion.

When family members and friends inquired as to his whereabouts, Peete offered a bizarre explanation, claiming that he had been shot in the arm by a mysterious "Spanish woman" and left town to recuperate after the limb was amputated. She then proceeded to forge checks in his name, pawn his diamond rings, draw money from his savings account, and attempt to access his safe-deposit box. By the time Denton's body was discovered beneath a load of dirt in his basement—a bullet to the back of his neck having severed his spinal column—Peete was reunited with her previous husband, Richard.

Arrested and convicted of Denton's murder, she was sentenced to life and spent eighteen years in prison before being paroled in April 1939. By then, Richard Peete had hanged himself in a Tucson

"Tiger Woman" Louise Peete on the stand

hotel room, the third of her husbands to take his own life. A few years after her release, Peete became the live-in housekeeper for a well-to-do couple, Margaret Logan and her seventy-three-year-old husband, Arthur, who was in the throes of Alzheimer's. Peete then married again, this time to an elderly bank employee, Lee Judson. On May 29, 1944, after Peete was caught forging checks in her employer's name, Margaret Logan disappeared.

After Arthur was consigned to a psychiatric hospital, Peete moved into the Logan home with her new husband. In the following months, she forged checks, had Margaret's clothes retailored to fit herself, redecorated the house, and—when Arthur died six months after his commitment—attempted to collect on his life insurance policy.

34 • 50 STATES OF MURDER

Alerted to Peete's financial shenanigans, police paid her a visit, during which they discovered Margaret's body buried in the yard and arrested Peete and her husband. Though the charges against Judson were dropped, he was unable to deal with the public disgrace and, like his three predecessors, died by suicide, jumping from a hotel window. Peete—dubbed the "Tiger Woman" in the press—was convicted of first-degree murder and died in the San Quentin gas chamber in April 1957.

A BOAT BOMBING IN NEWPORT

Newport Harbor, California
March 15, 1947

Just before midnight on March 15, 1947, the fifty-foot cabin cruiser belonging to financier Walter Overell blew up while moored in Newport Harbor, sending flaming debris a hundred feet in the air. The gathering crowd on shore speculated that the ship's butane gas tank had exploded, but one old tar among them sniffed something else in the air. "Butane, hell," he scoffed. "I know dynamite when I smell it."

He turned out to be right. When rescue workers reached the partially sunken wreck, they discovered the remnants of a crude time bomb in the debris of the engine room—a broken 12-volt battery, a detonator cap, and a shattered alarm clock all connected by wire—as well as thirty sticks of unexploded dynamite beneath a floorboard. They found something else, too: Overell's body impaled on a splintered plank and his wife's corpse in the forward cabin.

The couple had not, however, died in the explosion. Medical examiners determined that they had been killed an hour before the dynamite went off, bludgeoned to death with a ball-peen hammer. Within forty-eight hours, two suspects were under arrest: the Overells' seventeen-year-old daughter, Beulah Louise, and her twenty-one-year-old boyfriend, George "Bud" Gollum. An "ugly duckling daughter," as one newspaper put it, who had grown up "unwanted, misunderstood, and unloved," Beulah stood to inherit the entirety of her father's considerable estate. She had been swept off her feet by Gollum, a handsome premed student thought by many people, including Beulah's parents, to be a gold digger.

Placed under arrest, the young couple exchanged a series of jailhouse letters so shockingly graphic in that pre-sexting era that a judge later ordered them to be burned. ("I'll make you bend over me and place your nipples in my mouth and while I am sucking and biting on one of them. I'll tickle the other one and run my tongue over their naked loveliness," ran a typical passage in one of Gollum's love notes.)

Their seventeen-week trial generated such a nationwide media frenzy that it has been described as the "O. J. Simpson trial of its day." It also shares something else with the Simpson case. Despite overwhelming circumstantial evidence of their guilt—including a sales receipt for fifty sticks of dynamite purchased by Gollum under an assumed name, detonator wire found in his car, and the fact that he and Beulah were alone with her parents on the boat just before of the murders, then rowed to shore in a skiff before the explosion—the two were acquitted.

THE JESUS OF CHATSWORTH

CHATSWORTH, CALIFORNIA • DECEMBER 10, 1958

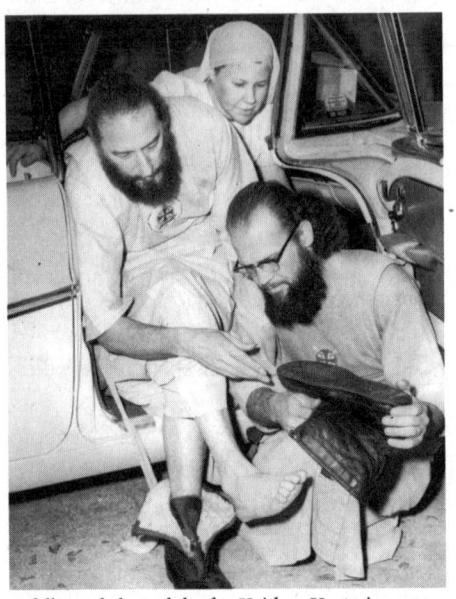

A follower helps cult leader Krishna Venta in 1957.

San Francisco–born Francis Herman Pencovic led a knockabout life in his youth, bumming around the country during the Great Depression, working odd jobs, committing petty crimes, and doing a stint in a mental institution. He discovered his true calling in 1948 when he decided that he was Christ, changed his name to Krishna Venta, and founded a cult called WKFL (Wisdom, Knowledge, Faith, and Love) Fountain in Simi Valley, California.

A handsome, charismatic thirty-eight-year-old who adopted a biblical style—shoulder-length hair, flowing beard, long robe, and bare feet—he claimed to be a 240,000-year-old native of the planet Neophrates and had no trouble attracting a group of gullible followers who bought into his hare-brained beliefs.

In the typical fashion of other doomsday cults, he told of a coming race war in which Black Americans, assisted by Russia, would rise up and conquer the white population, only to be betrayed by their communist sponsors, who would vanquish the Black Americans and take over the country. At this point, Venta and his followers—who had retreated from their Box Canyon commune to a secret location in the desert—would reemerge, overpower the Russians, and establish a new world order based on the cult's guiding principles.

Venta, however, never lived to see if his prophecy would be fulfilled. Availing himself of the perks that seem to come with cult leadership, he had not only bilked his followers of their worldly possessions but exercised his sexual prerogatives over the more attractive young women in his flock, married or otherwise. Two of these women were the wives of members Ralph Smith Muller and Peter Duma Kamenoff. In December 1958, Muller donned twenty sticks of dynamite and the two blew up the Box Canyon compound.

Besides themselves, the suicide bombers killed ten people, including Venta, a seven-year-old girl, and an eleven-month-old infant. The cult soon disbanded. Venta's apocalyptic prophecy is said to have inspired Charles Manson's ravings about an imminent race war he named "Helter Skelter."

BABY CRAZY IN LOS ANGELES

Los Angeles, California
May 16, 1975

Unmarried and expecting her fourth child, twenty-eight-year-old Kathryn Viramontes felt fortunate when she was befriended by a forty-seven-year-old obstetrics nurse, Norma Jean Armistead, who offered to help the overburdened younger woman in whatever way she could. In the months that followed, Armistead, already overweight, began putting on pounds and informing friends and co-workers that she was pregnant.

On May 16, 1975, when she was on the brink of giving birth, Viramontes summoned Armistead to her apartment to perform the delivery. After injecting her young friend with "anesthetic, muscle-relaxing, and labor-inducing drugs," Armistead taped her mouth shut, slit her throat with a scalpel, and cut the baby from the womb. A short time later, she showed up with the newborn at her workplace, the Kaiser Permanente Hospital, where she explained that she had gone into labor at home and given birth en route. When the examining physician discovered that she had no cervix or uterus—the result of a decade-old hysterectomy—Armistead grew hysterical, accusing him of "trying to take my baby away from me."

The following day, after Viramontes's bloody corpse was found by a neighbor, Armistead was arrested. It quickly emerged that the maniacal nurse—"suffering from an insatiable obsession to have a baby," as one forensic psychiatrist put it—had committed another, if less deadly, act of newborn-snatching eight months earlier. On the morning of September 21, 1974, twenty-six-year-old Mary Childs, who had been admitted to the maternity ward the previous evening, awoke from a profound slumber to find her oversized belly deflated and a stillborn fetus between her legs. Hospital officials determined that, during the night, Armistead had administered strong sedatives plus a labor-inducing drug to the sleeping Childs, delivered the baby, substituted a dead fetus from the hospital morgue, and walked away with the stolen child.

In the end, Childs's baby was returned to her, Viramontes's given over to the custody of its biological father, and Armistead convicted of first-degree murder and sentenced to life in prison.

Psychopathic "fetal-snatcher" Norma Jean Armistead

A VERY BAD MONDAY IN SAN DIEGO

San Diego, California
January 29, 1979

The product of a chaotic upbringing, during which she suffered extreme neglect from her divorced mother and alleged abuse at the hands of her father, Brenda Spencer had been arrested twice—for burglary and for vandalizing a public school—by the time she was sixteen. A chronic truant with confessed suicidal tendencies and a fondness for alcohol and drugs, she fantasized about killing policemen and doing "something big to get on TV." Her favorite pastime was target shooting with her pellet gun, a hobby encouraged by her father, who thought it was a good idea to give his manifestly troubled daughter a scoped, semiautomatic rifle and five hundred rounds of ammunition as a Christmas present in 1978.

One month later, Spencer barricaded herself in her house and opened fire on children arriving at the Grover Cleveland Elementary School across the street. By the time she surrendered several hours later, the school principal and custodian lay dead, and a policeman and eight children were shot and wounded. During a phone conversation with a local journalist during the standoff with the SWAT team, Spencer was asked about her motives. Thanks partly to a hit rock song that immortalized the phrase, her reply has taken on semilegendary status: "I just don't like Mondays," she said, adding that she thought it was a good way to "cheer up the day."

A cuffed Brenda Spencer, one of the nation's few female mass shooters

Charged as an adult, the teenage Spencer pleaded guilty to two counts of murder and was sentenced to twenty-five years to life. Her crime is now seen as a harbinger of the school shooting epidemic that has plagued the nation since the Columbine massacre twenty years later.

THE COVINA MASSACRE

Covina, California
December 24, 2008

In 2002, Bruce Pardo and his first wife, Elana, split up after their thirteen-month-old son fell into the backyard swimming pool under his father's watch and was left permanently disabled. Typical of the profoundly self-centered Pardo, he never saw his son again or paid a penny to help support him.

His second wife, Sylvia—fed up with their increasingly acrimonious fights over money—filed for divorce in June 2008 after two years of marriage. Ordered to pay $1,785 a month in spousal support, Pardo—who complained to friends that his ex was "taking him to the cleaners"—sent her one check that bounced and stopped payment on the second. The following month, he was fired from his electrical engineering job for billing fraudulent hours. Owing to his lack of employment, his monthly payments to Sylvia were suspended, though, under the terms of their divorce—finalized one week before Christmas 2008—he was required to pay her a lump sum of $10,000.

Just before midnight on Christmas Eve, dressed in a Santa Claus costume, he showed up at the home of his in-laws during their annual holiday party. In his arms he carried a gift-wrapped package containing several semiautomatic handguns and an air compressor rigged to spray gasoline. Stepping into the house he opened fire, killing Sylvia and her parents execution-style and wounding other partygoers, including his eight-year-old niece, who got shot in the face. With his homemade flamethrower, he then doused the home with gasoline and set it ablaze.

Altogether, nine people—Sylvia, her parents, a sister, two brothers and their wives, and a teenaged nephew—died in what became known as the Covina Massacre. Suffering third-degree burns on his arms and with part of his Santa suit melted onto his skin, Pardo drove to his brother's house and shot himself in the head.

Mass murderer Bruce Pardo admires himself in his Santa costume before carrying out his Christmas Eve massacre.

COLORADO

BROOMFIELD
THE BROOMFIELD TEEN WHO PUT A HIT ON HERSELF
43

MORRISON
A BEER SCION DISAPPEARS IN MORRISON
41

DENVER
SHOCK JOCK SHOT IN DENVER
42

A BEER SCION DISAPPEARS IN MORRISON

Morrison, Colorado • February 9, 1960

On the morning of February 9, 1960, forty-year-old Adolph Coors III, CEO of the beer company founded by his grandfather, bid good-bye to his wife and four children, got behind the wheel of his green and white station wagon, and set off for the brewery twelve miles away in Golden, Colorado. A few hours later, the car was discovered on a narrow wooden bridge not far from his home, motor running, radio playing, no driver in sight.

A search of the area turned up Coors's baseball cap and eyeglasses, along with blood stains on the bridge. The following day, Coors's wife, Mary, received a typewritten note demanding $500,000 in tens and twenties for the safe return of her husband and instructing her to place a classified newspaper ad as a signal that the ransom was ready to be paid. She never heard from the kidnapper—or saw her husband—again. Seven months would pass before the latter's skeletal remains were found near a remote garbage dump in the foothills of the Rockies.

The abduction-murder of Coors set off the largest FBI manhunt since the Lindbergh baby kidnapping. Witnesses reported seeing a yellow 1951 Mercury sedan in the vicinity of the bridge on several occasions. One man had even noted part of the license plate number. The car was traced to a paint factory employee going by the name of Walter Osborne, who had hurriedly decamped from his Denver apartment on the morning after Coors went missing.

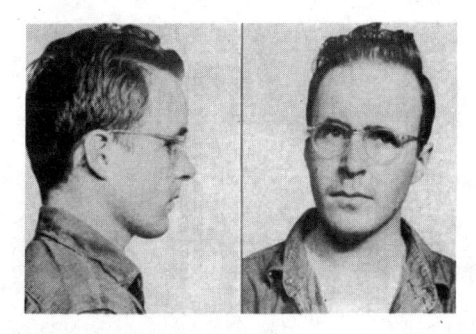

Mugshot of kidnapper-murderer John Corbett Jr.

A fingerprint retrieved during a search of his rooms revealed that "Osborne" was actually a thirty-one-year-old fugitive named Joseph Corbett Jr. A highly intelligent, widely read man undone by what prison psychologists would later diagnose as "schizoid and asocial tendencies," Corbett had gone from being a pre-med student at Berkeley to a convicted murderer after stealing a car and shooting a hitchhiker in the head in 1950. He had served only five years of his life sentence when he managed to escape prison and make his way to Colorado.

Tracked to Vancouver, Corbett was arrested without a struggle in late October. Sentenced to life at his March 1961 trial, he was paroled for good behavior in 1980 and settled down in Denver, where he worked as a Salvation Army truck driver. He died of a self-inflicted gunshot wound to the head in 2009.

Radio deejay Alan Berg

SHOCK JOCK SHOT IN DENVER

Denver, Colorado
June 18, 1984

Among the first generation of "shock jocks," Alan Berg kept his audience both captivated and enraged on his nightly call-in show on Denver's KOA radio station. Though his rants were often laced with humor, the "Wild Man of the Airwaves" (as he styled himself) did not suffer fools, racists, or bigots of any stripe, and often reduced his callers to sputtering rage before cutting them off mid-sentence by abruptly hanging up on them.

An unabashed liberal who made no secret of his Jewish identity, he was beloved by some for his razor-tongued, take-no-prisoners honesty and reviled by others for his scathing takedowns of white supremacists, antisemites, and members of various hate groups. He seemed fearless in the face of death threats.

At one point, when a local KKK leader stormed into the studio while Berg was on-air and threatened him with death, he continued broadcasting, calmly telling listeners that there was a gun pointed at him. On the night of June 18, 1984, those threats became a terrible reality when Berg was gunned down in the driveway of his apartment building by an assassin wielding a silenced .45-caliber machine pistol.

A massive manhunt led to the arrest of several members of The Order, a white supremacist terrorist group that had Berg high on its hit list because, as one member explained, "He was thought to be anti-white and he was Jewish." Sentenced to 252 years in prison, triggerman Bruce Pierce died of natural causes in a federal penitentiary in 2010. In death, the controversial talk radio host was acknowledged even by those put off by his abrasive style, as "a catalyst of the freedom of speech in America."

THE BROOMFIELD TEEN WHO PUT A HIT ON HERSELF

BROOMFIELD, COLORADO
DECEMBER 28, 2017

One day after nineteen-year-old Natalie Bollinger went missing, her body was found in a wooded area of a dairy farm not far from her home, a bullet to her head and a potentially lethal dose of heroin in her system. Suspicion immediately fell on a homeless man whom she had once befriended and who had begun stalking her so relentlessly that she had been granted a restraining order against him just two weeks prior.

The case took a bizarre turn, however, when a trace of Bollinger's phone and internet records led police to twenty-three-year-old pizza deliveryman Joseph Michael Lopez. According to Lopez, Bollinger—known to have struggled with drug abuse and depression—had posted an ad on Craigslist, titled "I want to put a hit on myself."

Lopez agreed to do the job, claiming that he had experience in such matters. Scouting several locations, they settled on the dairy farm, where—after purportedly trying and failing to talk her out of it—he shot Bollinger in the head as she knelt in prayer, using a 9mm handgun she had supplied. Lopez was allowed to enter into a plea agreement with prosecutors and was sentenced to forty-eight years in prison for second-degree murder.

Selfie of Natalie Bollinger, who hired her own murderer

CONNECTICUT

WINDSOR
THE WINDSOR MURDER FACTORY
46

NEW LONDON
A TWELVE-YEAR-OLD GOES TO THE GALLOWS
45

HARTFORD ★

NEWTON
A WOOD-CHIPPING IN NEWTON
47

CHESHIRE
CARNAGE IN CHESHIRE
48

BRIDGEPORT
THE CONNECTICUT CANNIBAL
49

A TWELVE-YEAR-OLD GOES TO THE GALLOWS

New London, Connecticut • July 21, 1786

The orphaned, biracial child of a Black father and Pequot mother, Hannah Ocuish possessed (as one contemporary put it) "a maliciousness of disposition that made other children in the neighborhood much afraid of her." At the age of six, she and an older brother ran afoul of the law after attacking a little girl, stripping her of her clothing and a gold necklace, then "beating the child until they almost killed her."

A drawing of the hanging of Hannah Ocuish

As punishment, Hannah was bound out in servitude to a widow. Six years later, on the morning of July 21, 1786, the body of little Eunice Bolles, six-year-old daughter of a wealthy farmer, was found lying at the base of a stone wall bordering a well-traveled road. Rocks lay on her arms, back, and head, as if a portion of the wall had collapsed on her. A closer examination, however, revealed that her death was no accident. Her skull had been battered in and, as deep fingernail marks on her throat attested, she had also been strangled.

Suspicion quickly alighted upon Hannah, who was known to bear a grudge against Eunice. Some weeks earlier, the little girl had publicly accused Hannah of stealing her basket of strawberries while the children of the town were out harvesting the fruit. Brought in for questioning about the death, Hannah initially fabricated a story about four boys she had ostensibly seen near the spot where Eunice's body was found. Unpersuaded, her interrogators brought her to the Bolleses' home and confronted her with the corpse of the little girl laid out in the parlor.

Bursting into tears, Hannah confessed to the murder. She had waylaid Eunice, who was on the way to school, then beat her unconscious with a stone, choked her to death, and placed rocks upon the body "to make people think that the wall fell upon her and killed her." At the end of her shocking tale, she promised that "if she could be forgiven, she would never do it again." The community, however, was in no mood for forgiveness. Found guilty at trial, the twelve-year-old girl was condemned to death and went to the gallows on December 20, 1786—the youngest person ever executed in the United States.

The Archer Private Home for the Elderly, site of a horrific series of murders

THE WINDSOR MURDER FACTORY

WINDSOR, CONNECTICUT
1910–1916

One of our nation's most prolific female serial killers, Amy Archer-Gilligan went into the nursing home business with her first husband, James H. Archer, in 1904. Six years later, after taking out a life insurance policy at his wife's behest, James died suddenly, supposedly of kidney disease.

In November 1913, Amy wed her second husband, Michael W. Gilligan, a wealthy widower nearly twenty years her senior. Three months later, having signed a will leaving his whole estate to his new wife, the seemingly healthy Mr. Gilligan suddenly fell ill and died, reportedly of "acute indigestion."

At her nursing home, the inmates (as Archer-Gilligan called them) were also dying at an alarming pace. Among them was Franklin R. Andrews, a vibrant sixty-one-year-old who spent the morning of May 29, 1914, working happily in the nursing home garden but was dead by evening after suffering a sudden onset of severe abdominal pain, nausea, and vomiting. Suspicious over the circumstances of his death, Andrews's sister reported her concerns to authorities.

On Tuesday, May 2, 1916, her brother's body was exhumed. An autopsy established that he had died not from gastric ulcers (as his doctor had concluded), but from arsenic poisoning. Other exhumations quickly followed. All revealed lethal quantities of arsenic in the stomachs of the deceased. The case became a nationwide sensation after the *Hartford Courant* ran a screaming banner headline on May 9, 1916: "POLICE BELIEVE ARCHER HOME FOR AGED A MURDER FACTORY." Including her two husbands, as many as forty victims may have died at Archer-Gilligan's hands.

Indicted on five counts of first-degree murder, she was tried, found guilty, and sentenced to be hanged. Two years later, after a successful appeal, she was granted another trial. It ended abruptly when she changed her plea from insanity to guilty of murder in the second degree and was sentenced to life in the state prison in Wethersfield. In July 1924, she was declared insane by the prison physician and transferred to the state mental hospital in Middletown, where she lived out the remaining thirty-eight years of her life, whiling away the days, as a 1962 obituary noted, "playing funeral marches on the piano and carrying on long telephone conversations with herself."

A WOOD-CHIPPING IN NEWTON

NEWTON, CONNECTICUT
NOVEMBER 19, 1986

Anyone who has watched the Coen brothers' Oscar-winning 1996 movie *Fargo* is bound to remember the sight of Steve Buscemi being fed into a woodchipper. What few people realize is that the scene was inspired by a real-life crime.

In fall 1986, Helle Crafts, a Danish-born flight attendant residing in Newton, Connecticut, became convinced that her husband, Richard, was having an affair. After a private investigator, Keith Mayo, confirmed her suspicions with photographic evidence, she filed for divorce. Not long afterward, she disappeared. When Helle's worried friend and co-workers tried contacting her, Richard told contradictory stories: that she was visiting her sick mother in Denmark, vacationing with a friend in the Canary Islands, or had simply left without telling him where she was going.

Convinced that his client had fallen victim to foul play, Mayo pressured the police to begin an investigation. Under questioning, the Crafts' au pair described a dark red stain she had spotted on the couple's bedroom carpet which Richard had subsequently cut out and discarded. Even more incriminating were Richard's credit card receipts for a freezer, a chainsaw, and a woodchipper.

After a witness came forward who said that he had seen Richard using a woodchipper by a local lake on the night of Helle's disappearance, police conducted a search that turned up bone fragments, strands of blonde hair, human tissue fiber, and part of a tooth with a metal crown that precisely matched Helle's dental records. Evidence indicated that her husband had bludgeoned her to death, kept her in the freezer, then chainsawed her body and fed the pieces through the woodchipper. In Connecticut's first murder conviction without a body, Richard Crafts was ultimately found guilty and sentenced to fifty years in prison. He was released for good behavior in 2020 at the age of eighty-two.

Wood-chip killer Richard Crafts on the witness stand

The fire-damaged home of the Petit family

CARNAGE IN CHESHIRE

Cheshire, Connecticut
July 23, 2007

One of the most heinous crimes in Connecticut history, the Petit home invasion took place in the bucolic, upscale town of Cheshire. The victims were fifty-year-old Dr. William Petit Jr., one of the nation's top diabetes specialists; his forty-eight-year-old wife, Jennifer Hawke-Petit, a pediatric nurse; and their two daughters, Hayley and Michaela, seventeen and eleven years old, respectively.

On the evening of July 23, 2007, Jennifer and Michaela were shopping for dinner provisions at a local supermarket when they caught the eye of Steven Hayes, a forty-four-year-old chronic thief who, beginning with his first conviction for burglary at the age of sixteen, had spent more than two decades in and out of prison for crimes ranging from purse snatching to weapons possession. Recently paroled, he was living at a halfway house where he had bonded with another small-time miscreant, twenty-seven-year-old Joshua Komisarjevsky, a drug-addicted, compulsive housebreaker described by one sentencing judge as "a calculated, cold-blooded predator."

The bedroom where the Petit sisters died

When Jennifer and Michaela left the store, Hayes trailed them to see where they lived, then contacted Komisarjevsky and made plans to burglarize the Petit home. In the middle of the night, they snuck inside through an unlocked cellar door. Finding Dr. Petit asleep in the sunroom, they battered him unconscious with a baseball bat, hogtied him, dragged him to the basement, and lashed him to a pole. Upstairs, they bound his wife and daughters to their bedposts.

After the two men ransacked the house, Hayes went off to a gas station and filled two cans he had taken from the garage. By then, it was morning. Driving Jennifer to her bank at 9:00 a.m., Hayes ordered her to withdraw $15,000 from her account, threatening to kill her daughters if she failed to comply. Inside, Jennifer managed to inform a teller that her family was being held hostage.

When she and Hayes returned with the money, Komisarjevsky announced that he had sexually assaulted eleven-year-old Michaela in their absence and goaded his partner into raping Jennifer. Roused from his semi-conscious stupor by his wife's screams, William managed to work free of his bonds and make it outside, shouting for help. Realizing that Dr. Petit had escaped, Hayes strangled Jennifer to death. Her body, along with the children's bedrooms, were then doused with the gasoline and set ablaze. Both sisters died of smoke inhalation.

Alerted by the bank, police captured the murderers as they fled. When Connecticut abolished the death penalty in August 2015, their death sentences were commuted to life in prison, where, in 2019, Hayes transitioned to a woman and took the name Linda.

THE CONNECTICUT CANNIBAL

Bridgeport, Connecticut
December 15, 2011

A onetime model psychiatric patient and aspiring author struggling to complete a book about murder, rape, and the Greek gods, Tyree Smith showed up at the apartment of his cousin, Nicole Rabb, on December 15, 2011, and announced that it was time for him "to get blood on his hands."

He reappeared the next day in blood-spattered clothes, carrying chopsticks and a small blood-caked hatchet. Sitting down to dinner, he explained that, after leaving Rabb's place the previous evening, he had gone to a former residence—a now-derelict home in Bridgeport—and murdered a homeless squatter, Angel Gonzalez. After smashing Gonzalez's skull with the hatchet, he had removed one of the dead man's eyes and some brain matter, which he consumed in a nearby cemetery, washing them down with sake. The eyeball, Smith told his cousin, "tasted like an oyster."

Rabb promptly kicked her cousin out of her house and contacted the police, but a month passed before Gonzalez's mutilated, decomposed corpse was discovered by a building inspector. Found not guilty by reason of insanity, the Connecticut cannibal was committed to a state mental hospital for a term of sixty years.

DELAWARE

NEW CASTLE
A FIERY EXECUTION IN NEW CASTLE
51

DOVER
THE JILTED PARAMOUR
51

OMAR
A SIBLING SLAUGHTER
53

A FIERY EXECUTION IN NEW CASTLE

NEW CASTLE, DELAWARE
JUNE 1731

Delaware was still a colony in 1731 when Catherine Bevan became the only woman in American history to be executed by burning. The unhappily married fifty-year-old Bevan had been carrying on an affair with the family servant, a much younger man named Peter Murphy. Neighbors whispered of their "too-familiar intimacy" and commiserated with her sixty-year-old husband, Henry, when he complained that "his wife and servant . . . abused him."

Henry's sudden death in June of that year struck many of them as suspicious, particularly when Catherine had her husband's coffin nailed shut before friends and family members could view the corpse. When a county magistrate, aware of the rumors, ordered the coffin pried open at the funeral, Henry's body was found to be covered in terrible bruises.

Taken into custody, the illicit lovers initially protested their innocence. It wasn't long, however, before Murphy broke down and confessed, telling his interrogators that, after a failed attempt at poisoning Henry, Catherine proposed that Murphy "beat his master well, especially about the breast, till he should grow so weak that she might be able to deal with him." Following her instructions, Murphy set upon Henry, thrashing him until he could no longer stand, at which point Catherine strangled him to death with a handkerchief.

Convicted of "petty treason"—a capital offense defined as "murdering someone to whom you owed obedience"—Murphy was sentenced to be hanged and Catherine to be burned alive. The executions took place on June 10, 1731. In an act of mercy, a rope was tied around Catherine's neck so that she would be hanged over the fire and strangled before the flames reached her. When the fire was lit, however, the rope burned and she fell into the flames, suffering an agonizing death.

THE JILTED PARAMOUR

DOVER, DELAWARE
AUGUST 11–12, 1898

On August 9, 1898, a package bearing no return address was delivered to Mrs. Mary Elizabeth Dunning, daughter of former Delaware congressman John B. Pennington. The wife of journalist John Dunning, Mary had had her fill of her husband's drinking, gambling, and philandering during their years in San Francisco and taken their little daughter to move

Mrs. Cordelia Botkin, the Chocolate Box Murderer

DELAWARE • 51

A newspaper illustration of Cordelia Botkin on trial

back to her parents' home in Dover two years earlier, leaving her fast-living husband back in California.

Inside the package was a box of chocolate bonbons, along with a note reading: "With love to yourself and baby—Mrs. C." That evening, after a dinner of trout and fritters, Mrs. Dunning sat on the porch and shared the treats with her older sister, Ida, her nephew and niece, and two female neighbors who had stopped by for a visit. A few hours later, all six became violently ill. The children and two young women eventually recovered, but Mrs. Dunning and her sister died painfully a few days later.

Chemical analysis of the candies revealed that they contained enough arsenic to "kill over a score of people." The investigation into what Governor Ebe Walter Tunnell called the "most horrible case that has ever occurred in Delaware" quickly focused on Mary's husband, John. Shown the note that had accompanied the lethal chocolates, John Dunning identified the handwriting as that of Mrs. Cordelia Botkin, a portly thirty-eight-year-old San Franciscan estranged from her husband and with whom he'd been conducting a lengthy affair.

Despite her protestations of innocence, overwhelming circumstantial evidence—including positive identifications by the druggist who sold her the arsenic and salesclerks at the candy shop where she purchased the chocolates—quickly led to Botkin's arrest. Because the murders had been perpetrated by mail between two states, a jurisdictional dispute had to be resolved before Botkin could be tried. While awaiting a decision, she was said to have been "on intimate terms with one or more of her guards, which accounted for the fact that she was surrounded with every comfort at the jail."

In the end, the proceedings took place in a San Francisco courtroom. Found guilty of first-degree murder, Botkin was sentenced to life imprisonment. When the conviction was overturned on appeal, she was tried again with the same result and sent to San Quentin. She died in 1910 of what the prison physician deemed "softening of the brain due to melancholy."

A SIBLING SLAUGHTER

OMAR, DELAWARE
NOVEMBER 7, 1927

At about 9:30 p.m. November 7, 1927, Robert R. Hitchens—a fifty-five-year-old bachelor who made his living as a house carpenter—returned home after buying a loaf of bread at his local general store. When a few days passed with no sign of him, his widowed sister, May Carey, who lived across the street, sent the oldest of her three sons, twenty-year-old Howard, to investigate.

The young man found his uncle's body lying in a dried puddle of blood in a corner of the kitchen. He had been shot twice in the head and bludgeoned so savagely that the mortician needed more than two hundred stitches to make the corpse presentable for viewing. Because $6 in cash was found in his pockets, police ruled out robbery as a motive. A number of empty whiskey bottles scattered on the floor led some detectives to speculate that the killer was an alcoholic, perhaps a bootlegger.

An investigation into the victim's finances revealed that he had a $2,000 life insurance policy to be paid out to his closest living relative, Mrs. Carey. The murder went unsolved until December 1934, when Carey's youngest son, Lawrence, was arrested for breaking and entering. Under questioning by police, he made a startling confession. Seven years earlier, Carey had enlisted her two older sons, Howard and James, in a plot to murder her brother for his insurance money.

On the evening of the crime, Carey and her sons Howard and James had snuck into Hitchens's house and lay in wait for him while he made his nightly visit to the general store. No sooner had Hitchens entered than May and James started clubbing him to death, the former with a three-pound sledgehammer, her son with a heavy oak cudgel. Ordered by his mother to deliver the coup de grâce, Howard then shot his uncle twice in the head. Before leaving, they doused his corpse in whiskey and poured some down his throat to make it appear that he had died in a drunken brawl.

Howard and his mother were both convicted of first-degree murder and executed on the same day, June 7, 1935. Mrs. Carey became (as newspapers declared) the "first white woman to be hanged in Delaware."

Robert Hitchens (top) and his sister, May Carey (bottom), who was hanged for his murder

FLORIDA

TALLAHASSEE

MALABAR
THE VAMPIRE RAPIST
55

PORT ST. LUCIE
THE HAMMER BOY STRIKES
58

SARASOTA
A CHILD SNATCHED IN SARASOTA
57

WESTON
A BULLY SLAYED IN WESTON
56

MIAMI
THE MIAMI ZOMBIE
59

Mug shot of John Brennan Crutchley in 1995 (inset) and shortly before his death in his prison cell

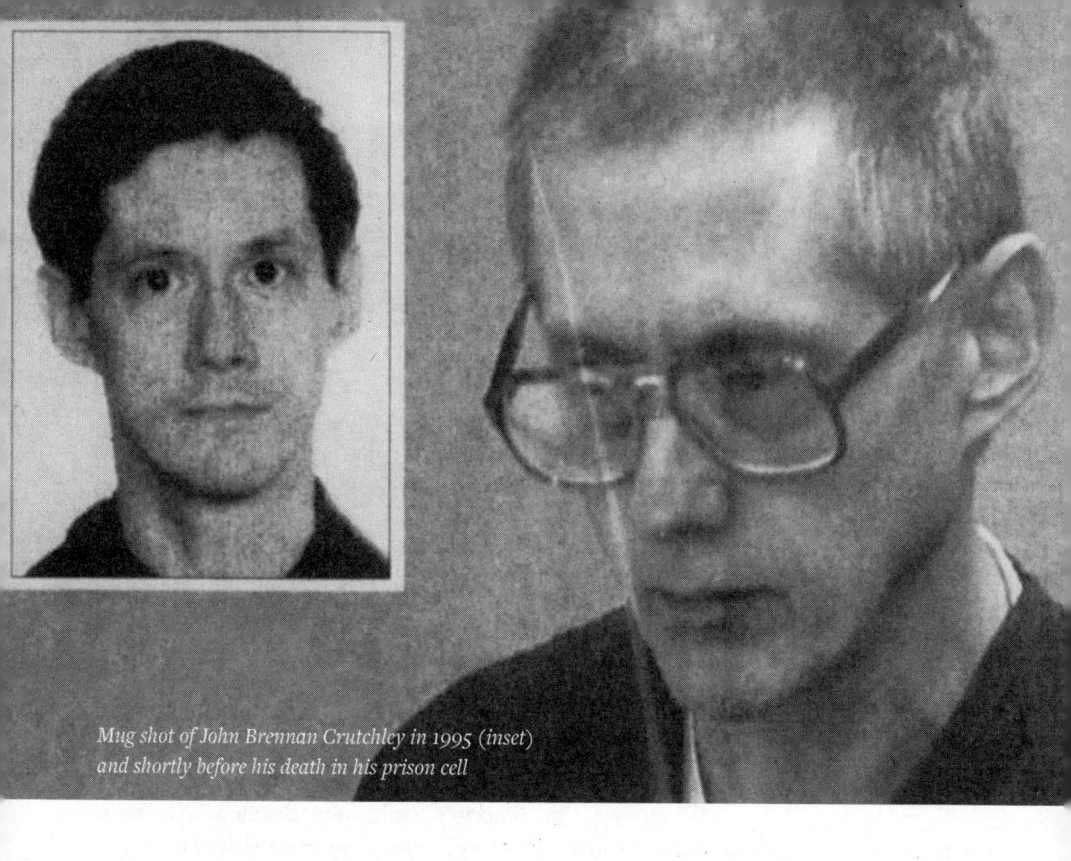

THE VAMPIRE RAPIST

Malabar, Florida
November 21, 1985

Though all signs pointed to him as a serial sex-killer responsible for the deaths of as many as thirty women in four states, John Brennan Crutchley was never charged with a single homicide. The crime that finally brought him down—and that earned him the nickname the "Vampire Rapist"—was the kidnap, rape, and torture of a nineteen-year-old hitchhiker in Brevard County, Florida, during Thanksgiving week in 1985.

Crutchley offered the young woman a lift, then strangled her into unconsciousness, dragged her into his home, stripped her naked, and strapped her to his kitchen counter. Over the next twenty-two hours, while a video setup recorded his assaults, he repeatedly raped her and used surgical equipment to drain her blood into a jar, drinking as much of it as he could before it became too clotted to swallow.

After she managed to escape during Crutchley's absence, the victim was taken to a hospital where doctors determined that she had lost nearly half her blood. Sentenced to twenty-five years, Crutchley was freed after ten for good behavior but almost immediately found himself back behind bars after testing positive for marijuana, a parole violation. Six years later, he was found dead in his cell, having accidentally killed himself while engaging in auto-erotic asphyxiation.

FLORIDA • 55

Bobby Kent preens for the camera (left); Marty Puccio, Kent's minion and murderer, at his sentencing hearing (right)

A BULLY SLAYED IN WESTON

WESTON, FLORIDA
JULY 14, 1993

According to his father, twenty-year-old Bobby Kent "was a kind person, happy, funny." In truth, he was a domineering sadist who got perverse pleasure from humiliating those closest to him, especially his best friend since elementary school, Marty Puccio. Exactly why, despite the near-constant physical and emotional mistreatment dished out to him, Puccio remained in such thrall to Kent is unclear, though there were distinctly homoerotic undercurrents in their relationship.

It was Kent who enlisted Puccio in a scheme to produce and peddle gay porn and—according to some reports—pressured him into prostituting himself to men. Everything changed when Puccio began seeing eighteen-year-old Lisa Connelly. Incensed at the bullying her new boyfriend endured, she tried to turn Kent's attention elsewhere by hooking him up with her friend, Ali Willis, a former teen sex worker. That relationship came to a quick end when Kent forced to her to watch a gay porn video while having sex with her, slapping her hard in the face when she tried to avert her eyes.

When Connelly became pregnant with Puccio's child, she decided that more extreme measures were necessary to get him away from Kent. Persuading Puccio that getting rid of Kent was the only way to set himself free, she enlisted the help of five other people: her cousin, Derek Dzvirko; Ali Willis and her current boyfriend, Donald Semenec; a friend named Heather Swales; and a hitman-wannabe, Derek Kaufman.

On the night of July 14, 1993, the seven-member group lured Kent to a remote canal where they stabbed him repeatedly, cut his throat, bashed his head in with a baseball bat, and dumped him in the water. Unable to keep quiet about the murder, Connelly quickly confided to her mother, and within days all seven conspirators were under arrest.

Six of them received sentences ranging from seven years to life. Puccio received the death penalty, though his sentence was later commuted to life.

A CHILD SNATCHED IN SARASOTA

SARASOTA, FLORIDA
FEBRUARY 1, 2004

A child of divorce, eleven-year-old Carlie Brucia lived most of the year with her mother and stepfather in Sarasota, Florida. Just after 6:00 p.m. on the evening of Super Bowl Sunday 2004, Brucia left a friend's house and set off on the one-mile walk back home to watch the big game with her family. She never arrived.

A search led police to a car wash along a busy commercial street. Spotting a motion-activated security camera overlooking the rear of the building, they secured the tape. The video—images from which would soon be released to a horrified world—showed a dark-haired man in a mechanic's uniform striding up to Brucia and pausing to say a few words before grabbing her by an arm and hurrying her away.

From viewers who had watched the chilling footage on the local news, police quickly identified the suspect as an unemployed auto mechanic named Joseph Smith, a Brooklyn-born drug addict with a long rap sheet for various narcotic-related felonies. Taken into custody, Smith refused to talk to investigators but confided in his brother that, while on a "far-out cocaine trip," he had killed the sixth grader during "rough sex" and left her body in a stand of trees behind a church a few miles away.

From cuts and bruises on her limbs, medical examiners concluded that she had put up a desperate struggle before being strangled. A semen stain on her shirt matched Smith's DNA profile. Sentenced to death, he died of unspecified causes in July 2021.

"I feel wonderful," Brucia's father said upon hearing the news of Smith's passing. "It's long overdue."

A security camera captured the kidnapping of eleven-year-old Carlie Brucia by her rapist-killer, Joseph Smith.

The bedroom where Tyler Hadley stashed his murdered parents before throwing a house party

THE HAMMER BOY STRIKES

Port St. Lucie, Florida • July 16, 2011

According to one childhood friend, Tyler Hadley first spoke about killing his parents when he was ten years old. He was in and out of trouble throughout his adolescence for crimes ranging from arson to burglary and did a brief stint in the county jail after an arrest for aggravated assault. Deeply worried about his erratic behavior, his mother, Mary Jo—a beloved elementary school teacher—had him admitted to a psychiatric clinic. Though he appeared much improved after a few weeks of counseling—"over the hurdle," in Mary Jo's words—he began telling friends via Facebook that he planned to kill his mother.

On the night of July 16, 2011, exactly five months shy of his eighteenth birthday, Tyler threw a raucous party that attracted roughly sixty teens who smoked pot, played beer pong, blared music, and left the house in shambles. Asked where his parents were, Tyler—stoned on various drugs—offered contradictory explanations before confiding to his friend Mike that, earlier in the day, he had snuck up on his mother as she worked on the family computer and smashed her in the head with a claw hammer. Her dying words were, "Why? Why?"

When his father, Blake, hearing her screams, ran into the room, Tyler killed him the same way, shattering his skull with the claw end of the hammer. When Mike seemed skeptical, Tyler led him to the master bedroom, where the bloodied corpses of his parents lay beneath a heap of household items. Rather than fleeing the murder scene, Mike stayed at the party for another forty-five minutes, at one point posing for selfies with Tyler. It would be four hours before he reported the killings to the police.

In jail while awaiting trial, Tyler is said to have signed autographs for fellow inmates, using his self-adopted nickname "Hammer Boy." Spared the death penalty because of his age, he was sentenced to life without parole.

THE MIAMI ZOMBIE

MIAMI BEACH, FLORIDA
MAY 26, 2012

A onetime promising student from an elite New York City high school, Ronald Poppo dropped out of college shortly after enrolling and embarked on the life of a drifter, cutting himself off so completely from his family that they eventually assumed he was dead.

For the next forty years, he lived on the streets, racking up two dozen arrests for a variety of offenses, among them public drinking, trespassing, burglary, and assault. By 2012, the now sixty-five-year-old Poppo was spending his nights in a Miami homeless encampment and hanging out during the days in the shade of a three-mile-long causeway. He was napping near an exit ramp on the afternoon of May 26 when Rudy Eugene came upon him.

A thirty-one-year-old car wash employee with a record of seven arrests, most for marijuana possession, Eugene had driven to South Beach for the Memorial Day festivities. About forty minutes after his arrival, witnesses saw him walking along the causeway, completely naked, a Bible clutched in one hand. Spotting the dozing Poppo, he launched into an appalling attack, stripping off the older man's pants, pummeling him, then hunching over him and biting into his face.

The horrific assault went on for eighteen minutes before the police—alerted by a 911 call from a passing bicyclist—arrived on the scene. Ordered to desist, Eugene looked up at the officers, growled through the strips of flesh hanging from his mouth, and went back to gnawing on Poppo. The cops then opened fire, shooting Eugene dead. The hideously disfigured Poppo—85 percent of his face chewed off, his left eye gouged out, his right eye blinded—survived.

Though lab tests turned up nothing but marijuana in Eugene's body, toxicologists remained convinced that Eugene—now known as the "Causeway Cannibal" and the "Miami Zombie"—must have ingested a far stronger substance, possibly the psychoactive street drug known as "bath salts." As one expert put it, "To say that marijuana could have induced this behavior is simply outrageous. No matter how sick mentally or physically a [marijuana smoker] is, they don't go around eating faces."

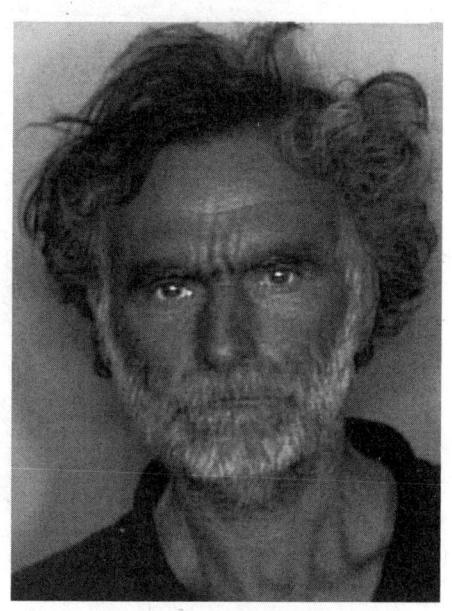

Ronald Poppo, the homeless man whose face was eaten off by Rudy Eugene. "For a very short amount of time, I thought he was a good guy," Poppo said of his attacker.

GEORGIA

ATLANTA
ATLANTA'S JACK THE RIPPER
61

FAYETTEVILLE
THE CRIPPLER OF FAYETTEVILLE
63

COWETA COUNTY
DOWNFALL OF A "KING"
62

ATLANTA'S JACK THE RIPPER

Atlanta, Georgia • January 1911 and January 1912

Owing to systemic racism, even the most heinous crimes committed against Black Americans tend to receive little attention in the United States. Between August and November 1888, London's Jack the Ripper murdered and mutilated five women. Nearly a quarter century later, a serial killer known as "Atlanta's Jack the Ripper" slaughtered as many as nineteen. While the Whitechapel butcher has become a mythological figure, his American counterpart has been almost entirely forgotten, largely because the victims, as well as the presumed perpetrator, were Black.

When the body of thirty-five-year-old Rosa Trice was discovered on Sunday, January 22, 1911—her skull crushed, her jaw stabbed, her throat slashed so viciously that she was nearly decapitated—the crime earned only a small notice on page five of a local paper. Perfunctory items about the equally savage slayings of two more Black women in May and June were similarly relegated to the inside pages. It wasn't until the mutilation-murder of the seventh victim—killed, like the others, on a Saturday night—that the case made the front pages, with headlines declaring that a "Negro 'Jack the Ripper'" was on the loose.

Victim Mary "Belle" Walker

With the Black population of the city in an uproar, police increased their efforts to track down the serial killer, and the governor posted a $250 reward for his capture. His attacks, however, continued with unabated ferocity. One victim was found with her excised heart lying beside her ravaged corpse. The only description of the madman came from a survivor who reported him as "tall, black, broad-shouldered, and wearing a broad-brimmed black hat."

Though police arrested various suspects, none were convicted, and the identity of "Atlanta's Jack the Ripper," like that of his legendary namesake, remains a mystery.

Police sketch of the Atlanta Ripper suspect

DOWNFALL OF A "KING"

Coweta County, Georgia • April 20, 1948

The head of a powerful clan that had dominated Meriwether County for decades, wealthy landowner John Wallace ruled over his "kingdom" (as he called it) like a feudal overlord, dispensing favors to his servile underlings and meting out vigilante justice to anyone who crossed him. Moonshine was a major source of his income. In 1948, a sharecropper named Wilson Turner, who helped operate the still, ran afoul of Wallace after he was denied payment for a dangerous job and stole two of his boss's prized cows in retaliation.

He was quickly arrested and, with the cooperation of the Meriwether sheriff—another of Wallace's lackeys—set up to be killed. Turner was to be set free at a precise time, supposedly for lack of evidence. As he drove away toward home, Wallace and his henchmen, who were waiting just outside of town, would waylay and shoot him down on the pretext that he had broken out of jail. Things didn't go as planned, however.

Released ahead of schedule, Turner led Wallace and his minions on a chase across the line to neighboring Coweta County, where his truck ran out of gas. In full view of several witnesses, he was set upon and clubbed to death with a shotgun. Wallace then drove the body onto his estate and dumped it in an abandoned well. Fearing that it might be discovered, he enlisted two of his Black tenants to help him remove the body, which was then carried to a pit and incinerated in a bonfire.

John Wallace (center), flanked by Sheriff Lamar Potts and defense attorney Fred New

With no corpse to be found, Wallace believed he had gotten away with murder. Thanks to the persistence of Coweta County Sheriff Lamar Potts, however, he was ultimately arrested. Though confident that, as he put it, "No one is going to convict me of killing white trash," he was found guilty, largely on the testimony of the two men forced to help him dispose of the body: the first time in Georgia history that a white man was convicted on the words of Black men.

Sentenced to death, Wallace remained certain that he would escape execution right up to the minute he was strapped into the chair and electrocuted on November 3, 1950.

THE CRIPPLER OF FAYETTEVILLE

FAYETTEVILLE, GEORGIA
JUNE 22–24, 2007

A wrestling fanatic from the age of eleven, Canadian-born Chris Benoit became a pro at eighteen. Over the course of his twenty-two-year career, he worked his way up the ranks of various organizations, winning thirty championships and achieving superstardom as the fearsome "Canadian Crippler," a nickname he earned after inadvertently breaking an opponent's neck.

His trademark move, the "Crippler Crossface"—in which he trapped one arm of a prostrate opponent with his legs, locked his hands beneath the chin, and pulled backward, straining the other man's neck almost to the breaking point—never failed to draw appreciative roars from his rabid fans. In 1997, he became romantically involved with Nancy Sullivan, then performing as a sinister femme fatale as part of her wrestler-husband's satanism shtick. She and Benoit married in November 2000, eight months after giving birth to their son, Daniel.

In the fall of 2005, after the sudden death of his closest friend and longtime wrestling partner, Benoit became increasingly despondent, short-tempered, and paranoid. On June 25, 2007, two days after Benoit missed a major wrestling show in Houston, the bodies of Benoit, his wife, and their seven-year-old son were discovered in their sprawling Fayetteville home.

As investigators would determine, the double murder and suicide had taken place over a three-day period. Nancy had been killed first, bound and strangled with a coaxial cable on June 22. The following day, Benoit had sedated his son with Xanax before snapping his neck with the "Crippler Crossface." One day later, he contrived to hang himself on one of his weight-lifting machines.

The tragedy, which sent shockwaves through the world of professional wrestling, would be attributed to Benoit's severe depression over the loss of his friend, compounded by his drug use and (as an autopsy would later reveal) extensive brain damage caused by another of his signature moves, the "Diving Headbutt."

Chris Benoit applies the Crippler Crossface to an opponent.

HAWAI‘I

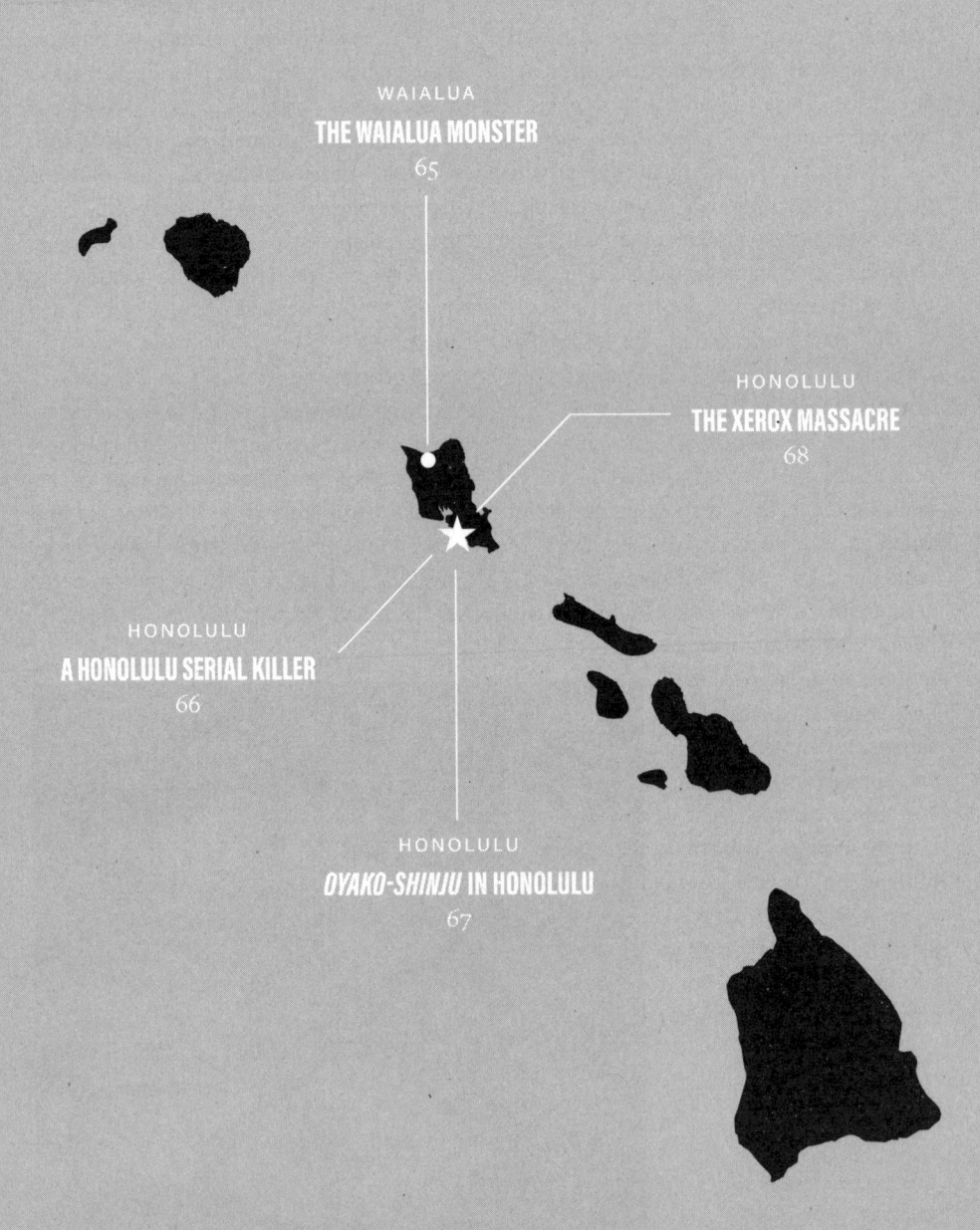

WAIALUA
THE WAIALUA MONSTER
65

HONOLULU
THE XEROX MASSACRE
68

HONOLULU
A HONOLULU SERIAL KILLER
66

HONOLULU
***OYAKO-SHINJU* IN HONOLULU**
67

Workers cutting sugarcane on an Oahu plantation.

THE WAIALUA MONSTER

Waialua, Hawai'i • January 3, 1906

In September 1905, Frank Johnson—"an undersized and altogether miserable specimen of humanity," as one newspaper described him—showed up at the home of an acquaintance, Henry Wharton, in the town of Waialua on the north shore of Oahu. Over the objections of Mrs. Wharton, an overworked housewife with four young children to care for and another on the way, the wizened little man was allowed to board at their house for $6.50 a month.

A native of Dublin, Ireland, Johnson—whose real name was John O'Connell—had settled in Hawai'i ten years earlier after deserting the merchant vessel on which he had arrived. He worked for a while as a coachman for a man named Kentwell in Honolulu before taking a job with another family, the Mossmans. It would later emerge that, during his latter employment, he had been accused of attempting to murder the Mossmans' prepubescent son with a scythe, though

HAWAI'I • 65

the charges were eventually dropped for unknown reasons.

On the morning of January 3, 1906, Mrs. Wharton was outside hanging the laundry when she spotted Johnson pushing her seven-year-old son, Simeon, on the swing that hung from a backyard mango tree. A short time later, after Mrs. Wharton had gone back inside, a Japanese girl named Yeta, who helped with the chores, saw the little man leading Simeon toward a cane field. When the boy failed to appear at lunchtime, everyone in the vicinity joined in a search.

It wasn't until 5:00 p.m. that a party of Japanese workmen from a nearby plantation made the shocking discovery: the little boy's hideously mutilated remains stuffed inside in a shallow, scooped-out grave in the cane field, the arms, legs, and head cut off, entrails torn out, eyes gouged from the sockets. Questioned by police, Johnson—wearing a ragged coat that he kept tightly pulled around his body—denied any knowledge of the murder.

When his questioners forced him to remove his outer garment, they found that his shirt was badly stained with blood. Dried blood was also caked under his fingernails and on the blade of the large jackknife he carried in his pocket. After two days of brutal interrogation, Johnson broke down and confessed, claiming that, after getting drunk on sake the previous night, he awoke on the morning of the murder "seized with the desire to kill." Leading the little boy into the cane field, he stabbed him to death, then "became frightened and started to dig a grave with his knife and hands."

Unable to "make it large enough owing to the gravel and rocks," he cut up the body, put the dismembered parts in the hole, and covered it with some brush. Asked about his motive, Johnson replied, "Something must have been the matter with me." Perpetrator of what newspapers called the "most revolting crime ever committed in these islands," Johnson was tried that spring. The jury needed just four minutes to convict him.

Though the presiding judge declared himself "unalterably opposed to the death penalty," he was duty bound to sentence the prisoner to hang. The "Waialua Monster," as he was branded in the press, went to the gallows on May 3, 1906.

A HONOLULU SERIAL KILLER

HONOLULU, HAWAIʻI
MARCH 1959–AUGUST 1995

Often referred to as Hawaiʻi's first known serial killer, Eugene Barrett murdered three women over a thirty-six-year period. In 1959, when his lover, Annie Phillips—a divorced mother of five young children—broke up with him, he shot her to death in the bedroom of her Honolulu apartment. Sentenced to fifty years in prison, he won parole after eight.

In 1971, four years after his release, Barrett married a woman named Roberta Ululani Averito, who filed for divorce a few months later. On December 27, 1972, he stabbed her to death with a kitchen knife in the courtyard of a Honolulu hotel. Pleading guilty to manslaughter, he was sentenced to ten years and was paroled after serving only three.

For the next two decades, he lived an uneventful life, working as a security guard and residing in an apartment complex. His neighbor across the hall was forty-one-year-old Roxanne Kastner, who—so he would claim—slept with him once, then rebuffed his further advances and began sexually taunting him by flaunting her affairs with other men. Increasingly obsessed with thoughts of harming her, he checked himself into a psychiatric hospital in August 1995.

On August 11, a few days after his release, he barged into Kastner's bedroom and shot her twice in the head with a semiautomatic pistol. Convicted of murder and three firearms violations, he was sent to prison for life, dying of natural causes in November 2003 at the age of seventy-two.

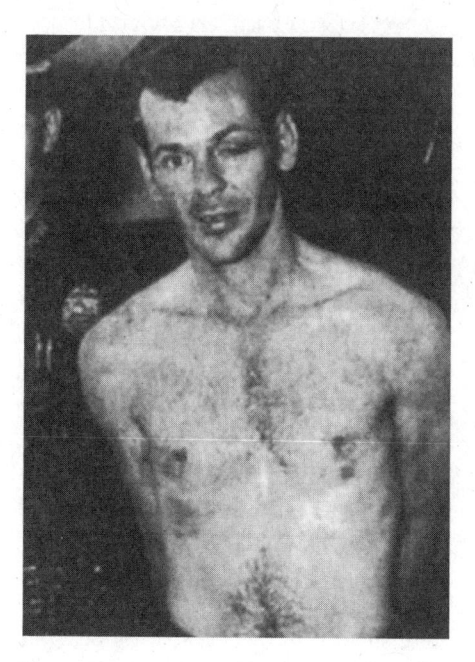

Eugene Barrett, Hawai'i's first known serial killer, under arrest

OYAKO-SHINJU IN HONOLULU

Honolulu, Hawai'i
August 18, 1988

In the United States, mothers who kill their children are typically viewed as "monster moms" (to use tabloid terminology). Things are different in Japan, where the custom of *oyako-shinju* persists as a cultural practice. In such cases, when a married woman suffers an unbearable shame—"loses face"—it is considered honorable for her to take her own life along with those of her young children, thus sparing them the hardships of a motherless upbringing. Because Japanese culture regards a child as part of the mother, the term *oyako-shinju* signifies parent-child suicide. In the West it is seen as something else: murder-suicide.

In the summer of 1988, a group of thirty Japanese tourists flew to Honolulu for a vacation at the Hilton Hawaiian Village. Travel arrangements for ten of them were made by forty-three-year-old Mariko Komiya, mother of three young sons. A few days into the trip, Komiya was informed that she had secured return tickets for only nine of the group. So mortified was she by this blunder that she felt driven to atone by an act of *oyako-shinju*.

Tying two pairs of pants into a makeshift backpack, she used it to strap her sleeping four-year-old son, Satoshi, onto her shoulders. She then woke up her other two sons, ten-year-old Hirouki and sixteen-year-old Naomichi, and led them onto the balcony of their seventh-story room. When she attempted to push the

The Hilton resort where Mariko Komiya committed ritual murder-suicide

older boy over the railing, he put up a struggle and fled back into the room. Hirouki, still half asleep, put up no resistance as he was lifted and thrown from the balcony but somehow managed to clutch onto the metal rails. With Satoshi on her back, Komiya then climbed over the railing, jumped, and plunged seventy feet onto the flagstone sidewalk, killing herself instantly. Her little boy died a short time later in the hospital.

Awakened by the commotion, a vacationer in the adjacent room, a California truck dispatcher named Don Garrison, ran out onto his balcony and saw the dangling ten-year-old. Climbing onto the Komiyas' balcony from his own, he reached over the railing and pulled the boy to safety. Later, police found a suicide note written on hotel stationery. "I cannot live in this world any longer," it read in part. "I caused many inconveniences; it is natural I'm doing this."

THE XEROX MASSACRE

HONOLULU, HAWAI'I
NOVEMBER 2, 1999

According to family members, Byran Koji Uyesugi—perpetrator of the worst mass shooting in Hawai'i history—was never the same after sustaining a severe concussion in a car crash on the night of his high school graduation. Possibly so; head injuries are not uncommon in the medical histories of mass and serial killers.

Still, it is clear that his affinity for firearms predated the accident. He was a member of his high school's rifle team and its army JROTC. By 1996, he had married, fathered a daughter, and assembled an arsenal of seventeen legally registered guns. His hobby was breeding rare goldfish and koi that he sold to local pet stores. His occupation was service technician for the Xerox company.

In the years leading up to his rampage, he had grown increasingly paranoid, accusing his co-workers of harassing him, tampering with his machines, and spreading rumors that caused him to be ostracized. He began making threats against other members of his team and was sent to an anger management course after flying into a fury and kicking in an elevator door at the company building.

A tipping point came when the type of photocopier he had always worked on was replaced by a new model whose technical complexities Uyesugi felt unequipped to handle. Fearing that he would be fired, he decided—as he later told a psychiatrist—"to give them a reason to fire me." Shortly after 8:00 a.m. on November 2, 1999, he entered the Xerox offices and gunned down his supervisor and six co-workers with a 9mm semiautomatic pistol. Fleeing in a company van, he parked in an upscale neighborhood and held the police at bay during a five-hour standoff until his brother talked him into surrendering.

His trial from May 15 to June 13, 2000, climaxed with his conviction. In a state without the death penalty, he was given a sentence commensurate with his crimes: 235 years without the possibility of parole.

Mass shooter Bryan Koji Uyesugi surrenders after an hours-long standoff. "He was contemplating suicide," said the crisis negotiator who talked him down.

HAWAI'I • 69

IDAHO

CALDWELL
AN EXPLOSIVE EPISODE IN CALDWELL
71

GARDEN CITY
IDAHO'S JACK THE RIPPER
74

BOISE

OWYHEE COUNTY
CLAUDE DALLAS: IDAHO OUTLAW
75

TWIN FALLS
FLYPAPER LYDA
72

Aftermath of the 1899 mineworkers revolt in Wardener, Idaho

AN EXPLOSIVE EPISODE IN CALDWELL

CALDWELL, IDAHO • DECEMBER 30, 1905

In the late 1800s, northern Idaho was the scene of bitter conflicts between powerful mining companies and unionized workers. A particularly dramatic episode occurred in April 1899 when nearly a thousand striking miners hijacked a train and rode it into the town of Wardner, where they dynamited machinery valued at the then-colossal sum of $250,000, burned down the company mill and office building, and shot a nonunion worker to death.

Although he had won election with support of organized labor and was regarded as a friend of the working class, Governor Frank Steunenberg declared martial law and appealed to President McKinley, who dispatched federal troops to the besieged town. Hundreds of miners were arrested and herded into stockaded warehouses—"bullpens," as they were called—where they languished for several months while the mines reopened with scabbing nonunion workers.

For his part in the suppression of the labor unrest, Steunenberg—branded a turncoat who had betrayed his one-time supporters—incurred the enmity of the powerful Western Federation of Miners. At about 4:00 p.m. on Saturday, December 30, 1905, the former Governor Steunenberg, five years out of office, set off from home by foot for the business district of Caldwell, the little country town where he resided with his wife and four children. He headed back at 6:00 p.m. after completing some errands.

Upon arriving at home, he passed through the wooden gate leading to his side door and turned to close it. In that instant, he was blown ten feet into the yard by a massive explosion. Mangled

IDAHO • 71

from the waist down, though still alive, he was carried inside the house, where he died an hour later. Suspicion immediately alighted on a stranger in town, a man who called himself Hogan. His real name was Harry Orchard and, as he ultimately confessed, he was a paid assassin who had previously carried out more than a dozen murders on behalf of the leadership of the Western Federation of Miners, allegedly among them labor organizer William "Big Bill" Haywood.

Tried, convicted, and sentenced to death, Orchard was eventually granted clemency and died in the Idaho State Penitentiary in 1954. Haywood was arrested and tried as a coconspirator. Defended by soon-to-be-legendary lawyer Clarence Darrow, he was ultimately acquitted.

Harry Orchard converted to Christianity soon after his arrest. In his later years, he wrote a book with the Seventh Day Adventist church, titled Harry Orchard: The Man God Made Again.

FLYPAPER LYDA

Twin Falls, Idaho
September 7, 1920

Being a pretty, blue-eyed redhead, Lyda Trueblood had no trouble attracting men. Over the course of her life, she had seven husbands, four of whom fell ill and died not long after the nuptials. Other people close to her perished in strikingly similar ways, including a brother-in-law and a two-year-old daughter. In every case, the deaths were initially attributed to natural causes: typhoid fever, diphtheria, acute gastroenteritis. Besides a strange propensity to drop dead shortly after she entered their lives, the five men had something else in common: Each, her brother-in-law included, had taken out life insurance policies naming Trueblood as a beneficiary.

It was not until the death of her fourth husband, Edward Meyer—a "sturdy ranch hand" who sickened and died a month after their wedding—that people began to notice a rather suspicious pattern. When the exhumed corpses of Meyer and his three predecessors were found to contain arsenic, a warrant was issued for Trueblood's arrest.

By then, however, she was already remarried and living in Honolulu with husband number five, a young navy petty officer stationed at Pearl Harbor. Waiving extradition, she was brought back to Twin Falls and tried for Meyer's murder. Unlike earlier "Black Widow" killers, who generally relied on easily obtainable rat poison to do away with their victims, Trueblood— as investigators were able to show—got her arsenic by extracting it from boiled flypaper, a method that earned her the tabloid nickname "Flypaper Lyda."

Convicted, she was sentenced to the state penitentiary in Boise for ten years to life. In May 1931, she engineered an escape with the assistance of a recently paroled ex-con who had become enamored of her. Making her way to Denver, she found work as a housekeeper for a well-off widower, who soon succumbed to her charms and became husband number six. With police hot on her trail, however, she absconded to Topeka, Kansas, where she was tracked down and arrested. She did another ten years in the Boise penitentiary before being paroled.

Relocating to Utah, she married her seventh husband, who vanished after two years under still-unknown circumstances. After Trueblood dropped dead of a heart attack on a Salt Lake City street on February 5, 1958, the mortician discovered that her body was completely hairless—"a symptom," as one biographer writes, "of long-term exposure to arsenic."

Serial poisoner "Flypaper Lyda" Trueblood got her nickname from her unique method of obtaining arsenic.

IDAHO'S JACK THE RIPPER

GARDEN CITY, IDAHO
SEPTEMBER 22, 1956

Forty-eight-year-old divorcée Cora Lucyle Dean of Boise typically spent her Saturday nights in the clubs of nearby Garden City, drinking, playing the slots, and looking for male companionship. She was in a spot called the HiHo Club on Saturday night, September 22, 1956, when she was approached by a slight, dark-haired man who chatted her up, asked her to dance, then left with her.

Early the next morning, a twelve-year-old boy in search of discarded beer bottles he could turn in for the deposit money was riding his bicycle through the neighborhood when he spotted a woman's bloody corpse sprawled on the sidewalk. The autopsy on Dean revealed that her voice box had been cut to keep her from making any noise. She had also been stabbed in the face and all over her body a total of twenty-nine times. Her right nipple was missing, and her vulva mutilated.

The cause of death was determined to be a stab wound to the back of her neck that severed her spinal cord. It was the latter detail that caught the attention of a Garden City detective who recalled that, a few years earlier, a woman reported that her common-law husband had menaced her with a knife, threatening to cut her spinal cord. His name was Raymond Snowden. A drifter with a lengthy police record extending back to his adolescence, Snowden had a history of violence against women.

In 1948, according to his subsequent confession, Snowden picked up a woman in a

Cora Lucyle Dean, victim of the Idaho Ripper

Texas café, led her to some nearby railroad tracks and stabbed her in the stomach, then left town before he could be identified. He was also a suspect in a sensational 1941 murder of a nineteen-year-old bookkeeper in Lynn, Massachusetts, who, as newspapers reported, "was attacked with maniacal violence."

Tracked to his fleabag hotel, Snowden was taken in for questioning on Monday, September 24, and, after a day of grilling, confessed to Cora Dean's murder. According to his story, they got into an argument after leaving the club. When she kneed him in the groin, he "blew his top," pulled out his pocketknife and cut her throat, and finished her off by shoving the two-inch blade into the base of her skull and severing her spinal cord. Then he went at her body in a frenzy of bloodlust.

He pleaded guilty to first-degree murder and was hanged in the Idaho State Penitentiary, slowly strangling to death when his neck failed to snap. Because of the sheer sadistic atrocity of his crime, he would go down in history as "Idaho's Jack the Ripper."

CLAUDE DALLAS:
IDAHO OUTLAW

OWYHEE COUNTY, IDAHO
JANUARY 5, 1981

In a nation with a long history of romanticizing frontier badmen, it's no surprise that some Idahoans view Claude Dallas as a folk hero, a throwback to the days of legendary outlaws such as Jesse James and Billy the Kid. To others, Dallas was nothing more than a psychopathic killer.

Obsessed from his earliest years with tales of the Old West, after high school Dallas made his way to Oregon after high school, where he worked part of the year as a cowboy and spent the winter months as a fur trapper. In December 1980, he set up camp in a remote area of Idaho and, ignoring state regulations, trapped bobcats and hunted deer out of season. The following month, having gotten wind of Dallas's illegal activities, two conservation officers from the Idaho Department of Fish and Game, William Pogue and Wilson Conley Elms, paid a visit to his camp, where they found a pair of bobcat pelts in his tent along with several hundred pounds of venison from poached deer.

Threatened with arrest, Dallas drew his .357 Magnum revolver and gunned down both game wardens, then bolted into his tent, emerging with a .22 rifle that he used to finish each of them off, execution style, with a bullet to the head. After disposing of the bodies—Elms's in a river, Pogue's in a coyote den—Dallas went on the run, eluding the law for fifteen months before FBI agents tracked him to Winnemucca, Nevada, where he was holed up in a friend's trailer.

Heavily armed officers converged on the trailer; Dallas made a desperate getaway attempt before being captured in a shootout that left him wounded in one leg. Tried, convicted of manslaughter, and sentenced to thirty years behind bars, he escaped three years later, adding to his legend as the "last outlaw" (or so crooned Canadian balladeer Ian Tyson). He remained on the loose for a year before being recaptured in Riverside, California. He then spent twenty-two years in prison before his early release for good behavior in February 2005.

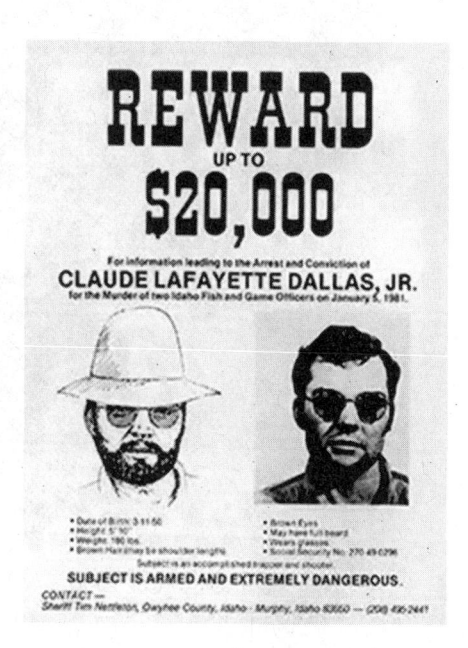

Mythologized as the last of the Western outlaws, Claude Dallas was, in the eyes of the law, nothing more than a cold-blooded killer.

ILLINOIS

CHICAGO
A CHI-TOWN LOVE QUADRANGLE
78

WAYNE
THE LAST TRAIN TO WAYNE
77

CHICAGO
CHICAGO'S MOST BEAUTIFUL MURDERESS
79

CHICAGO
A PEDOPHILE STRIKES IN CHICAGO
80

UTICA
CARNAGE IN A CAVE
81

SPRINGFIELD ★

URBANA-CHAMPAIGN
A LAST RIDE IN URBANA-CHAMPAIGN
82

THE LAST TRAIN TO WAYNE

Wayne, Illinois
September 26, 1913

A thirty-seven-year-old with a checkered past that included two ex-husbands and several suicide attempts, Mildred Rexroat was earning her living as a tango instructor in a Chicago dance hall in September 1913 when she met the man who called himself Henry Spencer. A classic sociopath who had gone by a half dozen aliases over the course of his long criminal career, his real name was Paul Skarupa. Orphaned at an early age when his father died by suicide, he was sent to a home for incorrigible boys by his adoptive parents and was in and out of prison for the next seventeen years for various felonies, including larceny, burglary, embezzlement, and parole violation.

Not long before he entered Rexroat's life, he had assaulted his landlady with a hammer. According to some accounts, Rexroat—ten years his senior—took him into her bed with the full expectation of marriage. What is certain is that, on the evening of September 26, wearing an expensive diamond ring and carrying a suitcase full of clothing and a handbag containing her $200 savings, she left with him for Wayne, Illinois, where, so he said, he had arranged for her to open her own dance school.

When they disembarked, he led her along the tracks a short distance from the depot, shot her in the head, collected her valuables, then laid her body on the tracks, where an approaching train ran over it, cutting it in two just above the hips. Arrested in Chicago nine

Tango teacher Mildred Rexroat and her murderer, Henry Spencer

days later, Spencer shocked the world with a detailed confession of "wholesale murder," professing to have killed as many as twenty-nine people, including two policemen. Though the bulk of these claims was pure fabrication—the kind of braggadocio not uncommon in psycho-killers—evidence linked him to four of the homicides.

Tried and convicted for Rexroat's murder, Spencer went to the gallows in July 1914 dressed in white shoes, white trousers, and a white silk shirt with a red carnation pinned to his breast. Having undergone a jailhouse conversion, he recited memorized psalms for ten minutes with the noose around his neck and expressed his belief that, for the first time in his orphaned life, he had a father waiting to receive him in heaven.

Among his final words: "This is the happiest day of my life."

A CHI-TOWN LOVE QUADRANGLE

Chicago, Illinois
March 13, 1923

According to the story they initially told police, Mrs. Annabelle McGinnis and her sister, Miss Myna Ploch, had been summoned by phone to their mother's home by Annabelle's husband, thirty-six-year-old Chicago fireman Michael McGinnis. When they arrived, Michael, who was armed with a handgun, accused his wife of infidelity. A bitter quarrel ensued that "led to a scuffle." Somehow, Ploch got hold of the gun and shot Michael in the head as he was attacking her sister. He died the next day.

Within two weeks, a very different and far more titillating story emerged. Both women, it turned out, were having affairs with Francis Nee and Charles Schade, two nineteen-year-olds whom the papers called "sheiks," the Jazz Age slang for slick, sexually available young men. When Annabelle told her teenaged lover that she "was tired of living with her husband," the four hatched a "love plot."

On the night Annabelle's husband was killed, Ploch and Schade showed up at the McGinnis home. Both women were carrying guns—Annabelle a revolver her husband had bought her for protection, Ploch a pistol borrowed from Schade. Sometime after Michael returned home from work, both his wife and sister-in-law opened fire on him, with one of Myna's shots hitting him in the back of the head.

At their sensational trial that summer—covered with lip-smacking gusto by the tabloids—the defense argued that Michael had come home drunk and been killed in self-defense when he had gotten into an altercation with Ploch and started choking her. The state argued that Annabelle's conjugal relations with her older, overworked husband had grown stale and that she contrived to get rid of him so she could freely pursue her sexual escapades.

Supposed proof of Annabelle's immorality was her hairstyle, the type of blonde bob regarded by the older generation as the hallmark of the cigarette-smoking, Charleston-dancing, loose-living "flapper." "Show these bobbed-hair women they can't kill their husbands and get away with it," the defense lawyer admonished the jury during his summation. The jury was not persuaded, acquitting both women.

Annabelle McGinnis (left) and Myna Ploch (right), members of the Jazz Age "Love Quadrangle"

78 • 50 STATES OF MURDER

Beulah Anna thanks the jury after her acquittal.

CHICAGO'S MOST BEAUTIFUL MURDERESS

CHICAGO, ILLINOIS • APRIL 3, 1924

Garage mechanic Albert Annan was at work on the afternoon of April 3, 1924, when he received a call from his much younger wife, Beulah May. "I've shot a man, Albert," she said. "He tried to make love to me." Rushing home in a cab, Albert found Beulah pacing the living room floor. Hunched against a wall in the bedroom was a young man in shirtsleeves, bleeding from a bullet hole in his back.

When the police arrived, Beulah fed them the same story her husband initially swallowed. The victim was a young man named Harry Kalstedt, a co-worker of Beulah's at the laundry where she had a part-time bookkeeping job. That afternoon he had shown up at her apartment, invited himself inside, and "made himself at home. Although I scarcely knew him," Beulah said through her tears, "he tried to make me love him. I told him I would shoot. He kept coming anyway and I—I did shoot him."

After a night of intense grilling by law officers, however, she broke down and poured out the truth. Beulah had been "fooling around" with the handsome Kalstedt for the past two months, while her husband slaved away at the garage. The previous morning, as Beulah told her interrogators, Harry had come over and announced that "he was through with me. . . . When I saw he meant what he said, my mind went into a whirl and I shot him."

The ravishing, redheaded Beulah became a tabloid sensation: "Chicago's

ILLINOIS • 79

Most Beautiful Murderess," as the newspapers branded her. At her May 1924 trial, her attorney, W. W. O'Brien—a flamboyant courtroom performer who spent twelve years as a theatrical promoter before taking up the law—portrayed his client as "a frail, little virtuous working girl" who had killed Kalstedt in self-defense when he showed up drunk at her apartment and made indecent advances.

It took the jury less than two hours to vote for acquittal. Thirty-six hours later, Beulah announced that she was divorcing her husband. "He doesn't want me to have a good time," she said. "He never wants to go out anywhere and he doesn't know how to dance. I'm not going to waste the rest of my life with him. . . . I want lights, music, and good times!"

Certain that she could parlay her notoriety and her looks into a career as a motion-picture actress, she was thinking of moving to Hollywood. Her starry-eyed dreams never materialized. Just four years later, in March 1928, she died of tuberculosis at the age of thirty-two. Though she never made it to Hollywood, she became a big-screen immortal, serving as the model for the character Roxie Hart in the hit show *Chicago*, which was twice turned into a movie.

A PEDOPHILE STRIKES IN CHICAGO

Chicago, Illinois
October 16, 1955

When a salesman on his lunch break spotted three strange figures sprawled in a ditch near the entrance to a Cook County forest preserve, he first took them for discarded department store mannequins. Upon closer inspection, they turned out to be the naked bodies of three young boys—brothers John and Anton Schuessler, thirteen and eleven, and their fourteen-year-old friend Robert Peterson—who had gone off to a movie two days earlier and never returned home.

The youngest Schuessler boy had been choked to death, his older brother killed with a "judo-type blow to the neck."

Peterson had been strangled and bore injuries—a fractured rib and eleven slashes to the head inflicted with a pitchfork or rake—that showed he had put up a ferocious struggle with the killer. The shocking triple murder, considered "one of [Chicago's] most heinous crimes," became a nationwide media sensation, generating headlines across the country and a two-page spread in *Life* magazine.

From left: Robert Peterson, John Schuessler, Anton Schuessler, victims of Kenneth Hansen

80 • 50 STATES OF MURDER

CARNAGE IN A CAVE

Utica, Illinois
March 14, 1960

On March 14, 1960, three middle-aged suburban women, all wives of Chicago business executives, drove to scenic Starved Rock State Park in downstate Utica, Illinois, for a four-day vacation. After checking in and lunching at the lodge, they went for a hike in a remote, picturesque canyon. Two days later, their bodies were found in a blood-spattered cave, their wrists and ankles bound with twine, their heads beaten in with a frozen tree limb that lay nearby. Two were naked from the waist down.

The savage crime generated nationwide media coverage, including a six-page spread in *Life* magazine. Investigators eventually focused their attention on twenty-three-year-old Chester Weger, a dishwasher at the lodge and a suspect in the recent assault of a teenaged girl who

Kenneth Hansen in custody, thirty-six years after committing his outrage

A massive year-long investigation involving 3,000 law officers, 43,000 interviews, and the interrogations of 3,270 suspects led nowhere. Thirty-six years passed before police, who were investigating the officially unsolved 1977 disappearance of candy heiress Helen Brach, got a tip that led them to the perpetrator of the 1955 triple murder. A onetime worker at a stable not far from where the bodies were found, Kenneth Hansen was a habitual pedophile who, as he confided to one acquaintance, dreamed of having "sex with two boys at the same time."

Picking up the trio as they hitchhiked home from their outing, he drove them to his employer's barn, sent the older one off to brush a horse, and proceeded to assault the two Schuessler boys. When Peterson returned and saw what was happening, Hansen grabbed him by the throat and choked him to death, then—as he told his friend—he "had no other choice but to kill the other two kids." Sentenced to two hundred to three hundred years in prison, he died of natural causes in 2007.

Chester Weger after being apprehended

had been bound and raped in another nearby state park. After a grueling interrogation, Weger broke down and confessed, providing a detailed account of the crime, which began as a botched robbery and climaxed in the horrific triple murder.

Though Weger would promptly recant his confession, calling it coerced, he was tried, convicted, and sentenced to life. Over the course of his nearly sixty years in prison—the second-longest stretch in Illinois history—he would continue to proclaim his innocence. Granted parole in November 2019 after twenty-three requests and denials, the eighty-three-year-old ex-con saw hope for vindication when DNA testing proved that a strand of male hair taken from the glove of one of the victims was not his.

A LAST RIDE IN URBANA-CHAMPAIGN

Urbana-Champaign, Illinois
JUNE 9, 2017

An academic superstar in her native China, where she graduated from college at the top of her class and went on to earn a master's in environmental engineering, twenty-six-year-old Yingying Zhang traveled to the United States in April 2017 to conduct research in crop fertility at the University of Illinois Urbana-Champaign. Two months later she was on her way to lease an off-campus apartment when she disappeared. Surveillance video footage showed her missing a bus connection before accepting a ride from someone driving a black Saturn Astra.

As word of Zhang's disappearance spread throughout the community, a student named Emily Hogan came forward to report that, on the morning of June 9, she had been approached by a man driving a black sedan who identified himself as an undercover cop and offered her a ride that she turned down—information that supported the growing suspicion that Zhang had been kidnapped.

Though the surveillance camera failed to capture the plate number of the Saturn, investigators determined that there were only eighteen cars of that make registered in the county and tracked the vehicle to twenty-nine-year-old Brendt Christensen, a graduate student in physics with a job as a teaching assistant. Shown a photo of Christensen, Emily Hogan immediately identified him as the man who had tried picking her up.

Questioned by police, Christensen initially claimed that he couldn't remember where he'd been when Zhang vanished—possibly at home in bed or playing a video game—before recalling that he had in fact given a ride to an Asian girl but had driven her only a few blocks when she insisted on leaving the car.

Though married, Christensen had a girlfriend he had met on a dating website who shared his interest in a BDSM relationship. Approached by FBI investigators, she agreed to wear a wire and secretly recorded Christensen admitting to the murder, explaining that he had taken Zhang back to his apartment, raped her, choked her, "broke her head open" with a baseball bat, and decapitated her with a knife. He also bragged that he was a serial killer and that Zhang was his

The black Saturn Astra that Yingying Zhang was seen entering on the day she disappeared.

thirteenth victim (a claim never verified and later dismissed by authorities).

In addition to his taped confession, investigators gathered other evidence, including the baseball bat with Zhang's DNA on it and internet data showing that, in the weeks before the murder, Christensen had visited a fetish website that linked to a forum called Abduction 101.

Arrested on his birthday, June 30, 2017, he was tried two years later, convicted after jury deliberations that lasted about ninety minutes, and sentenced to life without the possibility of parole. Zhang's body was never found. According to reports, it had ended up in a massive landfill after Christensen dismembered it in the bathtub and disposed of it in the dumpster behind his apartment complex.

Surveillance photo of Yingying Zhang

INDIANA

HARTFORD CITY
PRIINCIPAL REDDEN GOES ON A RAMPAGE
87

HAMMOND
A KLANSMEN KILLER
85

INDIANAPOLIS ★

YORKTOWN
A BUTCHER DIES IN YORKTOWN
86

A KLANSMEN KILLER

HAMMOND, INDIANA • MARCH 16, 1925

Disbanded after Reconstruction, the Ku Klux Klan (KKK) came roaring back to life in the wake of D. W. Griffith's 1915 cinematic epic, The Birth of a Nation, which glorified the hooded, white-robed vigilantes as heroic defenders of Southern honor against what Griffith portrayed as the depredations of corrupt Northern carpetbaggers and bestial newly freed slaves. By 1925, the Klan had more than three million members nationwide—typically, as one historian writes, "middle-class white American men and their families." A shocking scandal involving its most prominent figure, however, would soon lead to the rapid collapse of the organization's popularity.

As Grand Dragon of the Indiana Klan—the largest state branch of the KKK with an estimated quarter million members—D. C. Stephenson wielded enormous influence, hobnobbing with congressmen, governors, judges, and US senators and harboring his own ambitions for political office. He was also a man of unbridled, brutish appetites, particularly when drunk, with a sordid history of attempted rapes and sexual assaults.

In January 1925, Stephenson met and became fixated on Madge Oberholtzer, a demure twenty-nine-year-old state education program worker who still lived at home with her parents. On the night of March 15, she received an urgent call from Stephenson, asking her to come to his house. She arrived to find him drunk. He was going to Chicago, he said, and insisted that she accompany him. When she refused, his bodyguards showed her their guns. Forced into a car, she was driven to Union Station, dragged onto a Chicago-bound train, and shoved into a private compartment, where Stephenson subjected her to a sexual attack of such ferocity that she was left with bite wounds all over her face, neck, breasts, back, and legs.

The next morning, during a stopover at Hammond, Indiana, Oberholtzer—overwhelmed by shame and an unbearable sense of violation—bought a box of mercury bichloride tablets and swallowed a lethal dose. Before her agonizing death, she made a harrowing last statement, describing the outrages Stephenson had inflicted on her. Charged with rape, kidnapping, and second-degree murder, Stephenson was convicted and sentenced to life imprisonment.

Madge Oberholtzer's murder so outraged members of the Indiana Ku Klux Klan that membership dropped by tens of thousands following the news of the attack.

At a time when the Klan promoted itself as a bulwark against the breakdown of traditional morality and a fierce defender of what a later age would call "family values," his crime led to a widespread repudiation of the KKK among its ostensibly God-fearing, middle-class members. By 1927, membership had plummeted from several million to roughly 350,000. It would sink even lower in succeeding years. Never again would the Klan enjoy the degree of acceptance that it had achieved during its brief rebirth in the 1920s.

A BUTCHER DIES IN YORKTOWN

YORKTOWN, INDIANA
FEBRUARY 26, 1934

James Marvin Gleason (left) and his father, Lloyd (right)

The earliest newspaper stories about the death of Lloyd C. Gleason—a forty-year-old butcher whose body was found in the basement of his meat market, a .22-caliber revolver by his side—reported that he had killed himself. The cause of death was revised from suicide to homicide after an autopsy revealed two bullet wounds to his head, a savage blow to the back of his skull, and burn marks on one leg.

Within twenty-four hours, the gun had been traced to the presumed killer: Gleason's twenty-one-year-old son, Marvin, a bright but deeply troubled loner who blamed his problems on his alcoholic, womanizing father. His proclamations of innocence ended when investigators found his blood-stained clothing at home. According to his confession, he was working in the store when his father left briefly after lunch and returned with a bottle of whiskey.

Fed up with his old man's drinking, Marvin—who was carrying his gun in his belt—tried to wrestle the bottle away from him. In the ensuing scuffle, the young man "got excited" and shot his father twice in the head. He then dragged the body to the basement and tried to cremate it in the furnace but was able to get only one leg inside before he gave up, wiped his prints off the gun, and placed it near the corpse to make the death look like a suicide. Shortly after signing his confession, Marvin amended his statement, claiming that he had acted in concert with his mother, Dora, who was not only aware of his plan to shoot and incinerate his father but heartily approved.

Arrested as an accomplice, Dora was ultimately cleared, married a chiropractor, and lived a contented, affluent life. Her son, judged "mentally incapable of standing trial," spent the next six years in an institution for the criminally insane before being released back into the world.

PRINCIPAL REDDEN GOES ON A RAMPAGE

Hartford City, Indiana
February 2, 1960

School shootings by mentally unbalanced young men, often current or former students, have become an all-too-common occurrence in the United States. What made the infamous Indiana classroom slayings of 1960 so shocking was not just the appalling nature of the crime but the person who carried it out: the school principal, Leonard Redden.

To the outside world, forty-four-year-old Redden was a pillar of the community, a loving husband and father who owned a nice house, attended church every Sunday, and was devoted to his job as an elementary school principal. His wife, Hazel, however, saw a darker side to him. During World War II, he had seen heavy action in the South Pacific and returned home with a Purple Heart, shrapnel in his legs, and deep psychological scars. Though others would describe him as a "mild-mannered, very nice" man who "never had a nasty word for anyone," Hazel would later tell reporters that, ever since his return from the army, he felt "bitterness toward people in general."

It wasn't until the spring of 1959, however, that he began displaying symptoms of serious psychological disorder. He was concerned, he told Hazel, that people were gossiping about them, saying that their marriage was in trouble and that he was "romantically interested" in another woman—Harriet Robson, a fifth-grade teacher referred to in the press as a "fifty-two-year-old spinster." Though Hazel assured him that he was imagining things, his obsession continued to grow.

By Christmastime, he was in the grip of full-blown paranoia, ranting about taking revenge on the people responsible for his troubles, including Robson, who, he deludedly believed, was planning to sue him for character defamation. In a rare moment of lucidity, he recognized that he was losing touch with reality and desperately pleaded for help from his wife, parents, and the school superintendent, who made arrangements for him to see a psychiatrist. The appointment was scheduled for 2:30 p.m. on Tuesday, February 2.

That morning, Redden, who enjoyed hunting, drove to work with his 12-gauge shotgun. At about 10:30 a.m., he barged into Robson's classroom and, in full view of the students, aimed the gun at her chest and pulled the trigger. He then strode to the second-floor classroom of sixty-two-year-old Minnie McFerren—whom he blamed for starting the rumors of his infidelity—and killed her with a blast to her head before making his getaway. A massive manhunt climaxed with the discovery of his body in an isolated wooded tract, a self-inflicted gunshot wound to his chest.

As for his motives, his wife could offer only one explanation: "He was plain off his head."

IOWA

CEDAR FALLS
THE CAIN AND ABEL MURDERS
93

ESTHERVILLE
CORNFIELD KILLER
92

CLAYTON COUNTY
A BOY MURDERER IN CLAYTON COUNTY
89

VILLISCA
THE UNSOLVED AXE MURDERS OF VILLISCA
90

★ DES MOINES

A BOY MURDERER IN CLAYTON COUNTY

Clayton County, Iowa • July 16, 1889

On the morning of July 17, 1889, eleven-year-old Wesley Elkins, his shirt spattered with blood, showed up at the farm of a neighbor and calmly reported that his father, John, a forty-three-year-old sawmill operator, and his stepmother, Hattie, age twenty-three, had been killed by an intruder sometime during the night. Authorities summoned to the Elkinses' little house found what one reporter described as "a scene that tried the nerves of the strongest."

The couple lay sprawled on their bed in a room "splashed with [their] blood and brains." John had been killed with a rifle shot through the left eye socket; the exiting bullet blew off the top of his skull. His wife had been pounded to death, her face and head reduced "to jelly." The murder weapons—a single-barrel rifle that turned out to be John's and a heavy wooden club used as a threshing tool—were quickly discovered on the property. Nothing had been stolen from the house, and there were no other signs of a break-in.

According to his initial testimony, Wesley had gone to sleep in the barn after supper because it was cooler there than in the cramped house. He was awakened in the middle of the night by a gunshot and a woman's scream. After waiting a while because he was scared, he went to investigate and, by the moonlight filtering through the window, discovered the awful sight.

The sheer enormity of the murders—the "most brutal and atrocious ever committed in Iowa," according to one group of outraged citizens—created a statewide uproar. The case became an even greater sensation when, less than two weeks after the killings, the slight, well-spoken boy admitted to the horrific crime. With no

IOWA • 89

trace of emotion, he explained how he had taken his father's rifle, loaded it, then snuck into the bedroom where his parents lay sleeping and, placing the muzzle "about two feet off Father's face," pulled the trigger. He then seized the club that he had carried in from the barn and struck his stepmother on the head "until I was sure she was dead."

Though Wesley had suffered years of terrible neglect and abuse at the hands of his various caregivers, he was widely viewed as an innately evil creature beyond the hope of redemption—a "juvenile monster," a "young fiend," as the press branded him. At the advice of his lawyer, the eleven-year-old pleaded guilty to his father's murder and was sentenced to life of hard labor at the state penitentiary.

Thanks to sympathetic prison officials and other influential figures who understood his potential for rehabilitation—as well as to his own remarkable success at self-education—he won parole in 1902 and went on to live an upstanding, productive life, dying in 1961 at the age of eighty-one.

John Wesley Elkins was thought to be the youngest person to be sent to prison at the time of his sentencing.

THE UNSOLVED AXE MURDERS OF VILLISCA

VILLISCA, IOWA
JUNE 10, 1912

A respected businessman in the small Iowa town of Villisca, Josiah Moore was a happily married father of four children—three boys and a ten-year-old daughter, Katherine. On Sunday evening, June 9, the entire family attended a service at the Presbyterian church, along with two of Katherine's friends, Lena and Ina Stillinger, who had been invited to spend the night. The following morning, all eight were discovered in their beds, the victims of the most notorious mass murder in Iowa history.

Sometime after midnight, an unknown intruder, wielding an axe he had taken from the backyard, had bludgeoned their heads to unrecognizable pulp. Before leaving, he had performed the ritual of hanging cloths over all the mirrors in the house. He had also taken a slab of bacon from the icebox and placed it, along with the murder weapon, against a wall of the parlor bedroom where the Stillinger girls had slept. Investigators speculated that the killer used some of the bacon grease as a lubricant while masturbating over the little girls' corpses.

The identity of the killer would remain a mystery. Suspects included Frank Fernando Jones, Joe's former employee and subsequent competitor in the hardware business; Sam Moyer, husband of Joe's younger sister, who was said to bear a bitter grudge against his brother-in-law; another brother-in-law,

90 • 50 STATES OF MURDER

The Moore family home, site of the Villisca Axe Murders. Today, it is a tourist attraction for paranormal enthusiasts.

Roy Van Gilder, rumored to have "harbored hard feelings" against Joe; and a creepy itinerant minister, Rev. Lyn George Jacklin Kelly, a known sexual deviant who, after confessing to the murders, recanted at his trial and was ultimately acquitted.

There was also talk that the Villisca Axe Murders were perpetrated by a roving serial murderer—a "transient butcher" in the lingo of the time. Recent research has pointed to a psychopathic sex-killer, Paul Mueller, allegedly responsible for a string of similar atrocities around the country.

Josiah Moore and his wife, Sarah, two of the eight victims slaughtered in the massacre

IOWA • 91

CORNFIELD KILLER

ESTHERVILLE, IOWA • MARCH 16, 1933

In 1933, at the height of the Great Depression, more than fifteen million Americans—fully one quarter of the US workforce—were unemployed. Among them was thirty-three-year-old Joe Berven of Estherville, Iowa. Married and the father of three young children ranging in age from one to five years old, Berven and his family lived in a tenant house on the farm of his father-in-law, Olin Anderson. Increasingly moody after two years of joblessness, Berven kept himself busy by helping out with various chores.

At noon on Thursday, March 16, 1933, having worked up an appetite shelling corn all morning, he hauled the cobs into the barn and entered his house, expecting to find his lunch awaiting him. When he saw that his wife, twenty-five-year-old Edna, was just setting the table, he flew into a rage, grabbed his shotgun, and battered her to death with the barrel and butt. He then went after the children, inflicting fatal head injuries on all three. Still seething with fury, he marched over to his in-laws' house and announced that he had just killed his wife and children.

After a disbelieving Anderson hurried to the nearby home and found the four victims crumpled on the blood-splattered kitchen floor, the police were summoned, and Berven was arrested and locked in the county jail. The next morning, he was interrogated by police and the county attorney. To virtually every question put to him—"Do you realize you're in jail for the most serious crime a man can commit?" "Why did you kill your family?"

Edna Berven, slain by her husband

"When did you first realize what you had done?"—he gave the same answer: "I don't know."

Taken to the psychopathic hospital at Iowa City for examination, Berven claimed that, if in fact he had killed his wife, it was done "at the order of higher powers," that she was not really dead and would "rise again" and that "God [would] intervene on his behalf if they tried to hang him."

At his trial later that April, psychiatrists testified that he had paranoia and "*dementia praecox*," an obsolete term for schizophrenia. Judged to be insane, he was consigned to the mental ward at the Anamosa State Penitentiary, where he remained until his death in 1974, earning a place in Iowa criminal history as the perpetrator of one of the state's most notorious familicides.

THE CAIN AND ABEL MURDERS

CEDAR FALLS, IOWA • NOVEMBER 1, 1975

Iowa's infamous "Cain and Abel Murders"—one of the most shocking mass killings in the history of the state—first came to light on the morning of November 1, 1975, when farmer Clark Renner, concerned that something was amiss at the home of his neighbor Leslie Mark, alerted the latter's parents. Going to investigate, Leslie's mother, Dorothy, entered the house and made a horrifying discovery: the bullet-riddled bodies of her son, Leslie; his wife, Jorjean (both twenty-five); and their two children, five-year-old Julie and eighteen-month-old Jeff.

An autopsy revealed that Leslie and Jorjean were executed with bullets to the back of the head while kneeling on the floor in front of their bed. The little ones were shot in the head as they lay in their beds. Almost as shocking as the murders themselves was the person accused and convicted of the crime: Leslie's older brother, Jerry.

Jerry Mark at his appeal hearing

Following a stint in the Peace Corps in Brazil, Jerry, a legal aid lawyer, moved to the countercultural hotbed of Berkeley, California, where he embraced what his staid Midwestern parents derided as a "hippie lifestyle," living with his girlfriend, Mimi, and dabbling in radical left-wing politics. Leslie, meanwhile, dutifully stayed home to help work the family's 1,200-acre farm of corn and soybeans.

When it became clear that Leslie was slated to take over the family business and inherit his parents' seventeen-room farmhouse, Jerry seethed with resentment, telling a friend that "My little brother screwed me out of my farm." Inflamed—so prosecutors would argue—with "a combination of revenge, jealousy, rage, and greed," Jerry embarked on his murderous mission, setting out from Berkeley with a .38-caliber and a box of fifty Winchester Long Colt bullets.

Arriving on Halloween night, he entered the farmhouse and committed his fratricidal massacre sometime between 1:00 a.m. and 3:00 a.m. After throwing a potted plant through a window and ransacking several desk drawers to make it seem as if the family had died at the hands of a burglar, Jerry fled, leaving behind a number of the distinctive bullets—a key piece of incriminating evidence at his 1976 trial. Found guilty of the four murders, he was given a mandatory life sentence.

KANSAS

WOLCOTT
A HUSKY HORROR
96

JOHNSON COUNTY
A KID KILLER IN JOHNSON COUNTY
95

TOPEKA

OLATHE
A BOMBING IN OLATHE
99

WICHITA
THE WICHITA HOTEL SNIPER
98

A KID KILLER IN JOHNSON COUNTY

Johnson County, Kansas
September 28, 1953

The wayward son of wealth who squandered his inherited fortune on the stereotypical vices—fancy cars and clothing, high-stakes gambling, whiskey, and women—Carl Austin Hall was reduced to robbing cab drivers at gunpoint to support his addictions to alcohol and drugs. During a stint in the Missouri State Penitentiary, he hatched a scheme to get rich quick by kidnapping the son of millionaire auto dealer Robert Cosgrove Greenlease of Kansas City, Missouri.

Out on parole, Hall hooked up with Bonnie Emily Heady, a forty-one-year-old alcoholic, drug user, and sex worker who, like Hall, had grown up in a prosperous family before descending into a life of degradation. Putting Hall's plan into motion on the morning of September 28, 1953, Heady showed up at the school of their target—six-year-old Bobby Greenlease Jr.—and, posing as his aunt, took him by cab to a rendezvous point, where he was transferred into Hall's waiting car driven to a remote spot across the state line in Johnson County, Kansas, and killed with a bullet to the head. His body was then wrapped in a plastic sheet and buried in Heady's backyard.

Assuring the little boy's stricken parents that their son was still alive, Hall demanded and collected a ransom of $600,000, the largest such payment in American history up to that point.

It took a jury only 68 minutes of deliberations to recommend the death penalty for the murderers.

Absconding to St. Louis, the pair holed up in a seedy apartment where a drunken Heady immediately fell asleep. After slipping $2,000 into her purse, Hall made off with the rest of the money in two metal suitcases. His erratic behavior over the next twenty-four hours led to his arrest and conviction for what the presiding judge deemed the "most cold-blooded, brutal murder" he had ever tried. Hall and Heady went to the gas chamber together on December 18, 1953. Heady became only the third woman executed by the federal government, after Lincoln assassination conspirator Mary Surratt in 1865 and convicted spy Ethel Rosenberg in June 1953.

KANSAS • 95

A HUSKY HORROR

Wolcott, Kansas • November 28, 1958

Euphemistically described in the newspapers as "husky," Lowell Lee Andrews was an enormous eighteen-year-old, standing six feet two inches tall and weighing nearly three hundred pounds. With a soft, flaccid face framed by horn-rimmed glasses, he was, to all outward appearances, a stereotypical nerd: a studious schoolboy at the University of Kansas who played bassoon in the college band, never had a girlfriend, and was regarded by his neighbors as the "nicest boy" in town.

In his daydreams, however, the bookish zoology major imagined himself as a machine-gun-wielding gangster who led a playboy life complete with spiffy clothes and a snazzy sports car. Because he lacked the cash to realize this goal, he decided to murder his father, mother, and older sister and inherit the family estate, consisting of a 250-acre farm valued at $200,000 plus an $1,800 savings account.

Andrews's initial plan was to buy some arsenic and poison them, though he quickly abandoned the idea, fearing that the purchase might be traced. On the evening of November 28, while home for the

Lowell Lee Andrews with police near the Kansas River, where he disposed of his murder weapons

Thanksgiving holiday, he armed himself with a rifle and revolver, walked into the living room where his parents and sister were watching television, and shot them all to death, firing a total of twenty-four bullets into their bodies. After ransacking the house to make it appear that it had been burglarized, he disposed of the weapons in the Kansas River. Then—to establish an alibi—he drove to his campus boarding house and spoke to his landlady before proceeding to a movie theater, where he made sure to exchange a few words with an usher.

Returning home after the movie ended, he called the police to report the supposed break-in. Detectives were instantly suspicious of the young man, who displayed such utter nonchalance at the slaughter of his family that, when asked about funeral arrangements, he shrugged and replied: "I don't care what you do with them." Initially insisting on his innocence, Andrews soon confessed to his family minister who persuaded him that, if he were in fact guilty, it was "time to purge [his] soul."

Though diagnosed as schizophrenic, he was convicted and sentenced to be hanged. While awaiting execution he shared death row with Richard Hickock and Perry Smith, the Clutter family killers made famous by Truman Capote, who devotes several pages to the Andrews case in his classic *In Cold Blood*.

"I really liked Andy," Hickock told Capote. "He was always talking about breaking out of here and making his living as a hired gun. He liked to imagine himself roaming around Chicago or Los Angeles with a machine gun in a violin case. Cooling guys. Said he'd charge a thousand bucks per stiff."

Four years almost to the day of the family massacre, twenty-two-year-old Andrews went to the gallows after a last meal of two fried chickens, mashed potatoes, green beans, and pie à la mode.

Lowell Lee Andrews' jail mates: killers Richard Hickock and Perry Smith, subjects of Truman Capote's In Cold Blood

THE WICHITA HOTEL SNIPER

WICHITA, KANSAS
AUGUST 11, 1976

In the spring of 1976, nineteen-year-old Michael Ray Soles—described by relatives, neighbors, and acquaintances as a "nice," "quiet," "clean cut," and "deeply religious boy"—moved from his Oklahoma hometown to Wichita, Kansas, where he boarded at the home of a minister and sought work as a welder. Five months later, as he would tell police interrogators, "It came into my head to shoot somebody."

The following day, he armed himself with two rifles he had brought from Oklahoma, packed a lunch, and drove downtown to the twenty-six-story Holiday Inn Plaza, the tallest building in the state. Entering through the garage, he rode the elevator to the top floor. After failing to shoot out the lock of the door leading to the roof, he made his way to a vacant room, positioned himself on the balcony, and opened fire on pedestrians, workers, and motorists below. His shooting spree lasted eleven minutes, beginning at roughly 2:45 p.m.

The carnage ended when police entered the adjoining room and fired a barrage through the partition separating the two balconies, wounding the sniper in the legs. By then two people were dead—a glass company employee doing an installation on the roof of a nearby parking garage and a freelance news photographer killed by a shot through his windshield as he drove to the scene. Seven others were wounded, including one twenty-three-year-old bank loan officer who died the next day.

Asked about his motive by an arresting officer, Soles replied, "It makes me feel good to shoot people." His plea of not guilty by reason of insanity was rejected by jurors at his January 1977 trial. Sentenced to life, he was turned down each of the five times he came up for parole between 1991 and 2017.

Wichita sniper Michael Ray Soles conducted his shooting spree from the rooftop of the Holiday Inn Plaza, the tallest building in Kansas.

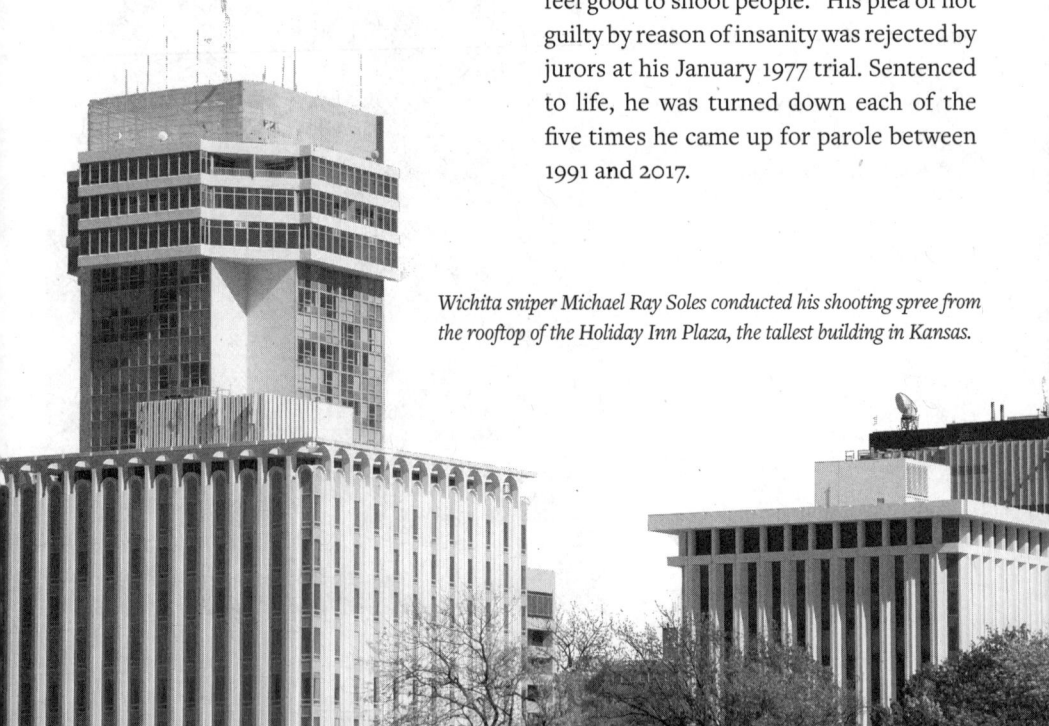

Booby-trap bomber, Danny Crump

A BOMBING IN OLATHE

OLATHE, KANSAS
SEPTEMBER 20, 1980

Danny Crump was twenty-six in the summer of 1979 when he met and fell in love with eighteen-year-old Diane Post in a grocery store parking lot. The two were married three months later and set up house in a trailer. By then, Diane was pregnant. Less than two months after giving birth to a boy they named Randy, Diane took the infant and left Crump, moving back home with her parents.

Announcing that "ain't nobody but . . . me gonna raise this kid," Danny was enraged when Diane, who had filed for divorce, was granted custody. At about 2:30 a.m. on Saturday, September 20, 1980, Danny drove to his in-laws' home and left a cardboard box addressed to Diane on the hood of the car in the driveway. Inside the box were ten sticks of dynamite hooked up to a motorcycle battery and booby-trapped to explode when the lid was removed.

Roughly seven hours later, someone in the household found the box sitting on the car, brought it back inside, and placed it on the dining room table where the entire family—Diane, her parents, two brothers, and a sister—were gathered for breakfast. When Diane lifted the lid, the explosion blew them all to pieces and reduced the house to rubble.

By evening, Danny was in custody. Convicted of six counts of murder, he was sentenced to six consecutive life terms.

KENTUCKY

OWENSBORO
THE LAST LEGAL HANGING IN KENTUCKY
103

FRANKFORT

PAINTSVILLE
THE SIX-YEAR-OLD SLAYER
102

ELIZABETHTOWN
A BROTHER'S VENGEANCE
101

A BROTHER'S VENGEANCE

Elizabethtown, Kentucky • April 27, 1891

Though they had wed only four months earlier, the marriage between young William Showers—a clerk at the Elizabethtown hotel run by his family—and Lena Moore was already in trouble. The two occupied separate rooms across the hall from each other on the hotel's second floor. The problem, it seemed, was Showers's addiction to the bottle, which—as newspapers would speculate—had plunged his "high-strung" young wife into a state of despair. Nevertheless, she seemed cheerful enough when she came down for breakfast on the morning of June 1, 1889.

Just moments after she returned to her room, however, other occupants of the hotel were startled by a pistol shot coming from upstairs. Exactly what happened next was never definitively established. According to his own story—confirmed by several eyewitnesses—William was getting dressed in his room when he heard the shot, rushed across the hall and found Lena crumpled on the floor, dead from a bullet to her right temple, the pistol beside her. Other witnesses testified that they had heard the couple quarreling violently in her room, then a scream followed by a pistol shot. Whether Lena—faced with the prospect of a degraded life with a drunkard—had died by suicide or been slain by a husband said to be insanely jealous of his beautiful wife became a topic of furious debate in the community.

Among the people most convinced of Showers's guilt was Lena's brother, Charles Moore, who pressured authorities for his brother-in-law's arrest. Though Showers was acquitted at his December trial, he seethed with resentment toward Moore and vowed to get even. The opportunity arose when Moore was indicted for forgery and fled the state. Not only was Showers instrumental in having Moore tracked down, arrested, and extradited, but when bail was set at $1,000, he was determined to persuade the judge to increase the amount.

He was at the Elizabethtown courthouse for that purpose on the morning of April 27, 1891, when he encountered Moore. Both men were armed, Showers with a pistol, Moore with a double-barreled shotgun that, without a word, he fired point-blank at his enemy's face, turning his head into "an unrecognizable bleeding mass."

Brought to trial, Moore was acquitted of murder on a plea of self-defense, to the great satisfaction of those who believed that Showers's death was nothing more than belated justice for the slaying of his wife.

Lena Moore: a victim of murder or suicide?

THE SIX-YEAR-OLD SLAYER

Paintsville, Kentucky
May 18, 1929

Two friends, Carl Mahan and Cecil Van Hoose—six and eight years old, respectively—were out scrounging for scrap metal they could sell to a junk dealer for a few pennies. When Carl came upon a "prize piece of iron," Cecil snatched it away, slapping the younger boy's face when he protested. A neighbor, Mrs. Manuel Fitzpatrick, later testified that she was standing by her open back door when she heard Carl warn the other boy that he would get a gun and shoot him if he didn't relinquish the iron.

Dismissing the threat as a "childish quarrel," she returned to her chores. In the meantime, Carl ran into his house, climbed on a chair, took his father's loaded 12-gauge shotgun from the wall, hurried back outside, and shot his friend in the chest. Hearing the blast, Mrs. Fitzpatrick ran outside, saw the wounded boy staggering around the backyard, loaded him into her car, and rushed him to the hospital, where he died soon afterward.

Less than a week later, Carl was put on trial—the youngest murder defendant in Kentucky history. After deliberating for thirty minutes, the jury found him guilty of manslaughter, and Carl—who had spent the one-day proceedings chewing gum, reading newspaper comics, and napping on the defense table—was sentenced to fifteen years in the reformatory.

Juvenile murderer Carl Mahan is the picture of innocence in this 1929 photograph.

The extreme youth of the defendant and the perceived harshness of the sentence set off a firestorm, bringing unwelcome media attention to the formerly obscure mining town. Legendary lawyer Clarence Darrow denounced the judgment, calling it "too stringent" and a throwback to the "Dark Ages."

After much legal wrangling, the conviction was set aside, and Carl was returned to the custody of his parents. He lived until the age of thirty-five, killing himself with a bullet to the head in 1958.

THE LAST LEGAL HANGING IN KENTUCKY

Owensboro, Kentucky • June 7, 1936

In the early morning hours of Sunday, June 7, 1936, twenty-six-year-old Rainey Bethea, who had been in and out of prison for crimes ranging from drunk and disorderly conduct to breaking and entering to grand larceny, snuck into the bedroom of a former employer, seventy-year-old widow Lischia Edwards, intent on burglary. When Mrs. Edwards awoke, Bethea strangled and raped her, then rummaged through her bureau drawers for jewelry.

Before making off with the loot, he tried on one of her rings, first removing the black celluloid one he had fashioned for himself in prison and then forgetting to retrieve it. He was arrested within days. Confessing to the rape-murder, he was sentenced to the gallows, the jury taking less than five minutes to convict him.

The case generated widespread media attention when it became known that the person tasked with the hanging was a woman, Florence Thompson, who had replaced her husband as town sheriff after his sudden death a few months earlier. Reluctant to become known as the first woman in US history to perform an execution, she accepted the offer of an ex-policeman, A. L. Hash, who wrote to her, volunteering his services free of charge.

Bethea's public hanging turned into an event that would spark revulsion throughout the nation. Thousands of eager spectators flooded into Owensboro by cars, trains, and farm wagons. Hotels were filled to capacity and, as one newspaper reported, some town residents hosted "all-night 'hanging parties.'"

An estimated twenty thousand spectators, comporting themselves as if at a county fair, watched Bethea die, an execution messily performed by Hash, who had shown up drunk. Eighteen months later, as a direct result of the nationwide outrage over the carnivalesque spectacle, Kentucky—the last state still conducting public hangings—outlawed the practice.

LOUISIANA

LAKE CHARLES
TONI JO GOES TO THE ELECTRIC CHAIR
106

BATON ROUGE

ST. MARTINVILLE
"LUCKY" WILLIE AND "GRUESOME GERTIE"
107

NEW ORLEANS
A PHENOMENALLY DEPRAVED SCOUNDREL
105

A PHENOMENALLY DEPRAVED SCOUNDREL

NEW ORLEANS, LOUISIANA
JANUARY 30, 1889

Born in Rennes, France, in 1830, Etienne Deschamps emigrated to America in his thirties, settling in New Orleans, where he practiced dentistry before embracing the pseudoscience of "animal magnetism," a form of quackery that claimed it could cure all ailments through a combination of hypnotism and the application of magnets to the body. He was also obsessed with a rumored trove of gold and silver coins reputedly buried by buccaneer Jean Lafitte.

Failing in his initial attempts to locate the hoard, he decided that what he needed was a young girl, "pure of heart and body," who, under hypnosis, would manifest mediumistic powers that would guide him to the treasure. The person he settled on was a beautiful twelve-year-old named Juliette Dietsh, daughter of a French upholsterer who lived nearby.

On January 30, 1889—in a crime that would dominate the front pages and rivet the city for months—the nude bodies of the fifty-nine-year-old "magnetic doctor" and the prepubescent girl were found together in his bed. Despite three self-inflicted stab wounds to the chest, Deschamps was still alive. Juliette was dead from a fatal dose of chloroform. An autopsy performed the following day concluded that she had been raped both vaginally and anally, possibly post-mortem.

Under arrest for murder, Deschamps proclaimed his innocence. According to

An "animal magnetism" hypnotist at work

his story, he had decided to kill himself after discovering that Juliette was not, in fact, a virgin. Apprised of his plan, Juliette—who was ostensibly mad about the wizened, nearly sixty-year-old fraud and felt she could not live without him—died by suicide. Denounced in the press as "a beast in human shape," "a phenomenally depraved scoundrel," perpetrator "of one of the most revolting crimes ever committed in this city," Deschamps would make another failed suicide attempt, throwing himself headfirst from the second-floor gallery of the prison to the brick-paved yard below.

His conviction at his April 1889 trial was overturned on appeal. Tried a second time, he was found guilty again and went to the gallows on May 12, 1892, still insisting that he was "as innocent as an unborn babe."

Toni Jo Hood behind bars

TONI JO GOES TO THE ELECTRIC CHAIR

Lake Charles, Louisiana
February 14, 1940

Beaten by her father after being fired from her job at a Shreveport macaroni factory, thirteen-year-old Annie Beatrice McQuiston ran away from home and was soon making her living as an underage sex worker. By sixteen, now going by the name Toni Jo Hood, she was addicted to cocaine, marijuana, and booze and was plying her trade in brothels in Louisiana and south Texas.

In 1939, at the age of twenty-three, she fell in love with and married one of her customers, Claude "Cowboy" Henry, a small-time palooka out on bail after killing a former San Antonio police officer in a barroom brawl. When Claude was tried, convicted, and sentenced to fifty years in the Huntsville penitentiary, his new bride vowed to get him out.

Her first step was to recruit an accomplice, an ex-con named Harold "Arkie" Burk, who had done time in the prison and was familiar with its layout. Hitching along a Louisiana highway on their way to Texas, they were picked up by a forty-three-year-old tire salesman, Joseph P. Calloway. Somewhere in the countryside past St. Charles, Toni drew a .38-caliber pistol and commanded Calloway to pull onto a dirt road, where the couple stripped him naked and shoved him into the trunk.

Burk took the wheel and drove Calloway to a remote field. Ordering him out of the trunk, Hood led him behind a haystack at gunpoint and shot him between the eyes as he knelt in prayer. When his body was autopsied, the medical examiner found evidence that pliers had been clamped around his penis, suggesting that Hood had tortured him before executing him. Burk, who had signed on for a jailbreak but not cold-blooded murder, soon absconded with the car.

Making her way by bus to Shreveport, Hood took refuge at the home of an aunt who—hearing enough from her niece to know that she was in serious trouble—contacted the state police. Taken in for questioning, Hood made a full confession. Three separate trials ended in convictions, the first two were overturned on appeal and the last upheld. Hood was put to death on November 28, 1942, the only woman executed in Louisiana's electric chair.

"LUCKY" WILLIE AND "GRUESOME GERTIE"

St. Martinville, Louisiana • November 8, 1944

Nine months after the murder of pharmacist Andrew Thomas—shot dead outside his home with a .38-caliber pistol—fifteen-year-old Willie Francis, a onetime employee of the druggist, was arrested for the crime. Under interrogation, the frightened teenager confessed that he had killed Thomas during a robbery that netted him $4 and a watch. At his trial, his court-appointed defense lawyers did not conduct a single cross-examination or raise an objection and rested their case without offering any testimony or evidence on behalf of the accused.

What turned the Francis case into a media sensation was neither the murder itself nor the travesty of his trial. On May 3, 1946, Francis was strapped to "Gruesome Gertie," the state's portable electric chair, which had been set up by a prison guard and an inmate, both drunk at the time. When the switch was thrown, the teenager writhed in agony and screamed "I am n-n-not dying!" before being removed, still alive, from the malfunctioning chair. "It felt like a hundred thousand needles and pins were pricking in me all over," Francis told reporters, "and my left leg felt like somebody was cutting it with a razor blade."

The first survivor of an electrocution in the United States, Francis would be dubbed "Lucky" Willie in the press, a nickname that would come to seem bitterly ironical. With his son still under a sentence of death, Francis's father retained a lawyer who believed that making someone go to the chair twice constituted "cruel and unusual punishment," pursuant to the Eighth Amendment. The appeal went all the way to the US Supreme Court, which ultimately rejected it. On May 9, 1947, Willie Francis was electrocuted again. This time, "Gruesome Gertie" worked.

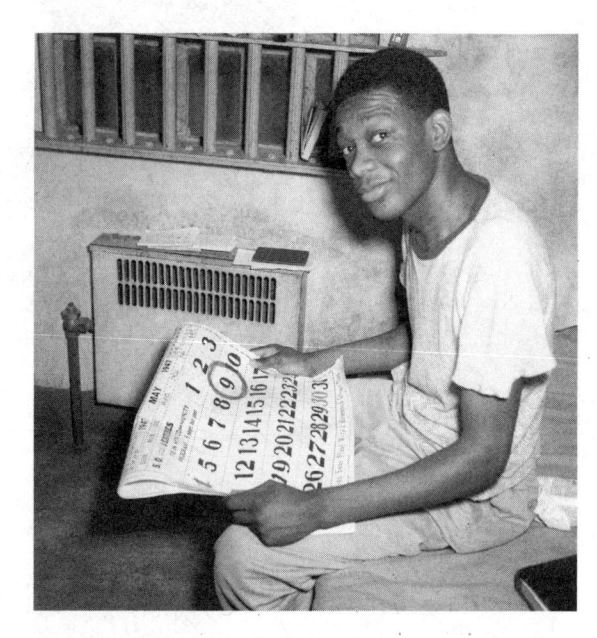

Willie Francis, who went to the chair twice

MAINE

AUGUSTA
THE PURRINGTON FAMILY MASSACRE
109

WATERVILLE
A MURDEROUS MADWOMAN
111

NEWRY
A COOK RAMPAGES IN NEWRY
113

BRUNSWICK
BRUTALITY IN BRUNSWICK
110

Horrid Murder!

Headline from a local broadside, dated July 11, 1906

THE PURRINGTON FAMILY MASSACRE

Augusta, Maine
July 9, 1806

In the early morning hours of July 9, 1806, seventeen-year-old James Purrington Jr. was awakened by the piercing shrieks of his mother. As he leaped from his bed and made for the door, his father suddenly appeared, axe in hand. The elder Purrington swung at his son but, in the cramped space of the room, the blade passed over the boy's shoulder, inflicting a slight wound on his back.

When James's twelve-year-old brother, Benjamin, who shared his bed, woke up and tried to run, Purrington Sr. went after the boy, allowing the teenager to escape. Still in his nightshirt, he raced to the farmhouse of his nearest neighbor, a Mr. Wyman, and, barely coherent with terror, told of the terrible scene he had just fled. Wyman alerted another neighbor and the two hurried to the Purrington home where, in the words of one contemporary account, "A scene was presented which beggar[ed] all description."

Purrington's wife, Betsy, lay in bed, her head "almost severed from her body." On the floor nearby was the corpse of her ten-year-old daughter, Anna, who had apparently run into the room upon hearing her mother's screams and been axed to death beside her. Her three sisters—nineteen-year-old Polly; fifteen-year-old Martha; and eighteen-month-old Louisa—had been set upon in another room. Martha was clinging to life, though she would die of her wounds three weeks later. A "dreadfully mangled" Benjamin, still clutching the trousers he had grabbed when attempting to flee, was sprawled by the hearth, while his younger brothers,

MAINE • 109

Nathaniel and Nathan, ages eight and six, respectively, lay beside each other in bed, their throats slit with a razor.

Purrington Sr.—who "lay prostrate on his face and weltering in his gore"—had used the same implement to cut his own throat. The stunned community struggled to make sense of the atrocity. Evidence emerged that Purrington—a forty-six-year-old Revolutionary War veteran "of good character and fair reputation"—had sunk into despair when his farm crops failed. Fearing that he and his loved ones would be left "destitute of bread" and believing in the principle of universal salvation, he had slaughtered them all and did away with himself in the most infamous case of familicide in early American history.

BRUTALITY IN BRUNSWICK

Brunswick, Maine
May 26, 1951

With three marriages behind her by the age of twenty-four—two ending in divorce, one in an annulment—Brunswick waitress Shirley Coolen seemed eager to reconcile with her most recent ex: Guy Coolen, a thirty-one-year-old shipyard worker living in Dorchester, Massachusetts. On Thursday, May 24, she mailed him a special delivery letter, inviting him to visit her. She was going to see a movie on Saturday night, she wrote, and would meet him outside the theater when the show let out at 10:30 p.m.

As planned, Shirley attended the movies with a girlfriend that Saturday, then stopped by her workplace, the Bowdoin Hotel, to chat with some acquaintances for a few minutes. Then she disappeared. Her body was not found until the following Tuesday, May 29, when a housekeeper spotted it in her employer's backyard flower garden. Face badly bruised, skirt hiked up, a red scarf tightly pulled around Shirley's neck, she had died of strangulation.

Initially the prime suspect, Guy Coolen was cleared after passing a lie detector test, though he was promptly arrested on a statutory rape charge when authorities learned that he was cohabiting with a fourteen-year-old girl. Other suspects were quickly brought in for questioning: two army airmen stationed at a nearby base; the son of a prominent Brunswick businessman; a pair of students recently expelled from Bowdoin; and various men that the "comely victim" had dated. All were eventually released when their alibis checked out.

For a while police focused their attention on Charles E. Terry, a "towering," six-foot-five-inch twenty-one-year-old with a long history of lawless behavior. In April 1951—following his dishonorable discharge from the marine corps for stealing a car while on leave—he was arrested for sexually attacking two women on the same night in Augusta, Maine. Given his criminal past—and his admitted "uncontrollable sex urges"—he seemed a likely suspect in the Coolen murder, but he was cleared after an intensive investigation.

Shirley Mae Murray Coolen

Mug shot of Charles Terry, who was convicted for murdering a woman with a scarf

Paroled after eight years in prison for the rape conviction, he was back behind bars within months for assaulting a forty-six-year-old woman and breaking her jaw in two places. Though diagnosed by prison psychiatrists as a sexually sadistic psychopath, he was back on the streets by 1961.

Two years later, Mrs. Zenovia Clegg, a cancer-stricken, sixty-two-year-old California divorcée who had come to New York City for a final "fling," was found dead in her Times Square hotel room. She had been strangled with the red scarf she wore to hide her surgical scars and raped after death with a liquor bottle. Tracked down and arrested in a Greenwich Village bar, Terry admitted that he had murdered the dying woman after she had picked him up "during a night on the town," taken him back to her hotel room, then mocked him when he proved impotent.

He also confessed to strangling three other women, one of them Shirley Coolen. Suspected of committing at least three murders attributed to the Boston Strangler, Terry, whose death sentence for the Clegg homicide was later commuted to life, died in prison of natural causes in April 1981.

A MURDEROUS MADWOMAN

WATERVILLE, MAINE
MARCH 8, 1954, AND
JUNE 30, 1966

When twenty-five-year-old Constance Fisher fell into a black mood following the birth of her third child in March 1953, doctors diagnosed her condition as postpartum depression and treated her accordingly. Her mental state, however, was far more dire than they imagined. Within months she began hearing voices advising her to kill herself and her whole family.

Fisher's first attempt happened in early January 1954 when she nearly strangled her infant daughter to death with a scarf before coming to her senses. At the advice of her doctors, her husband moved the family from their remote lakeside home—a cramped, primitive

Filicidal killer Constance Fisher

MAINE • 111

The Kennebec River, Waterville, Maine

cabin without indoor plumbing or running water—to a more congenial environment, a duplex apartment close to Constance's parents' house. It wasn't very long, however, before her suicidal thoughts returned.

After attempting to kill herself with an overdose of sedatives, she saw a local psychiatrist who, as with her previous physicians, failed to perceive the extent of her psychopathology. On March 8, 1954—heeding a voice that told her that killing her children was the only way to save them from the evils of the world—Constance drowned each in turn in the bathtub, then made a half-hearted attempt at suicide by swallowing a bottleful of caustic medicated shampoo.

Declared insane, she spent the next five years in a mental hospital before being returned to the care of her remarkably forgiving husband, Carl. Between 1960 and 1965, Constance gave birth to three more children, two daughters and a son. On Thursday, June 30, 1966, she drowned them all and made another failed suicide attempt, leaving a note for her husband explaining that killing their children was the "only way I could be sure they would go to heaven." Diagnosed as a paranoid schizophrenic, she was consigned to a state hospital for the insane, where she remained for the next seven years.

On October 1, 1973, she walked off the grounds and drowned herself in the Kennebec River, bringing to an end what the *Boston Herald* called "one of the most bizarre tragedies in New England history."

A COOK RAMPAGES IN NEWRY

NEWRY, MAINE • SEPTEMBER 1–4, 2006

Apart from a number of motor vehicle violations, including one for operating under the influence, thirty-one-year-old restaurant cook Christian Nielsen had no criminal record, though he admitted to investigators that he'd been thinking about killing someone for at least five years.

On September 1, 2006, he went fishing with fifty-year-old James Whitehurst—a handyman and fellow boarder at the Black Bear Bed & Breakfast—and shot him three times in the head and body before going off to work. He returned the next day with a can of gasoline, doused the corpse, and set it on fire. The following morning, he broke into the bedroom of the inn's owner, sixty-five-year-old Julie Bullard, shot her to death with his handgun, dragged the body into the woods, and dismembered it with a hacksaw.

Co-workers noticed nothing out of the ordinary about Nielsen when he worked his regular shift that night. When Bullard's thirty-year-old daughter, Selby—accompanied by a friend, Cindy Beatson—showed up the next day to check on her mother, Nielsen shot them both and dismembered them with a chainsaw he had borrowed from his father, Charles. He also cut off their fingers to get at their rings and killed the Bullards' two pet dogs.

That same afternoon—September 4—Christian Nielsen and his wife arrived for a Labor Day visit. Noticing a bloody trail leading from a bedroom, Christian followed it outside and toward the back of the property, where he came upon the remains of Selby Bullard and Beatson and immediately called the police. When responding state trooper Dan Hanson asked, "What's going on," a nonchalant Nielsen, after checking the officer's nametag, replied, "Well, I killed some people, Dan. I shot them all."

Despite being diagnosed as a schizoid personality, Nielsen was found competent to stand trial. Pleading guilty, he was sentenced to four consecutive life terms.

An investigator outside the Black Bear Bed & Breakfast, the site of Christian Nielsen's four-day killing spree over Labor Day weekend

MARYLAND

BALTIMORE
THE UNSOLVED MURDER OF SISTER CATHY
116

BALTIMORE
THE NOT-QUITE-PERFECT CRIME
115

ANNAPOLIS

ST. MICHAELS
LIFE IMITATES ART IN ST. MICHAELS
117

THE NOT-QUITE-PERFECT CRIME

BALTIMORE, MARYLAND
AUGUST 20, 1952

Just after midnight on August 20, 1952, two Baltimore policemen were sitting in their cruiser when a blue Chrysler sedan came swerving down the street, nearly hit their car, ran up an embankment, struck a utility pole, and rolled over onto its passenger side. Inside the overturned vehicle, the driver—a woman who had presumably fallen asleep at the wheel—lay beneath the dashboard, dead from severe head injuries.

She was quickly identified as thirty-three-year-old Dorothy Grammer, mother of three and wife of her high school sweetheart, office manager G. Edward (Ed) Grammer. From the first, there were things about the case that aroused official suspicion. The damage to the vehicle was relatively minor, not nearly extensive enough to account for the deep, fatal wounds to Dorothy's skull. And a small rock had been wedged beneath the gas pedal, keeping the engine racing even after the car flipped over.

It didn't take long for Baltimore's chief medical examiner to conclude that the victim had been bludgeoned to death with a heavy object. Brought in for questioning, Ed Grammer soon confessed, claiming that he had killed his wife in a blind rage during a marital quarrel. He then staged her death to look like a tragic accident, placing her body in the car, sticking the stone beneath the accelerator, and sending the vehicle careening

The killing of Dorothy Grammer became a national media spectacle.

through the streets until it collided with the pole. "The Not-Quite-Perfect Crime" (as *Life* magazine called it) went from local to nationwide sensation when the true motive for the murder came to light: Dorothy's unwillingness to grant her husband a divorce so he could marry his twenty-two-year-old mistress, a secretary who worked for the United Nations.

Grammer went to the gallows on June 11, 1954, a hanging so botched that he strangled for fifteen minutes before doctors declared him dead. The Grammer case fascinated author Vladimir Nabokov, whose pedophiliac protagonist, Humbert Humbert, muses on the crime in the novel *Lolita*.

Sister Cathy Cesnik

THE UNSOLVED MURDER OF SISTER CATHY

BALTIMORE, MARYLAND • NOVEMBER 7, 1969

On the evening of November 7, 1969, twenty-nine-year-old Sister Catherine Anne Cesnik, an English and drama teacher at the all-girls Archbishop Keough High School, set out on an errand and never returned. Two months later, on January 3, 1970, her decomposed corpse was found in a garbage dump at the outskirts of the city. An autopsy determined that she had been killed by a blow to the back of her skull with a blunt object, most likely a ball-peen hammer. Police efforts to find a motive for and suspect in the slaying came to nothing.

A possible answer finally emerged in 1995, when two former students of the much-beloved "Sister Cathy," now grown women, came forward with highly disturbing accusations against the one-time school chaplain Father Joseph Maskell. Maskell, so they asserted, had systematically subjected them to sexual abuse. When Sister Cathy learned what was happening to the teenagers, she promised to bring the situation to the attention of the Archdiocese of Baltimore but was murdered before she could do so.

According to one of the women, Maskell had driven her out to the dump just a week after Cesnik's disappearance, showed her the maggot-infested corpse, and warned her to keep her mouth shut if she didn't want to end up the same way. Maskell vehemently denied the charges and went to his death in 2001 protesting his innocence. In 2017, investigators exhumed his body to procure a DNA sample that was compared with DNA preserved from the crime scene. The two DNA profiles did not match, and Sister Cathy's murder remains one of Baltimore's most famous cold cases.

LIFE IMITATES ART IN ST. MICHAELS

St. Michaels, Maryland
February 14, 1998

To rekindle his failing marriage, thirty-five-year-old Stephen Hricko took his wife, Kimberly, a hospital surgical technologist, on what was supposed to be a romantic Valentine's Day getaway at a resort hotel. The highlight of the weekend was an interactive dinner-theater murder mystery, *The Bride Who Cried*, about a groom poisoned at his wedding reception. About three hours after the show ended, Kimberly appeared in the hotel lobby and calmly reported that her room was on fire.

Stephen was found dead inside the room, burned from the chest up, his pajama bottoms pulled down low enough to expose his penis. Lying on the bed were a *Playboy* magazine open to the centerfold and a pack of cigars. According to the story from which Kimberly would never deviate, she and Steve—who was already intoxicated from the champagne and wine he had consumed during the evening—had gone back to the room after the show, where they watched a movie while he downed a few bottles of beer. By now "sloppy drunk," he began to pressure her for sex, something that Kimberly, who hadn't slept with her husband for months, wasn't interested in. When he became even more insistent, she stormed out of the room, got in their car, and drove around "for what felt like hours" before returning and finding the room in flames. Evidently, the inebriated Steve had been masturbating while puffing on a cigar and accidentally set himself on fire.

Newspapers had a field day with the story of the murder-mystery weekend that ended with a real death. It wasn't long, however, before investigators found gaping holes in Kimberly's account. Steve, as friends testified, was not a smoker, drinker, or consumer of pornography. An autopsy turned up no traces of alcohol in his system, and the absence of any soot in his lungs indicated that he was dead before the fire started. Other witnesses, including some of Kimberly's closest friends, came forward to report that she was having an affair with a younger man and had talked openly of killing her husband and collecting his $400,000 life insurance policy.

As a hospital worker, Kimberly had easy access to succinylcholine, a powerful, undetectable muscle-relaxing anesthetic capable of causing rapid death. There seemed little doubt that she had managed to inject Steve with a fatal dose, set him on fire to conceal the puncture mark, and staged the scene to conform to her preplanned alibi. Found guilty at her five-day trial, she was sentenced to life for the murder and thirty years for arson.

Kimberly and Stephen Hricko in happier times

MASSACHUSETTS

BOSTON
THE BOSTON BELFRY SLAYER
119

BOSTON
ANOTHER MONSTER IN THE MYSTIC
123

NEWTON
"KILLER NANNY" GOES FREE
125

BOSTON
THE BOSTON GIGGLER
122

YARMOUTH
A MISCREANT IN YARMOUTH
120

CATAUMET
JOLLY JANE LAYS WASTE
121

THE BOSTON BELFRY SLAYER

Boston, Massachusetts
May 23, 1875

An intelligent, well-read twenty-four-year-old who served as the sexton of his Baptist church, Thomas Piper was a classic serial sex-murderer. He earned his infamous nickname—the "Boston Belfry Slayer"—on May 23, 1875, when, following the Sunday services, he lured a five-year-old girl named Mabel Young into the belfry by promising to show her his pet pigeons.

Once there, he bludgeoned her with a cricket bat he had brought to church that morning with murder on his mind. "He intended to outrage her after death," the *Chicago Tribune* reported, but—seeing that she was still alive—carried her farther up the tower and left her lying by the trapdoor, brains oozing from her crushed skull. Hearing the agonized shrieks she was still able to produce, passersby rushed into the church, climbed up to the belfry, and made the appalling discovery.

Witnesses, meanwhile, saw a young man—quickly identified as Piper—jump through a window twelve feet from the ground and hurry into the sexton's quarters next door. Mabel was carried to a nearby home where she languished for twenty-eight hours before dying. Promptly arrested, Piper stubbornly proclaimed his innocence. Not until he was convicted and sentenced to hang did he finally confess, admitting not only to the Young murder but to two other brutal crimes.

In December 1873, gripped by a sudden "desire to kill," he "nerved himself by drinking a compound of opium and whiskey," then, wielding a sawed-off piece of

Thomas Piper leads Mabel Young to her death.

wagon-shaft, went out in search of a victim. Spotting a young domestic servant named Bridget Landregan as she walked home alone, he came up behind her and crushed her skull with the club. Before he could sexually violate her corpse, however, he was scared away by a man coming down the street.

One year later, he picked up a sex worker named Mary Tyner and, after having a few drinks with her in a saloon, accompanied her back to her room, where the two went to bed and fell asleep. Upon awakening in the middle of the night, he was "seized with desire to kill her." Using a hammer belonging to her carpenter boyfriend, he battered her head. Tyner survived, but with such serious brain injuries that she was consigned to an insane asylum, where she lived out the rest of her days.

On May 26, 1876—one year almost to the day after Mabel Young's murder—Piper went to the gallows.

A MISCREANT IN YARMOUTH

Yarmouth, Massachusetts • September 13, 1899

Residents of the tight-knit Cape Cod town of Yarmouth tended to cast a wary eye on outsiders—by which they meant anyone who hadn't been born there. Though he'd lived in Yarmouth from early infancy and grew up in the household of a family deeply rooted in the community, Edwin Ray Snow—a Boston foundling adopted by a much-respected Yarmouth couple—was never made to feel as if he fully belonged. Even as an adult, headlines would refer to him as a "Boston waif" whose lawless behavior had nothing to do with his irreproachable upbringing but rather sprang from the "bad blood" he'd inherited from the dissolute mother who had abandoned the newborn on a doorstep.

Whatever its source, his criminality manifested itself at an early age. At sixteen, he was arrested and charged with larceny after breaking into a general merchandise store in Barnstable and stealing a razor and pistol. One month later, while free on bail, he and a companion burglarized another shop, making off with $1.80 in coins, ten ounces of cologne, and three pounds of candy. Convicted of breaking and entering, he was consigned to the Concord Reformatory.

Released ten months later in the spring of 1899, Snow returned to Yarmouth, where he became even more of a pariah. The town's view of him as an incorrigible miscreant was confirmed at the end of that summer. On the morning of September 13, twenty-one-year-old Jimmy Whittemore, a distant cousin of Snow's who worked as the deliveryman for a local baker, set off in his wagon to make his daily rounds. He hadn't gone far when he came upon Snow, who climbed aboard the vehicle and accompanied him on his errands.

120 • 50 STATES OF MURDER

Late that afternoon, as they were passing through a lonely stretch of woods, Snow pulled out a pistol, shot his cousin in the back of the head, and made off with the cash that Whittemore had collected from his customers.

Identified by witnesses who saw him riding on the wagon, Snow had already fled town by train but was quickly tracked down and taken into custody. Pleading guilty to first-degree murder, he earned the dubious distinction of becoming the first person in Massachusetts sentenced to the electric chair, the execution method adopted by the state just a year earlier. He avoided that fate when, by prearrangement, the governor commuted the seventeen-year-old killer's sentence to life.

JOLLY JANE LAYS WASTE

Cataumet, Massachusetts
July–August 1901

Until police dug up the decomposed remains of dozens of teenaged boys in the basement of John Wayne Gacy's suburban home in 1978, America's most prolific serial killer, according to *The Guinness Book of World Records*, was Jane Toppan. A trained nurse known as "Jolly Jane" for her lively personality, Toppan, by her own admission, derived perverse sexual pleasure ("voluptuous delight," as she put it) from subjecting her victims—patients, friends, and family members—to lingering deaths by feeding them carefully doled-out measures of atropine and morphine. She achieved her highest ecstasy when she climbed into bed with them and held their bodies tight while they suffered their final convulsions.

Toppan's undoing came in the summer of 1901, while she was vacationing in Cape Cod at a cottage owned by an old friend, Alden Davis. Within a six-week span, Jane murdered Davis, his wife, and their two married daughters. The shocking obliteration of the entire family aroused suspicion, and Jane was soon arrested. In custody, she cheerfully confessed to thirty-one murders. Diagnosed as "morally insane"—the Victorian term for a criminal psychopath—she was sentenced to spend the rest of her life in a mental asylum.

According to legend, she would occasionally beckon to one of the nurses and, with a conspiratorial smile, say, "Get the morphine, dearie, and we'll go out into the ward. You and I will have a lot of fun seeing them die."

Until John Wayne Gacy broke her record, Nurse Jane Toppan, who confessed to thirty-one murders, was America's most prolific serial killer.

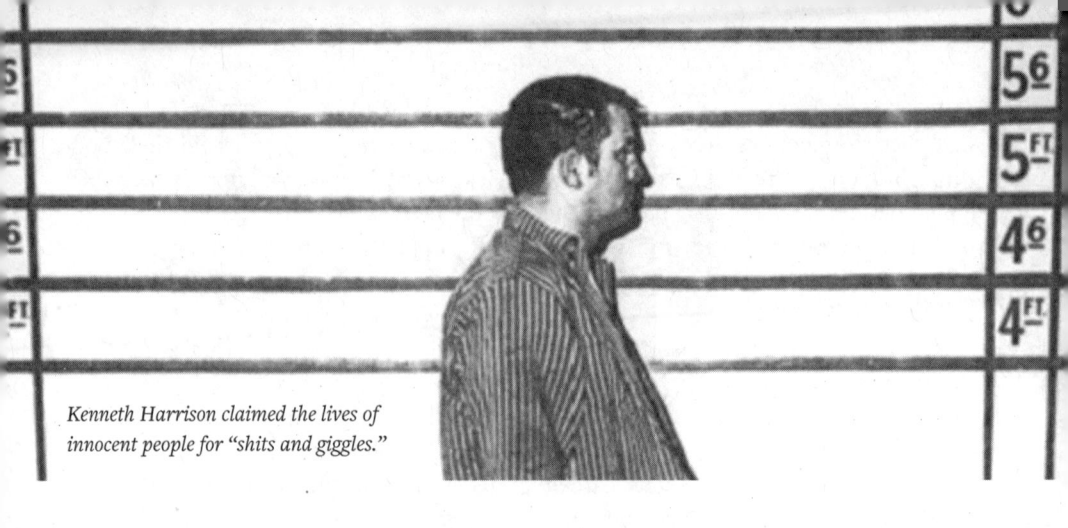

Kenneth Harrison claimed the lives of innocent people for "shits and giggles."

THE BOSTON GIGGLER

BOSTON, MASSACHUSETTS
APRIL 1967–NOVEMBER 1969

It's impossible to know if Kenneth Harrison had Batman's arch-foe The Joker in mind when he christened himself The Giggler. He first identified himself by that moniker in a phone call to the Boston police at about 1:30 a.m. on June 16, 1969. Earlier that evening, Harrison—a thirty-one-year-old drifter eking out a living as a short-order cook—met a man named Joseph Breen in a downtown dive bar. At closing time, having bonded over shuffleboard, they left together in search of more liquor.

When they got into a drunken brawl with each other a short time later over the cost of a bottle of whiskey, Harrison pushed Breen into a water-filled pit in a construction site and bashed his head in with a rock. He then found a nearby phone booth and called the police, giving them the location of the site and informing them that there was "a man down in the water, dead." When police asked who was calling, Harrison replied, "This is The Giggler," then tee-heed and hung up.

Five months later, Harrison was unemployed and living in the abandoned transit tunnels beneath a train station. On the day after Christmas, he approached nine-year-old Kenneth Martin, who was waiting on the platform for a downtown train. Luring the boy into a tunnel, Harrison strangled him to death with a rope and hid the body beneath a sheet of canvas. Over the following days, Harrison put in several calls to his sister, admitting to the child's murder. Tipped off by the sister, police found the body following a daylong search through the underground labyrinth.

Under arrest, Harrison not only admitted to Martin's murder but confessed to the killings of Joseph Breen and two other victims. The first was six-year-old Lucy Palmarin, whom he had lured into his cab while working as a taxi driver in April 1967, then driven to Fort Point Channel and drowned. The second was a seventy-five-year-old woman, Clover Parker, whom he had tossed into the same channel in November 1969.

Sentenced to life for Martin's murder, the "Giggler" died by suicide in 1989, deliberately overdosing on a prescribed antidepressant.

ANOTHER MONSTER IN THE MYSTIC

Boston, Massachusetts • October 23, 1989

Charles Stuart was a unique combination of two different types of murderer. Like California's Scott Peterson, he exemplified the so-called eraser killer: the man who—deciding to rid himself of an "inconvenient" (often pregnant) wife so he can indulge in a carefree bachelor life without the hassle and expense of divorce—coolly sets out to do away with her. At the same time, he bore a striking similarity to South Carolina's Susan Smith, the notorious "Monster Mom" who drowned her own kids, then blamed the heinous crime on a make-believe Black predator.

The general manager for a prominent Boston furrier, Stuart seemed to enjoy an idyllic suburban existence with his tax attorney wife, Carol. As his thirtieth birthday approached, however, he grew increasingly bitter about his circumstances, particularly after Carol became pregnant and announced her intention to be a stay-at-home mom. The loss of her income threatened to dash his dream of quitting his job and becoming a restaurateur. He had also become smitten with a much younger woman, a pretty, twenty-one-year-old office assistant at his workplace.

In his psychopathic calculations, the solution to his problems was obvious—get rid of his wife, collect on her hefty insurance policy, and enjoy the upscale, unfettered life he felt entitled to. When his idea of hiring a hitman was laughed off by a friend he confided in, Stuart concocted a sinister plan that he put into action on the night of October 23, 1989. After attending a childbirth class with Carol, he drove her to a dark, deserted street in a poor, primarily Black neighborhood, shot her in the head, then turned the gun on himself, inadvertently inflicting a much more serious wound to his internal organs than he intended. His younger brother, Matthew, who had agreed to assist in the plan for a cut of the insurance money, got rid of the murder weapon.

The manhunt for Carol Stuart's murderer unleashed a wave of police brutality against Black Boston residents.

Charles Stuart's body is fished from the Mystic River.

Carol would die in the hospital. Her premature child, delivered by Caesarean, would survive only seventeen days. Stuart himself would remain hospitalized for six weeks. His story—that his wife was killed and he himself gravely wounded by a Black male in a black jogging suit who had jumped into the rear seat of the car and shot them during a robbery—inflamed tensions in a city already plagued with a long, troubled history of intense racism toward its Black citizens.

In early July 1990, overcome with guilt, Stuart's brother Matthew broke down and confessed. Before police could arrest him, Charles killed himself by jumping off a bridge into the Mystic River.

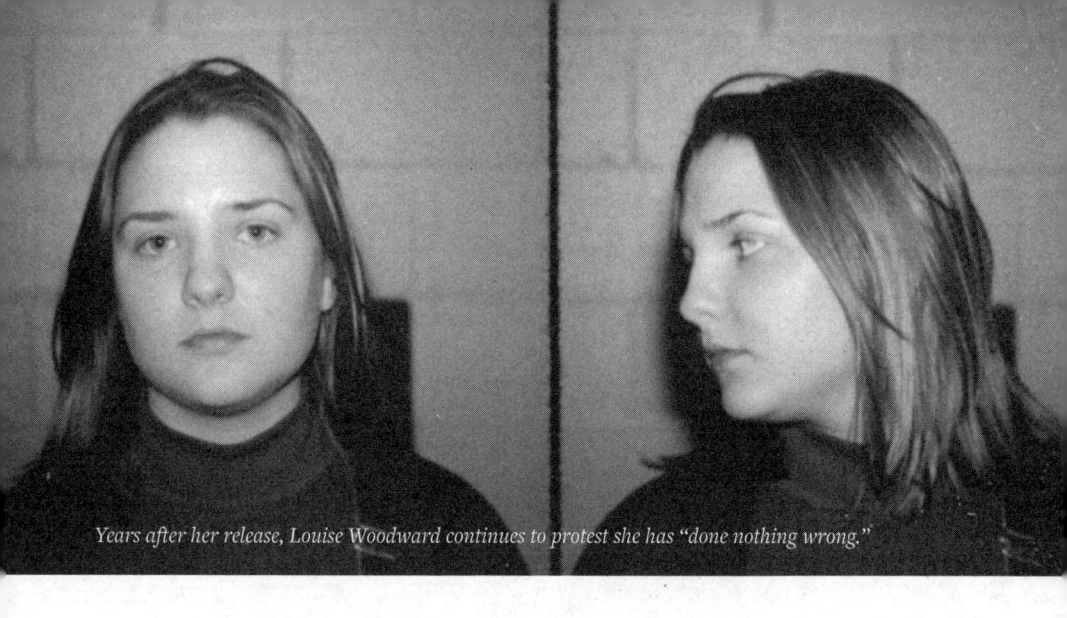

Years after her release, Louise Woodward continues to protest she has "done nothing wrong."

"KILLER NANNY" GOES FREE

NEWTON, MASSACHUSETTS
FEBRUARY 4, 1997

In February 1997, eight-month-old Matthew Eappen suffered fatal head injuries while under the care of eighteen-year-old British au pair Louise Woodward, soon to be known in the tabloids as the "Killer Nanny." Accused of having caused Matthew's death by violently shaking him in a fit of frustration, Woodward was arrested and charged with first-degree murder.

Woodward's televised trial in October transfixed viewers both here and in Great Britain, where much of the public rallied to her support. While Woodward denied manhandling the baby, the prosecution summoned medical experts who testified that little Matthew had died not only from "shaken-baby syndrome" but from a fractured skull, evidently sustained when his head was slammed against a hard surface, most likely the bathroom floor.

Defense experts countered that the infant had suffered his head injuries weeks before, probably from an accidental fall. When Woodward shook him to wake him for his bath—as she admitted doing—his already damaged brain hemorrhaged, killing him. Certain that the jury would set their client free rather than convict her of premeditated murder, the defense insisted on a "go-for-broke" strategy: Woodward would either be found guilty of first- or second-degree murder or acquitted.

The risky gambit did not pay off. She was convicted of second-degree murder, a verdict that meant a minimum of fifteen years imprisonment. Less than two weeks later, however, the presiding judge reduced her conviction to involuntary manslaughter and sentenced her to time served, 279 days—a judgment that elicited widespread outrage in the United States and unfettered celebration in her English hometown.

MICHIGAN

GROSSE POINTE
MASTER BOB IN GROSSE POINTE
129

DETROIT
THE ST. AUBIN AVENUE MASSACRE
127

LANSING ★

YPSILANTI
THE YPSILANTI RIPPER
128

The Evangelist family: Benjamin and his wife Santina with thirteen-month-old Mario on her lap (center), Angelina and Margaret, seven and five (inset top right), Jean, four (bottom right)

THE ST. AUBIN AVENUE MASSACRE

DETROIT, MICHIGAN
JULY 3, 1929

Sometime between midnight and 3:00 a.m. on July 3, 1929, an unknown killer snuck into the St. Aubin Avenue home of Benny Evangelist in Detroit's "Little Italy" neighborhood. An immigrant carpenter from Naples, Evangelist had made a prosperous life for himself and his family as a real estate agent. He was also a self-proclaimed "Divine Prophet": a faith-healing cult leader who had published his own 300-page Bible and led well-attended services in his basement temple, which was decorated with a dozen grotesque wax effigies representing his mystical deities and a giant electrically lit eyeball.

A business associate who arrived at the house that summer morning made the appalling discovery: a decapitated Evangelist seated at his desk, his severed head on the floor beside him. Quickly summoned to the scene, detectives found the rest of the family—Evangelist's wife and four young children—horribly butchered upstairs. Following a massive investigation, police were left with several possible theories. They suspected that the slaughter had been perpetrated by: an unhinged member of Evangelist's cult; an assassin connected to the notorious Black Hand extortion ring that preyed on Italian immigrants; or a real estate client named Umberto Tecchio, who had been involved in a recent dispute with Evangelist over a mortgage payment and who was known for his violent temper (he had stabbed his brother-in-law to death three months earlier during a quarrel over money). There was also speculation, as the *Detroit Free Press* reported, that the murders may "have been the work of a madman who believed himself an instrument of the powers of good and conceived it his duty to wipe out Evangelist."

In the end, however, no arrests were made, and the atrocity known alternatively as the "St. Aubin Avenue Massacre" and the "Evangelist Occult Murders" remains unsolved.

THE YPSILANTI RIPPER

Ypsilanti and
Ann Arbor, Michigan
July 9, 1967–July 23, 1969

Over a two-year period beginning in July 1967, a serial sex-killer committed a string of atrocities in the Ypsilanti/Ann Arbor area of Michigan. His six victims ranged in age from thirteen to twenty-two. Four were coeds at Eastern Michigan University (EMU) or the University of Michigan, the two youngest an eighth grader and a sixteen-year-old high schooler. That his crimes were fueled by extreme sadistic rage was clear from the inordinately savage injuries he inflicted.

All the victims were subjected to frenzied overkill: raped, strangled, stabbed, whipped, sexually mutilated, and in one instance, doused with a corrosive liquid, either acid or lye. Such was the ferocity of his assaults that the press dubbed him the "Ypsilanti Ripper." Despite intensive efforts by the local police, including the establishment of a fifty-man task force, the investigation went nowhere. At one point, a publicity-hungry celebrity psychic, Peter Hurkos, was brought in to assist in the search. Though he impressed a few lawmen with some of his guesses, Hurkos never managed to come up with a name, let alone a consistent description of the killer during his weeklong stay.

It was the proprietor of an Ypsilanti wig shop who helped bring the Ripper's reign of terror to an end, providing police with a description of the young man who had given the murderer's last victim a ride to the store on his motorcycle. He was quickly identified as twenty-year-old EMU English major John Norman Collins. A former high school honor student and star athlete, Collins assumed a mask of clean-cut affability that occasionally slipped, revealing his true face beneath.

With his good looks and easy charm, Collins had no trouble attracting women. But a number of his girlfriends quickly realized that their handsome catch was a deeply troubled young man—moody, sullen, prone to violent tirades against women. He had also been kicked out of his fraternity for theft and unsettled one of his professors by declaring in an essay that a man was beholden to no law but his own desires.

Physical evidence tying him to the basement where the last victim had been tortured and killed left no doubt of his guilt. Convicted in August 1970, he was sentenced to life imprisonment in solitary confinement at Southern Michigan Prison.

John Norman Collins lured women into danger by exploiting the common practice of hitchhiking and offering rides.

MASTER BOB IN GROSSE POINTE

Grosse Pointe, Michigan • January 24, 2012

In his affluent Grosse Pointe community, Bob Bashara, son of an esteemed state judge, was seen as a paragon of suburban upper-middle-class propriety. A churchgoing family man who served as president of the Rotary Club, he passed himself off as a successful businessman and real estate investor. None of his neighbors suspected that his finances were in a shambles and his marriage was on the rocks. Nor did they have any inkling about all the other secrets that would come to light when Bashara became the central figure in one of the most sensational crimes in Michigan history.

To start, there were the charges filed against him in 1995, when he was accused of sexually molesting his five-year-old niece. Then came his deepening involvement in the BDSM world where, despite—or because of—his chronic impotence, he lived a second life as the dominant "Master Bob," who converted a basement room in one of his properties into a "sex dungeon" and forged relationships with female submissives eager to be his "slaves." When Bashara became passionately attached to one of those women, he envisioned a new life with her in their own home, where they would add a second live-in female submissive to create a happy BDSM throuple.

The only obstacle to the realization of this fantasy was his wife, Jane. On January 24, 2012, her body, throat crushed, was found slumped in the back of her abandoned Mercedes-Benz in a desolate Detroit neighborhood. A few weeks later, Joe Gentz, a handyman who did work for

Bob Bashara and his wife Jane on vacation in Hawai'i the year before he killed her.

Bashara, confessed to police that the latter had offered him several thousand dollars and a used car to kill Bashara's wife. According to his account, later supported by forensic evidence, he had been summoned by phone to the Bashara house to help "clean the garage." Once there, Bob had brought Jane into the garage and ordered Gentz at gunpoint to "take her out." Gentz complied, knocking her down with a blow to her face, then stomping on her throat with his boot, breaking her neck. He eventually accepted a plea deal and was sentenced to seventeen to twenty-eight years in prison.

Bashara was ultimately sentenced to life without parole.

MINNESOTA

ST. CLOUD
THE WANNABE VAMPIRE OF ST. CLOUD
133

MINNEAPOLIS
THE MINNEAPOLIS SVENGALI
131

ST. PAUL
A HITMAN HIRED IN ST. PAUL
131

MINNEAPOLIS
VERSACE KILLER STARTS HIS SPREE
134

Harry Haywood became the second to last person to be hanged in Minnesota.

THE MINNEAPOLIS SVENGALI

MINNEAPOLIS, MINNESOTA
DECEMBER 3, 1894

A dashing twenty-nine-year-old sociopath from a wealthy family, Harry Hayward exerted his seductive charm on a young woman named Kitty Ging, who agreed to bankroll his gambling habits for a share of the profits. When she backed out of the deal after he incurred serious losses at the card tables, Harry—soon to be known as the "Minneapolis Svengali" for the seemingly irresistible power he wielded over her—persuaded Kitty to make him the beneficiary of two life insurance policies totaling $10,000.

Not long afterward, her body, with a bullet hole behind the right ear, was found on a road after being dumped from a fast-moving buggy. Although Harry was a prime suspect, he had an airtight alibi, having been at the theater at the time of her murder. Within days, however, authorities learned the truth from his brother, Adry, to whom Harry had confided his nefarious scheme.

Employing a combination of bribery and blackmail, Harry had compelled an accomplice, a "dimwitted" handyman named Claus Blixt, to commit the murder. Sentenced to death at the climax of a sensational seven-week trial that made headlines across the country, Harry eventually confessed not only to his role in the Ging murder but to three other homicides as well, making him—if his claims are true—one of nineteenth-century America's most infamous serial killers.

Blixt was given a life sentence and died in prison, reportedly after going insane.

A HITMAN HIRED IN ST. PAUL

ST. PAUL, MINNESOTA
MARCH 6, 1963

When he died at the age of eighty-eight in August 2015, obituaries remembered T. Eugene Thompson as the "man behind one of Minnesota's most infamous crimes of the twentieth century."

It happened on a near-freezing morning in the upscale neighborhood of Highland Park, while Thompson—a highly respected attorney—was at his downtown law office, having arrived for work that day at an unusually early hour. Shortly before 9:00 a.m., his thirty-five-year-old wife, Carol—barefoot, clad only in a bathrobe, blood streaming from her face, scalp, and neck—staggered to the home of neighbor, pleading for help. "A man did it," she managed to gasp.

Brutally beaten and stabbed repeatedly in the throat, she died in the hospital a few hours later. The savage murder of the lawyer's devoted wife—an almost stereotypical specimen of the happy, wholesome, stay-at-home mom held up as an ideal for women of that era—sent shockwaves throughout the city and beyond. Newspapers speculated that she been killed either by an intruder she had surprised in the act of burglarizing the house or by a grudge-filled former client of her husband bent on revenge.

Over the following weeks, however, investigators turned up information that cast a suspicious light on her seemingly upstanding husband. Not only had Thompson been conducting an affair with a former secretary he hoped to marry, but, in the previous year, he had taken out eight insurance policies on Carol's life that, together, would pay him more than $1,000,000 in the event of her death.

The case was finally broken thanks to a key piece of evidence: fragments of a pistol grip found at the crime scene were ultimately traced to an ex-con who confessed that Thompson had hired him to kill his wife. The hitman described in gruesome detail the ferocious struggle his victim had put up as he battered her face and head with the pistol butt, then stabbed her repeatedly in the throat with a paring knife he pulled from a kitchen drawer.

Convicted and sentenced to life imprisonment at the end of a sensational six-week trial, Thompson was paroled nineteen years later, remarried, and lived out his days earning a comfortable living from stock investments and real estate.

T. Eugene Thompson and his wife, Carol, were both "pillars of the community" before he had her killed by a hit man.

Timothy Erickson (left) and his brother, Mark (right), are led into court.

THE WANNABE VAMPIRE OF ST. CLOUD

St. Cloud, Minnesota
March 21, 1988

Timothy Erickson and his brother, Mark, eighteen and nineteen, respectively, shared a squalid apartment they turned into a "flophouse" for homeless and runaway adolescents. After watching the 1987 teen horror film *The Lost Boys*, Timothy got it into his head to start his own "vampire cult." On the evening of March 21, 1988, the two brothers along with a few of their friends and a thirty-year-old hanger-on, Donald Gall—a learning-disabled alcoholic recently released from jail after pleading guilty to assaulting his girlfriend—decided to camp out in Riverside Park near St. Cloud.

After doing drugs, drinking beer, eating hot dogs, and shooting the breeze until 4:30 a.m., Gall passed out by the campfire. Taking the others aside, Timothy proposed that they make Gall their "first victim," a suggestion endorsed by all except Mark, who refused to participate. Returning to the campsite, Timothy and his three younger cohorts set upon the sleeping Gall.

After clubbing him with a log, Timothy slit his throat, drank from the wound, and licked his hands clean of blood, then, with the help of the others, dumped the body into the Mississippi River. The next day, he bragged about the killing to a friend, Bill Benedict, giggling as he related the ghoulish details of the crime and saying that Gall's death was "not really that big of a deal." Two days later, a drunken Benedict reported the murder to police, who arrested Erickson after finding the corpse floating in the river.

His defense attorney claimed that his client was insane, arguing, "Only a nut would do something like this. Can a person who wants to be a vampire choose between right and wrong?" Erickson was nonethless convicted and sentenced to life.

VERSACE KILLER STARTS HIS SPREE

Minneapolis and Chisago County, Minnesota
April 26–May 2, 1997

Andrew Cunanan achieved international notoriety for murdering famed fashion designer Gianni Versace on the front steps of the latter's Miami Beach mansion in July 1997. Three months earlier, however, his homicidal rampage began with two killings in Minnesota.

A charismatic young man who enjoyed a glitzy, hedonistic life thanks to the largesse of his wealthy closeted lovers, Cunanan was plunged into an increasingly desperate existence after being dumped by his latest sugar daddy in September 1996. Virtually overnight, he went from a life of comfort and glamor to a sordid, hand-to-mouth existence. Maxing out his credit card, dealing (and consuming) drugs, indulging his growing appetite for hardcore BDSM porn, he came to fit the profile of the classic spree killer: the profoundly embittered individual who—seething with rage and resentment when his world falls apart—decides to go out with a bang and take others along with him.

In April 1997, Cunanan flew from California to Minneapolis, home of the two men he felt closest to. One was Jeff Trail, a former naval officer Cunanan referred to as "my brother," though the exact nature of their relationship—romantic or platonic—remains unclear. The other was Cunanan's ex-lover, architect David Madson, whom Cunanan regarded as the "love of my life." Neither was happy about the visit.

Trail, who was seeing another man, wanted as little to do with Cunanan as possible, particularly after the two had a nasty falling out when he rebuffed Cunanan's suggestion that they go into the drug-dealing business together. As for Madson, he'd grown increasingly uncomfortable around his former lover, suspecting that he was "into something shady," though, in his typically generous way, he allowed Cunanan to stay in his apartment.

On the night of April 26, Trail arrived at the apartment in response to a telephone summons from Cunanan. Three days later, his decomposed body was found rolled up in an Oriental rug stashed behind the living room sofa. He had been beaten to death with a claw hammer, smashed in the head, face, and upper torso more than two dozen times. By then, Cunanan and Madson—who had spent two days in the apartment with the rotting corpse—had taken off in Madson's Jeep.

On May 2, Madson's body was found beside a lake forty-five miles north of Minneapolis. Cunanan had shot him three times, in the eye, cheek, and upper back, with a gun he had stolen from Trail. Cunanan would murder two more victims on his way to Miami: Chicago real estate developer Lee Miglin, slain in a particularly gruesome way, and New Jersey cemetery caretaker William Reese, killed for his Chevy pickup truck.

By assassinating Versace, Cunanan achieved the dream of every malignant narcissist: becoming the center of the world's attention. Two weeks later, holed up in a houseboat, he shot himself in the head with the gun he'd used to kill Madson.

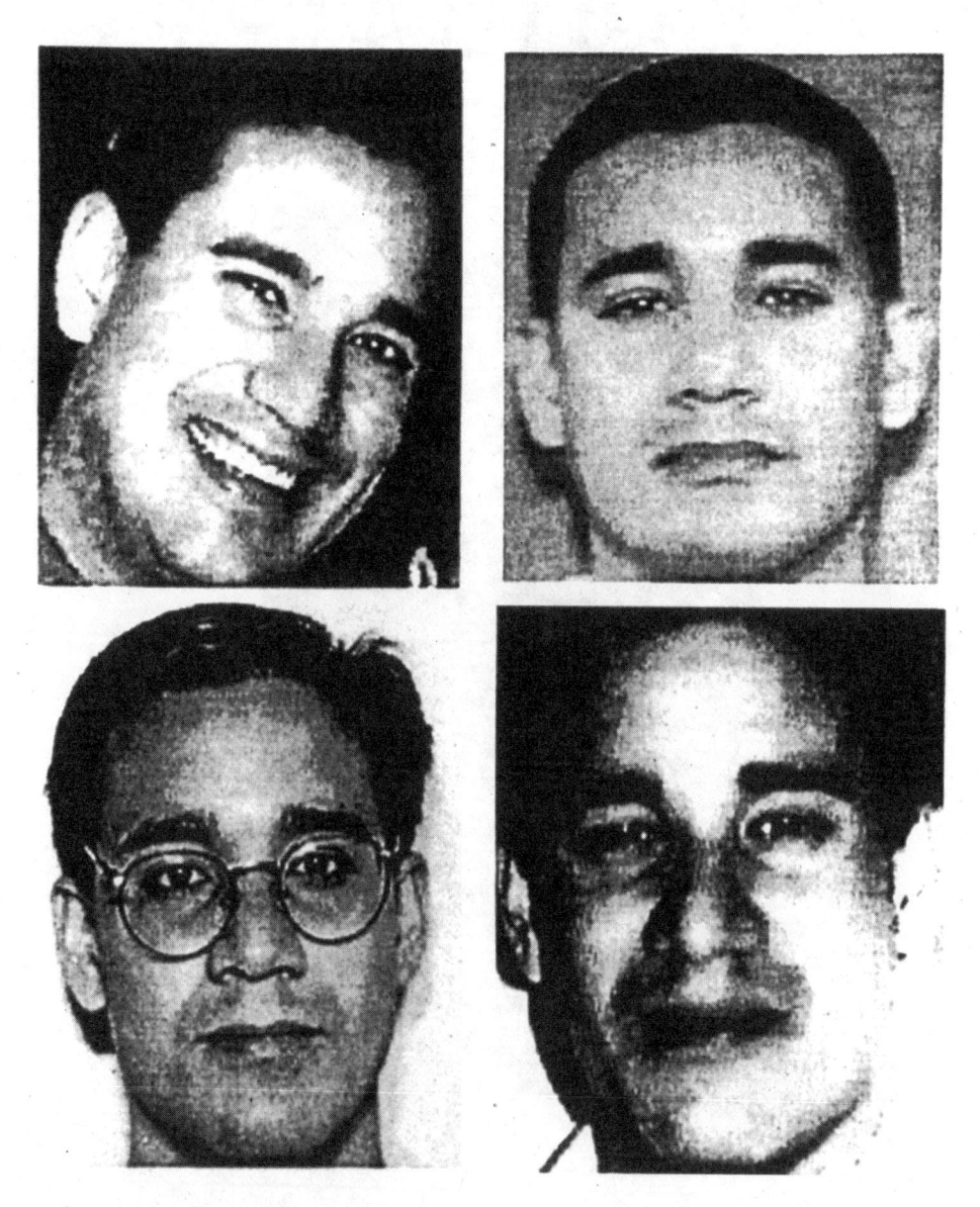

Andrew Cunanan, man of many faces

MINNESOTA • 135

MISSISSIPPI

MONROE COUNTY
"WERE MURDERED DECEMBER 17, 1880"
137

LELAND
SOCIALITE KILLED BY SAME
139

LAUREL
THE LEGS MURDER
138

JACKSON ★

LEETOWN
THE DEVIL HIMSELF DID IT?
139

"WERE MURDERED DECEMBER 17, 1880"

MONROE COUNTY, MISSISSIPPI
DECEMBER 17, 1880

In a small cemetery in Monroe County, Mississippi, there stands a weatherworn triple tombstone memorializing three members of the Ridings family: twenty-five-year-old Henry B., his sixteen-year-old wife, Florence (identified by the initials "A. F."), and their daughter, Creola, who was two years, four months, and fourteen days old. Little is known about the family apart from the information recorded on the base of their shared marker: "Were murdered December 17, 1880."

Early that day, Ridings drove his buckboard to the town of Eureka to sell some cotton, returning home with a few silver dollars. That evening, an itinerant laborer named Alvin McKenna, who had been in the neighborhood for a week or so, came to the door and asked if he could be put up for the night. Ridings welcomed him in. A few hours later, David Ridings, Henry's father, who lived a short distance away, spotted flames coming from his son's house. By the time he rushed over, the house and its occupants were past saving.

The following morning, searchers found the charred remains of Henry, Florence, and Creola in the smoking ruins. The skulls of the parents had been crushed with an axe. The absence of head wounds on the child suggested she had died in the conflagration. Suspicion immediately fell upon McKenna, who was swiftly tracked down and captured. Taken back to the scene of the crime, he made a chilling confession that revealed him to be one of the nation's early serial killers.

A thirty-two-year-old native of Ohio, he had received a ninety-nine-year sentence for robbing and murdering a man near Terre Haute, Indiana, then been transferred to an insane asylum by convincingly feigning madness, and promptly escaped. Along with an accomplice named Gilmore, McKenna had traveled through Illinois, Kentucky, Tennessee, and Alabama passing himself off as a farmhand in need of work "but really hunting victims" (as a contemporary newspaper reported). Stopping at a town, he would stay long enough to learn which of the residents was said to have the most money. He would then beg lodging for a night, chloroform his hosts as they slept, burglarize the premises, murder the occupants, and set the house ablaze before making off with his loot.

McKenna had killed eight men and women that way before he showed up at the Ridings' farm. In their case, he had murdered Henry first with an axe blow to the head, then raped Florence before dispatching her in the same way. He then doused their bodies, the bedding, walls, and floor with kerosene oil and set it ablaze, pouring a little extra on the sleeping two-year-old before fleeing. He admitted that before he "left the scene," he "heard the screams of the little burning infant."

No sooner had he made this appalling confession than a rope was produced, and he was strung up from a tree limb. He was still strangling to death when the rope snapped. To give him a taste of his own medicine, wood and kindling were piled on his "writhing body" and he was burned alive.

THE LEGS MURDER

Laurel, Mississippi • January 20, 1935

On Monday, January 21, 1935, a farmer named Dale Evans Jr. was out hunting rabbits in the woods when his dogs, trotting ahead of him, came to a sudden halt and began growling. When Evans drew closer, he saw that they were sniffing at two bundles wrapped in sugar sacks. Inside, as he discovered when he lifted part of the cloth with a stick, were the upper portions of a woman's legs, still attached to the hips.

Quickly summoned to the scene, police found tire track evidence suggesting that a car had recently driven up to the site, gotten stuck in the mud, then been pulled out by another, larger vehicle. Within days, a local garage mechanic came forward to report that, earlier that Monday, he had towed a mired car from a spot close to where the severed legs had been found. Its owner, he said, was a local woman, Ouida Keeton.

The "Legs Murder" case, as it came to be known, entered into local legend. At its center was Juanita "Ouida" Keeton, a beautiful, intelligent, mentally unstable woman who lived under the domination of her widowed mother, Daisy. Exactly what happened between them on the fatal night of January 20 remains a mystery. The likeliest scenario, according to students of the crime, is that, after striking her mother with a poker during a violent quarrel, Keeton finished her off with three bullets to the head. She then dismembered the body in the bathtub, flushed some of the flesh down the toilet, incinerated other parts in the fireplace, then wrapped the rest—a portion consisting of the thighs, buttocks, and genitalia—in the burlap sacks and dumped them in the woods.

Keeton herself told a very different story, however, laying blame for the murder on her former employer and lover, a philandering businessman named W. M. Carter. Both were tried and found guilty, though Carter was eventually freed after his conviction was overturned on appeal. Sentenced to life imprisonment, the increasingly psychotic Keeton spent the rest of her days in state mental institutions, dying on November 11, 1973.

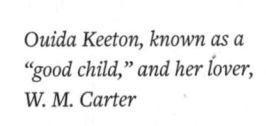

Ouida Keeton, known as a "good child," and her lover, W. M. Carter

138 • 50 STATES OF MURDER

SOCIALITE KILLED BY SAME

Leland, Mississippi
November 17, 1948

On the morning of November 17, 1948, sixty-eight-year-old Idella Thompson, matriarch of a socially prominent family in the Mississippi Delta town of Leland, was released from the hospital after a weeklong stay for high blood pressure. She was taken home by her daughter, Ruth Dickins, the socialite wife of a well-known cotton broker and a mother of two. A few hours later, police were summoned to the Thompson home, where they found Idella dead in the bathroom.

She had been slain in a frenzy of overkill, her face slashed to pulp, her head crushed, her body covered with more than 150 stab wounds. The murder weapon, a pair of pruning shears, lay by her side.

According to Dickins, who had scratches and bruises on her forehead, arms, and shins, she had run some errands, then returned to find her mother lying in the gore-drenched bathroom. As Dickins rushed to Thompson's side, a "young, slightly built, dark-skinned Negro" came at her with the clippers. In the ensuing struggle, Dickins managed to wrestle the gardening tool out of his hands. When she slipped in the blood and went face down on the floor, the intruder fled.

A thorough investigation by forensic experts, however, could turn up no trace of an intruder, while a wealth of physical evidence pointed to Dickins as the perpetrator. Authorities speculated that she and her hot-tempered mother had gotten into a rapidly escalating argument over family finances that climaxed when Dickins flew into an uncontrolled rage and butchered Thompson with the shears. She was found guilty of first-degree murder and sentenced to life, but—owing largely to her husband's political pull—was paroled after just six years.

THE DEVIL HIMSELF DID IT?

Leetown, Mississippi
November 26, 1981

By the time he was twenty, James Billiot had been arrested for assaulting his grandfather and done four stretches in state mental institutions. He was back home in the fall of 1981, living with his mother, Audrey; stepfather, Wallace Croll; and stepsiblings, Cheryl Ann and Stephen, fourteen and twelve, respectively.

Early on Thanksgiving morning, a neighbor who knew that Billiot was forbidden from driving the family car saw him speeding away in the vehicle. Going over to investigate, he found the bodies of Wallace, Audrey, and Cheryl Ann, their skulls "beaten to a mush" with a six-pound sledgehammer. Arrested two days later, Billiot claimed that he had watched from behind as the devil, wearing a black cloak, fetched the sledgehammer from the barn and murdered his family members. Stephen would have been killed, too, said Billiot, if he hadn't spent the night at a friend's house.

Though diagnosed as a paranoid schizophrenic who, at various times, claimed to be Jesus Christ, Hitler, "Romeo Machiavelli," and the entire rock band Led Zeppelin, Billiot was declared competent to stand trial, convicted of the murder of Wallace Croll, and sentenced to die in the gas chamber.

MISSOURI

KANSAS CITY
THE UNION STATION MASSACRE
143

ST. LOUIS
THE ORIGINAL FRANKIE AND JOHNNY
142

★ JEFFERSON CITY

JOPLIN
THE HITCHHIKING KILLER
144

ST. LOUIS
STACK LEE BECOMES LEGEND
141

SPRINGFIELD
GYPSY-ROSE GETS HER REVENGE
145

STACK LEE BECOMES LEGEND

St. Louis, Missouri • December 25, 1895

Recorded in countless versions by artists ranging from Duke Ellington to Woody Guthrie, Neil Diamond to Bob Dylan, Ma Rainey to the Grateful Dead, the ballad of Stackolee (also known as Stack Lee, Staggerlee, Stagolee, and Stackalee) tells the story of the titular Black badman who shoots down an acquaintance, Billy Lyons, in an argument over a Stetson hat. Though the fatal encounter between the two men has entered the realm of myth, it was based on a real-life crime that happened in St. Louis on Christmas night, 1895.

A flamboyantly dressed pimp of a type known as a "mack," Lee Shelton had apparently acquired the nickname "Stack" from his time working the riverboat *Stack Lee*, where the amenities included onboard prostitution. By 1895, he owned a notorious nightclub in East St. Louis's red-light district. On that fateful December evening, levee worker Billy Lyons—"a stout man in a derby"—was drinking at a Tenderloin saloon when Stack entered in one of his typically flashy outfits: gray-striped pants, red velvet vest, yellow embroidered shirt, high celluloid collar, custom-made shoes with gray spats, and a milk-white Stetson with a fancy hatband.

Striding up to the bar, Stack engaged Lyons in a friendly conversation that became heated when the subject turned to local politics. Soon blows were exchanged and Stack struck Lyons on the head, denting his derby. When Lyons, in retaliation, grabbed Stack's Stetson and refused to return it, the latter drew his .44 Smith & Wesson revolver from his coat pocket, pointed it at Lyon's stomach, and promised to shoot him if he didn't hand over the hat at once. Lyons responded by pulling a knife, whereupon Stack made good on his threat, putting a bullet in Lyons's gut, then snatching his hat from the dying man's fingers and striding from the saloon.

Tried, convicted, and sentenced to twenty-five years in the Missouri State Penitentiary, Stack was paroled in 1909 but imprisoned again two years later for assault and robbery. He died behind bars in March 1912 but lives on in song and story as the mythic embodiment of unrepentant outlaw swagger.

The mythic Stackolee

Frankie Baker, whose life became legend

THE ORIGINAL FRANKIE AND JOHNNY

St. Louis, Missouri
October 15, 1899

Four years after Lee Shelton killed Billy Lyon, another St. Louis shooting became the inspiration for a famous murder ballad. Its principal figures were twenty-three-year-old sex worker Frankie Baker and her seventeen-year-old live-in lover and pimp, Allen Britt. A snappy dresser and talented pianist who played ragtime at a neighborhood brothel, Britt had been cheating on Baker with a young "sporting girl," Alice Pryor.

Though accounts vary, most historians of the case agree that, on the night of October 14, 1899, Baker caught her lover and Pryor slow dancing at a hotel and, following a furious argument, stormed back to their apartment and went to bed. When Britt showed up early the next morning—having spent the night with Pryor—the two resumed their fight. According to Baker's version of events, when Britt drew a pocketknife and threatened to "cut her," she reached for the gun beneath her pillow and shot him once in the stomach. Britt managed to stagger to the home of his mother a few houses away and died four days later in the city hospital.

Within forty-eight hours of the shooting, a St. Louis street musician named Bill Dooley had composed a murder ballad, "Frankie Killed Allen." A sheet music version, renamed "Frankie and Albert," was published in 1904. Under its eventual title, "Frankie and Johnny," the ballad became a standard part of the American folksong repertoire.

Tried in November, Baker was acquitted on the grounds of "justifiable homicide for self-defense." She subsequently moved to Portland, Oregon, where she operated a "shoe-shining parlor" for a few years. When the 1933 Mae West film *She Done Him Wrong* opened in 1933, Baker sued Paramount Pictures for ripping off her life story. She lost the suit, as well as another one five years later over the alleged "wrongful, wanton, willful, and malicious" portrayal of her life in Republic Pictures's 1936 movie *Frankie and Johnnie*.

With her physical and mental health in decline, she was admitted to a state hospital in the spring of 1950 and died there two years later at the age of seventy-six.

The bloody aftermath of the Union Station Massacre

THE UNION STATION MASSACRE

Kansas City, Missouri • June 17, 1933

A silver-tongued gangster who once talked his way out of prison by persuading the warden that, if paroled, he would volunteer for combat duty in World War I, Frank "Jelly" Nash found himself back behind bars in 1924, sentenced to twenty-five years in Leavenworth for his part in an armed train robbery. He escaped six years later but was ultimately tracked down and apprehended in Hot Springs, Arkansas, by a pair of FBI agents with the help of an Oklahoma police chief.

The handcuffed prisoner was driven to Fort Smith and ushered onto a train bound for Kansas City, Missouri. Four additional lawmen were waiting on the platform when the train pulled into the Union Station depot the following morning at 7:15 a.m. So were a group of Nash's underworld confederates. Likely among them was the notorious gangster Charles Arthur "Pretty Boy" Floyd.

As Nash was being loaded into a car waiting to take him back to Leavenworth, the Tommy-gun-wielding Floyd and two of his armed associates approached the vehicle and shouted "Get 'em up!" Some accounts say that one of the lawmen fired first, hitting Floyd in the shoulder with a pistol shot. Others claim that Floyd simply yelled "Let 'em have it!" and opened fire.

What is certain is that, in the next ninety seconds, the gunmen let loose with a blazing fusillade that left five men dead—four of the lawmen and Nash, hit in the head by a bullet fired by Floyd and his cohorts. The "Union Station Massacre" (as it was immediately dubbed) made front pages across the nation and led to a massive FBI investigation. Floyd was ultimately tracked to a farm in Ohio and killed in a shootout, though, like other Depression-era badmen, he lives on in American legend.

MISSOURI • 143

THE HITCHHIKING KILLER

JOPLIN, MISSOURI
JANUARY 1951

Billy Cook had the kind of background virtually guaranteed to produce a sociopathic personality. He was five when his mother died, leaving him and his seven siblings in the hands of their father, who promptly drove them to an abandoned mine shaft, supplied them with a few provisions, then drove away, never to be seen again. The half-starved children were discovered a few days later and farmed out to foster families.

Already showing symptoms of his future psychopathology, Billy proved too much of a handful for any of his prospective guardians and was shipped off to a grim reform school. At fourteen, briefly released from the reformatory, he got hold of a blackjack and robbed a Joplin cab driver of $11. Back in custody, he proved such an incorrigible troublemaker that he was eventually transferred to the Missouri State Penitentiary, where he quickly earned a reputation for his violent and erratic behavior.

Released in 1950, the twenty-two-year-old Cook embarked on the spree that would gain him nationwide notoriety as the "Hitchhiking Killer." When an automobile he had carjacked broke down in Oklahoma, a Good Samaritan named Carl Mosser—on a family trip with his wife, three small children, and dog—offered the stranded young man a lift. No sooner had Cook gotten into the rear seat than he pulled out his gun, stuck it into Mrs. Mosser's side, and ordered her husband to drive.

For the next seventy-two hours, he kept them moving on a nightmarish, zigzag ride through four states. Too exhausted to go on, Mosser pulled off the highway outside of Joplin, Missouri, where Cook shot all five of his hostages, along with the family dog. After dumping their bodies down a mine shaft, he fled to Tulsa, Oklahoma, left the car in a ditch, and caught a westbound Greyhound bus.

When the car was discovered shortly afterward—its seats riddled with bullets and caked in blood—a nationwide all-points bulletin was issued for Cook. Despite the thousands of lawmen hunting him, Cook managed to hitchhike his way to Blythe, California, where he took a deputy sheriff captive and, after leaving him alive in the desert, made off with his patrol car. A few miles up the road, the young killer turned on his siren and pulled over a Buick driven by a vacationing salesman, Robert Dewey.

Executing Dewey with a shot to the head, Cook then sped off in the dead man's car toward Mexico. When the Buick broke down a hundred or so miles south of the border, Cook was offered a ride by two passing motorists. Taken hostage at gunpoint, they were forced to drive their young kidnapper on a 450-mile journey through the Baja California desert. Cook and his captives were eventually spotted at a café in Santa Rosalia, six hundred miles south of the border. He was arrested without a struggle.

Returned to the United States, Cook was tried and convicted for the kidnap-murders of the five Mossers and given five consecutive sixty-year terms, for a total of three hundred years. He was then turned over to California authorities, tried for the murder of Robert Dewey, and sentenced to death in the San Quentin gas chamber, where he was executed on December 12, 1932.

GYPSY-ROSE GETS HER REVENGE

Springfield, Missouri
June 14, 2015

To her neighbors, Dee Dee Blanchard was a woman to be both admired and pitied—a mother whose entire life had been sacrificed to the 24-7 care of her severely disabled daughter, Gypsy-Rose. From the time of her birth, so Dee Dee would explain, Gypsy had been stricken with an array of dire ailments—everything from leukemia to muscular dystrophy, epilepsy to asthma—that had left her confined to a wheelchair.

She received nutrients and medications through a feeding tube and slept with a breathing machine because of her apnea. At her mother's insistence, doctors removed Gypsy's salivary glands to cure her uncontrollable drooling, an operation that eventually caused her teeth to rot, necessitating their removal. Informed by her mother that she had cancer, Gypsy allowed Dee Dee to shave her bald since her hair was going to fall out anyway.

In truth, there was nothing wrong with Gypsy. It was Dee Dee who was sick, afflicted with Munchausen syndrome by proxy, a mental disorder in which a caregiver, typically a mother, generates attention and sympathy for herself by convincing the world that her child is suffering from a serious disease. As in Dee Dee's case, this type of abuse involves not simply pretending that the child is ill, but actually inducing symptoms in the little victim—in effect, subjecting them to incessant torture.

By 2015, Gyspy was twenty-four, no longer little, and had grown tired of being a victim. On Sunday, June 14, visitors to the Facebook page she shared with her mother saw an alarming post: "That Bitch is dead!" Worried neighbors alerted the police, who found Dee Dee lying face down on her blood-soaked mattress, dead from seventeen stab wounds. Gypsy was gone.

She was tracked down and arrested a few days later in the company of the killer—her boyfriend, Nicholas Godejohn. A "loner with autism spectrum disorder and a low-average IQ," as one psychiatrist described him, Godejohn had met Gypsy on a Christian dating website and the two quickly established an intense online relationship involving shared BDSM fantasies.

He agreed to kill Dee Dee when Gypsy persuaded him that, once her controlling mother was out of the way, they could run off and be together. On the night of the murder, Godejohn, who traveled from his home in Wisconsin, was let into the Blanchard house by Gypsy, who then handed him a knife and hid in the bathroom while her boyfriend crept into Dee Dee's bedroom and stabbed her to death as she slept.

Godejohn was convicted of first-degree murder and sentenced to life. Gypsy was allowed to plead guilty of second-degree murder and was sentenced to ten years in prison. Paroled in December 2023, she became a media darling and, beginning in 2024, the star of her own cable reality show, *Gypsy-Rose: Life After Lock Up*.

MONTANA

GLACIER NATIONAL PARK
A MARRIAGE GONE BAD IN GLACIER
149

MISSOULA
THE MISSOULA MAULER
148

HELENA ★

GALLATIN COUNTY
A LONER KILLER IN GALLATIN
147

A LONER KILLER IN GALLATIN

GALLATIN COUNTY, MONTANA
1967–1974

The search for Sandra Smallegan (left) and Susan Jaeger (right) was the largest manhunt in Montana's history.

On March 19, 1967, thirteen-year-old Bernie Poelman climbed the girders of a bridge outside his small Montana hometown and prepared to dive into the Gallatin River below. All at once, he clutched his chest and plunged into the water. Three weeks passed before his body was retrieved. An autopsy revealed that he died from a gunshot wound to his heart.

Fourteen months later, in May 1968, during a Boy Scout "camporee," twelve-year-old Michael Raney was murdered in his sleep by someone who sliced open the back of his pup tent, stabbed him in the chest, and delivered a fatal blow to his head. An eerily similar crime occurred in June 1973 when seven-year-old Susie Jaeger, camping with her family in a Gallatin state park, was snatched from her slit-open tent in the middle of the night.

Another person from the area disappeared the following February: Nineteen-year-old waitress Sandy Smallegan left a local bar at about midnight and was never seen again. Officers searched a remote, abandoned ranch where, hidden in the barn, they found the young woman's car. They also found hundreds of human bone fragments, some scattered around the property, others among the ashes in an oil drum used for burning trash.

In consultation with several pioneering FBI profilers, investigators zeroed in on a local man, David Meirhofer, a twenty-five-year-old carpenter and ex-marine with a reputation as a "quiet loner." He was arrested after authorities determined that he was the man who had made repeated taunting phone calls to Jaeger's mother. A search of his home turned up a human hand and several packages of meat in his freezer, one labeled with Smallegan's initials. Meirhofer confessed that he had molested Susie Jaeger, then choked her to death, cut up her body, put her head in an outhouse, and burned the rest in the oil drum. Smallegan was likewise asphyxiated, dismembered, and—except for the parts he stored in his freezer—incinerated.

Under a plea deal, Meirhofer also admitted to the murders of Poelman and Raney. Four hours after making his confession, he hanged himself with a towel in his jail cell.

Psycho-killer David Meirhofer

Wayne Nance, known as "Montana's baby-faced serial sex murderer"

THE MISSOULA MAULER

Missoula, Montana
1974–1986

Despite his obsessive fascination with the occult, the pentagram he had carved on one forearm, his boasts about skinning cats alive, and his professed desire to perform a human sacrifice, eighteen-year-old Wayne Nance was generally seen to be nothing more than a high school oddball caught up in the satanism craze of the time. Then, in April 1974, someone broke into the home of thirty-nine-year-old Donna Pounds—wife of a fundamentalist minister and mother of one of Nance's friends—raped her at gunpoint, shot her five times in the back of the head, and defiled the corpse, shoving the gun barrel into her vagina.

Seen by several eyewitness on the Pounds property at the time of the slaying, Nance became a prime suspect but remained unindicted for lack of evidence. Following a three-year stint in the navy, he returned to Missoula, where he worked in a furniture warehouse by day and as a bouncer at night. Having shed his reputation as a teenaged menace, he seemed to have matured into a caring and considerate friend, neighbor, and romantic partner: a testament to his skill at feigning normal human behavior, typical of psychopathic sex-murderers.

Exactly how many people Nance killed is unclear, though three young women whose decomposed remains were found dumped on the roadside or buried in a shallow grave between 1980 and 1985 were almost certainly among his victims. Two weeks before Christmas in 1985, Nance broke into the home of a family named Shook, stabbed the husband to death, bound, raped, and killed the wife, then set the house on fire. The three sleeping children barely survived.

Attributed to a shadowy home invader dubbed the "Missoula Mauler" in the press, the atrocity set off a panic in the city. Nance's end came on September 4, 1986. Talking himself into the home of his warehouse manager, Kris Wells, he bashed her husband, Doug, on the head with a billy club, tied him up, dragged him to the basement, and stabbed him in the chest. While Nance was upstairs with Kris—now bound to her bed—Doug, though badly wounded, managed to free himself and get hold of his hunting rifle.

Staggering upstairs, Doug shot Nance in the side, then battered him so ferociously with the rifle that the wooden stock shattered. Despite his injuries, Nance managed to grab hold of a pistol and get off three shots, one of which—apparently deflected by a swipe from Doug's weapon—struck the killer in the head. Nance died in the hospital the next day.

A MARRIAGE GONE BAD IN GLACIER

GLACIER NATIONAL PARK, MONTANA • JULY 7, 2013

Exactly why twenty-two-year-old Jordan Graham felt her marriage was a mistake from the start is unclear, though sex certainly had something to do with it. Raised in a strict Baptist household, she had saved her virginity for wedlock. Her new husband, twenty-five-year-old Cody Lee Johnson—by all accounts deeply besotted with Graham—had abided by her wishes. Once they were wed, he expected that they would embark on an active, mutually satisfying sex life.

From their first night together, however, she was repelled by his sexual avidity. As she texted a friend, his eagerness to "do stuff" in bed made her so miserable that she "didn't feel like living." On July 7, 2013, eight days after their wedding, Johnson went missing. Questioned by police, Graham initially claimed that her husband had gone on a joyride with some friends on the night of his disappearance and she hadn't seen him since. A day later, she produced an email supposedly sent by a mysterious "Tony," informing her that, after driving with his buddies to Glacier National Park, Graham had gotten out of the car, gone for a hike, and fallen off a cliff.

The message, as investigators quickly determined, was written by Graham, who soon led searchers to Johnson's body at the bottom of a three-hundred-foot cliff. Under interrogation, she admitted that she killed him but claimed that she had done so by accident when they went to the park to talk about their marriage and got into an argument. When Johnson grabbed her arm angrily, she had pushed him away and he had gone "face-first over the cliff."

At her March 2014 trial, the prosecution convinced the jury that Graham had lured her trusting husband to the cliff with the promise of a "big surprise," then, as he turned his back to her, shoved him from behind with both hands.

Found guilty of murdering her husband of eight days, Graham—who at no point displayed a trace of remorse—was sentenced to thirty years in prison.

Jordan Graham with her future husband—and victim—Cody Johnson

NEBRASKA

OMAHA
THE MANIAC SNIPER OF OMAHA
155

LINCOLN
A JUDGE GUNNED DOWN IN LINCOLN
153

KEARNEY COUNTY
THE NEBRASKA FIEND
151

JULIAN
A GUILTY KILLER CONFESSES
152

Kearney in the late 1800s

THE NEBRASKA FIEND

Kearney County, Nebraska
1876–1878

One of our nation's earliest documented serial killers, Stephen D. Richards—aka the "Nebraska Fiend"—was twenty years old in 1876 when he headed west from his family home in Ohio. During a yearlong stay in Iowa, he worked at a mental asylum where his job involved burying dead inmates. Decamping for Nebraska, he committed his first two murders shortly after arriving in the state.

Traveling by horseback through the countryside, he came upon a stranger and the two rode on together until dark, when they pitched a camp and played cards around a fire. When the man accused him of cheating and demanded his money back, Richards shot him in the forehead, then dumped his body into a river. A few days later, he encountered another stranger, this one on foot, who turned out to be the murdered man's business associate. The man had seen Richards riding alongside his now-missing business associate days before, and began "ask[ing] me so many questions that I got nervous," Richards wrote, "and it seemed to me it would be safest to kill him to stop his mouth." At the first opportunity, Richards drew his pistol, shot the man in the back of the head, and rode on.

Victim number three was a young man who had sold Richards a horse and buggy. When he discovered that he had been paid in counterfeit bills, he tracked Richards down and threatened to have him arrested. The end result, wrote Richards, "was that I shot him." Not long afterward, he killed another traveling companion, a man named Gemge, who—angry at Richards for waking him up in the middle of the night—called him an insulting name and ended up with a .32-caliber bullet behind one ear.

But the crimes that earned him nationwide notoriety were the murders of a female acquaintance, Mary L. Harlson, and her three children, two daughters and one son, ranging in age from two to ten years old. While staying at the Harlson home, where he "told the woman a good deal about myself," Richards decided that his

NEBRASKA • 151

hostess "talked too much" and was likely to "give me away" unless he silenced her.

On the morning of November 3, 1878, while mother and children slept, he murdered all four with crushing blows to their skulls with the flat side of an axe, then buried the bodies in a pre-dug hole. One month later, he killed fellow lodger Peter Anderson during an argument by shattering his skull with a hammer. Fleeing east, he was eventually captured, tried, and sentenced to hang.

Before his execution on April 26, 1879, a reporter asked the twenty-three-year-old "multi-murderer" if he felt any remorse for killing the three children. "Not a damn bit," Richards replied. "When I was a boy, I was sent out to kill a litter of kittens, and I did it by striking their heads against a tree—smashing out their brains, one by one. I didn't feel bad about it at all—it was fun. I experienced the same sort of feeling when I killed these little Harlson kids."

Serial killer Stephen D. Richards was known to the media by many names: the Nebraska Fiend, Kearney County Murderer, and the Ohio Monster.

A GUILTY KILLER CONFESSES

JULIAN, NEBRASKA
JUNE 16, 1899

In June 1899, the mutilated and decomposed body of Julian Behaud—described as a "rich old miser" who hoarded "large sums of money"—was found in his cabin outside the town of Julian, Nebraska. Burns on his hands and feet indicated that he had been tortured to reveal the location of his cash. The mystery of his murder remained unsolved for fourteen years.

In the summer of 1913, a man named Fuller Shallenberger, residing in Burlington, Kansas, collapsed of heat exhaustion. Believing that he was about to die, he decided to unburden his soul and confessed that he and an accomplice named Charles Kopf had committed the crime, killing Behaud before stealing the money they found stashed in an old tin can. Though Shallenberger retracted his statement after making an unexpected recovery, Kopf was tracked down and arrested in Vallejo, California, where he lived with his wife and children, an employee of the Mare Island Naval Shipyard and a respected member of the community.

The case became a forensic landmark when Omaha police officials, working with scientists from the University of Nebraska medical school, administered one of the earliest recorded lie detector tests, hooking Kopf up to an electrocardiograph machine, the recent invention of Dutch physiologist Willem Einthoven,

Willem Einthoven, inventor of the lie detector

who would go on to win the Nobel Prize for his device.

In the end, the case against Kopf was dismissed for lack of evidence after Shallenberger refused to testify against him. Though Shallenberger's attorney argued that his client had "a mania for confessing crimes of which he was not guilty," he was convicted and sentenced to life. In 1925, newspapers reported that "because he 'talked himself into prison,' confessing a murder when he thought he was dying only to recover and be convicted," Shallenberger hadn't "spoken one word in fourteen years," answering "all questions by shaking or nodding his head."

A JUDGE GUNNED DOWN IN LINCOLN

LINCOLN, NEBRASKA
FEBRUARY 18, 1924

A much-respected judge known for his sharp wit and blunt, no-nonsense language, William McClellan Morning had been in charge of Lincoln's court of domestic relations since his elevation to the bench in 1918. In July 1923, he granted a divorce on the grounds of cruelty to Mrs. Malinda Wallick, who testified that her husband, Wallace, had "held a gun on her and choked her on at least one occasion." Wallace was ordered to pay alimony and child support of $25 a month.

In October, having received no money from her ex-husband, Malinda sued him for nonpayment. Charged with contempt for ignoring the court's ruling, he spent four days in jail, though the experience did nothing to alter his behavior. "She'll never get a penny from me," Wallace told his brother-in-law after his release. "I don't care what they do to me." When he proved as good as his word, Malinda took him to court again.

On the morning of Monday, February 18, 1924, he appeared before Judge Morning. Seated in the spectator section were his ex-wife and her lawyer, Clifford Rein. When his case was called, Wallace rose and faced Judge Morning, who asked if he wanted an attorney. Wallace replied that he "didn't need one." Morning then told him to be seated. At that moment, Wallace drew a revolver from his coat pocket and shot the judge in the chest. After firing at the court reporter, Minor Bacon—whose life was saved by a leather card wallet in his vest pocket that blunted the bullet's impact—Wallace whirled around and began shooting wildly in the direction of his ex-wife and her attorney, missing both though they sat frozen in shock.

He then stuck the gun muzzle into his mouth and pulled the trigger, dying instantly. By then, Morning had staggered from his bench and made his way into his chambers. By the time the doctor arrived, he was dead, victim of one of Nebraska's most infamous crimes.

Judge William M. Morning (top) and the body of killer Wallace Wallick (below)

THE MANIAC SNIPER OF OMAHA

Omaha, Nebraska • February 1926

Seven decades before the residents of Washington, DC, and the surrounding communities were terrorized by the random shootings of the so-called Beltway Snipers, John Allen Muhammad and John Lee Malvo, a madman nicknamed the "Maniac Sniper" created a panic among the citizenry of Omaha, Nebraska.

The murder spree began on Sunday, February 14, 1926, when William McDevitt, a dairyman out for an evening stroll, was killed with a .22-caliber bullet to the back of his head a short distance from his house. Two nights later, Miss Esther Mauthe was in a drugstore two blocks from the murder scene when a bullet crashed through the window, narrowly missing her. In an alley across the street, police found an empty cartridge identical to ones found near McDevitt's body.

The following night, sixty-two-year-old physician Dr. Austin Searles was slain in his office, killed—like McDevitt—with a .22-caliber bullet that entered behind his left ear and lodged behind his eyes. By Thursday night, as the *New York Times* reported, Omaha had become "a closed town." People were afraid to leave their houses or stand in front of lighted windows, theaters played to empty houses, and department stores were devoid of shoppers. At one church, normally attended by up to three hundred congregants, only three people were present for evening services, one of them the pastor.

The killer struck again on Friday, when railroad detective Ross W. Johnson was ambushed while inspecting boxcars in a freight yard. Shot six times, he miraculously survived and was able to provide a description of his attacker. On Monday, February 22, a railroad worker named C. C. Bruce spotted a man matching the description walking along the railroad track in Bartlett, Iowa, thirty miles south of Omaha. He alerted the marshal, who gathered up some deputies, and the stranger—who was carrying a silenced .22-caliber semiautomatic pistol quickly identified as the murder weapon—soon found himself under arrest.

The suspect was an Irish immigrant named Patrick Murphy going by the name Frank Carter, who had done time for killing a small herd of dairy cattle belonging to a farmer who had fired him after a quarrel. Murphy spoke openly, even proudly, about his slayings, boasting about his marksmanship and casually explaining that his motive was a simple "desire to kill." He said that he had murdered forty-three people over the years, a claim that would have made him the most prolific serial killer in US history up to that point—had there been any truth to it. Sentenced to death, he declared that he was "anxious to see how it feels to be electrocuted."

He found out on June 24, 1927. His last words: "Turn on the juice."

A seasoned police offer called Frank Carter "the most cold-blooded and dangerous man I have ever known."

NEVADA

JARBRIDGE
A FORENSIC FIRST
158

VIRGINIA CITY
MURDER OF "THE COMSTOCK QUEEN"
157

CARSON CITY

ELKO
LOVELESS IN ELKO
159

Virginia City, silver-mining boomtown

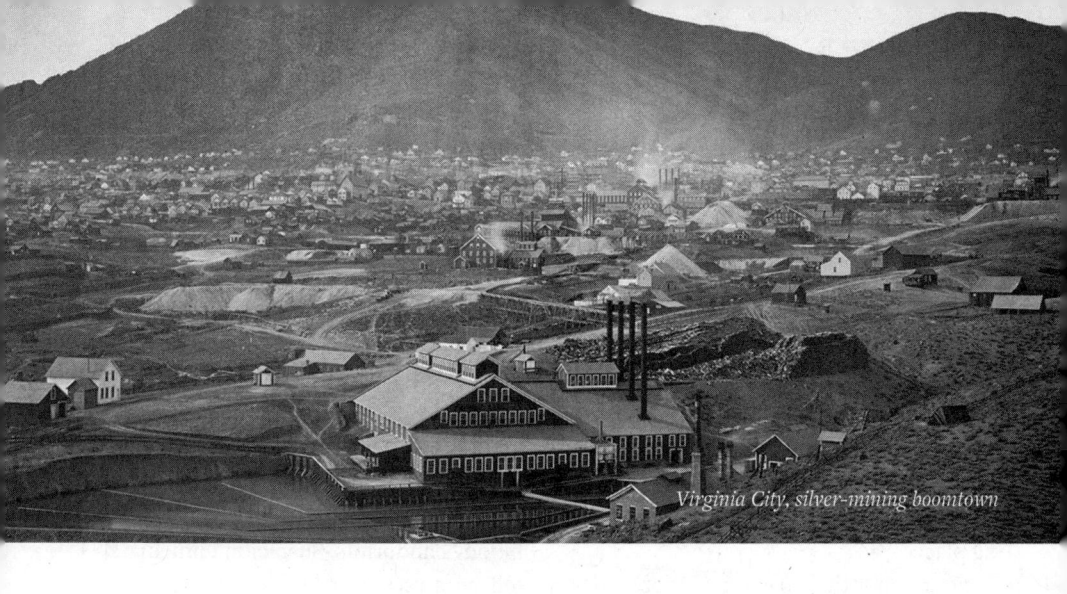

MURDER OF "THE COMSTOCK QUEEN"

Virginia City, Nevada • January 20, 1867

Following the 1859 discovery of the Comstock Lode—the richest deposit of high-grade silver ever found in North America—Virginia City, Nevada, grew virtually overnight from what one historian describes as "a rude collection of shanties housing about 500 people" to a vibrant metropolis with 25,000 inhabitants, dozens of theaters, several fire companies, five police precincts, four banks, a newspaper (at which Mark Twain worked as a reporter), and a bustling commercial district with a wide variety of stores.

Like other frontier boomtowns populated largely by men, it also had a dizzying number of saloons—as many as 130—and a large contingent of sex workers. The most celebrated of whom was Julia Bulette. Though later romanticized as a dark-haired beauty, she was in truth "a rather plain Englishwoman in her mid-thirties" who had plied her trade in New Orleans and various California mining camps before arriving in Virginia City in the early 1860s when its population consisted of 2,026 men and 30 women.

Living and working in a small two-room cottage, she became a beloved figure in the community. Dubbed "The Comstock Queen," she was known for ministering to sick and injured miners, donating money to the needy, and offering such unstinting financial support to the town's fire brigade that she was made an honorary member, complete with her own uniform, helmet, and badge. She was last seen alive on the night of January 19, 1867, when she went to the opera house, was denied entrance by the front door because of a new town ordinance, and—"refusing to sit in the section reserved for women of ill repute"—returned home in a huff. The next morning, she was found strangled

NEVADA • 157

and bludgeoned to death in her bed, her jewelry and other belongings stolen.

Her brutal slaying—"the most cruel, outrageous, and revolting murder ever committed in this city," as newspapers described it—provoked an outpouring of grief. Mines and saloons closed in her honor on the day of her funeral. Marching behind a procession of sixty firefighters, the Nevada militia band played a mournful tune while a black-plumed hearse bore her silver-handled casket to its final resting place.

Four months passed before her killer—a Frenchman named John Millian—was identified and arrested. Convicted after a one-day trial, he was hanged on April 24, 1868, before an enormous crowd of spectators that included Mark Twain. In succeeding years, Julia became a folk legend, celebrated in story and song, commemorated in local artworks and gift shop souvenirs, and even appeared as the title character in an episode of the classic TV Western *Bonanza*, "The Julia Bulette Story."

A FORENSIC FIRST

JARBRIDGE, NEVADA
DECEMBER 5, 1916

Though generally referred to as the Old West's last stagecoach robbery, the vehicle involved in this legendary crime was actually a horse-drawn "buckboard-like wagon" carrying bags of mail and nearly $3,000 in cash from Rogerson, Idaho, to the gold-mining town of Jarbridge, Nebraska. When it failed to arrive, a search party set out and found the rig a quarter mile outside of town, its driver, Fred Searcy, slumped on his seat, shot through the back of his head at close range with a .44-caliber revolver. Some of the mail sacks were slit open and the money pouch was missing.

Returning to the spot the next morning, searchers came upon a wadded-up black overcoat with torn sleeves, a shirt with the letter K inked below the collar, and another slashed mailbag with its letters scattered around, some bearing bloody handprints. Suspicion immediately fell on a recent arrival to town, a drifter named Ben Kuhl, often seen wearing an overcoat identical to the one found at the crime scene. An inveterate troublemaker, Kuhn had been jailed in California for petty larceny, done time in the Oregon State Prison for horse theft, and was currently awaiting trial in Jarbridge on a trespassing charge.

Searching his tent, lawmen found several incriminating items, including a .44-caliber revolver with one spent cartridge under the hammer. Kuhl's trial in September 1917 proved to be a milestone in US jurisprudence. Although most of the evidence against him was circumstantial, prosecutors brought in a pair of fingerprint experts from California who testified that the bloody palm print on one of the letters was unquestionably left by Kuhl.

When the jury returned a guilty verdict, Kuhl earned his spot in criminal history as the first American convicted on the basis of a palm print. His death sentence commuted to life, he spent twenty-six years in prison before being paroled in 1943.

LOVELESS IN ELKO

Elko, Nevada
August 20, 1942

Floyd Loveless was three years old when he watched his despondent mother throw herself in front of an oncoming freight train. A few years later, his father married a woman who, as one biographer notes, "simply didn't like" her stepson and made his home life miserable. Before he reached adolescence, the troubled boy was an inveterate thief, swiping jars of pennies from neighboring farmhouses and pocketing items from the local five-and-dime.

He was fifteen in the summer of 1942, when he carried out a six-week spree of shoplifting, stealing cars, and burglarizing homes. Late on the night of June 20, a handkerchief tied over his lower face, he entered the house of seventy-two-year-old Mary Soller, struck her on the head with a milk bottle he had taken from the front porch, then relieved the stunned and terrified woman of all the cash she had on hand—two $20 bills—before making his escape.

Ten days later, on the afternoon of June 30, he snuck into the home of a family named Knoth. Searching the bedroom closet while Mrs. Francis Knoth ironed clothes in the kitchen, he found a loaded .38-caliber pistol. Upon hearing a noise, Knoth came in to investigate and Loveless proceeded to rape her at gunpoint. Arrested soon afterward, Loveless—"the most dangerous criminal the local police have encountered in recent years," as one newspaper wrote—was given the maximum sentence for a juvenile: committed to the Indiana reformatory until he reached the age of twenty-one. One month after he entered the facility, he and another delinquent escaped.

Stealing cars and burglarizing homes as they made their way west, the pair split up in Elko, Nevada, where Loveless took off in a stolen truck. About twenty miles outside of town, he was flagged down by a constable, Dolph Berning. When Berning attempted to take him in, Loveless shot him in the neck and groin, dragged him into the truck, then sped off, abandoning the vehicle and the mortally wounded lawman a few miles down the road. Berning died in the hospital thirty-six hours later.

Arrested, tried, and convicted twice, Loveless was seventeen when he went to the gas chamber in September 1944—the youngest person ever executed in Nevada.

Fifteen-year-old killer Floyd Loveless. His execution sparked nationwide controversy over juvenile capital punishment.

NEW HAMPSHIRE

ETNA
STUDENT KILLERS IN ETNA
165

PEMBROKE
A GRIM MEMORIAL IN PEMBROKE
161

HANOVER
AN OBSESSION TURNS DEADLY
162

ALLENSTOWN
THE BEAR BROOK MURDERS
163

CONCORD

A GRIM MEMORIAL IN PEMBROKE

Pembroke, New Hampshire
October 4, 1875

Fleeing the law after raping his wife's young sister, French Canadian woodcutter Joseph LaPage left Quebec and made his way to the village of St. Albans, Vermont. Shortly after his arrival, a young teacher disappeared as she walked home along a lonely stretch of woods. Her naked corpse—"hideously violated and mangled in the most fiendish manner," as one newspaper reporter wrote—was discovered the next day. Arrested for the crime, LaPage managed to come up with an alibi convincing enough to secure his release.

Promptly relocating to the town of Pembroke, New Hampshire, he soon set his sights on a new victim. On the morning of Monday, October 4, 1875, a seventeen-year-old student at the Pembroke Academy named Josie Langmaid disappeared on her way to school. Her headless, sexually mutilated body was discovered in the woods that evening. Clues quickly pointed to Joseph LaPage.

This time, justice caught up with him. Convicted of first-degree murder, he was hanged in Concord, New Hampshire, on March 15, 1878. In honor of Josie Langmaid, the people of Pembroke erected a memorial to the slain schoolgirl that has since become a macabre tourist attraction for true-crime aficionados.

A fifteen-foot stone obelisk, it is inscribed with directions to the spot where her decapitated head was found the day after her murder.

Joseph LaPage, "The French Monster" (top), the Josie Langmaid Memorial (bottom)

AN OBSESSION TURNS DEADLY

Hanover, New Hampshire • July 17, 1891

The black sheep of a prominent New England family, George Abbott was burglarizing houses while still a schoolboy. By fourteen, he had accumulated so much loot—jewelry, tools, farm implements—that he had to stash it in a cave. Arrested at sixteen for stealing a neighbor's stove, he was spared punishment thanks to his father's influence. Not long afterward, encountering the neighbor out walking his dog, Abbott—simmering with resentment at the man for filing charges against him—drew a pistol and shot the dog dead.

He began his first stretch in prison the following year after robbing several homes with an accomplice. Released after serving his four-year sentence, Abbott took a stab at going straight before reverting to his old habits and joining a gang of house thieves operating in the Connecticut River Valley. Wounded in a gunfight with lawmen, he was arrested and sentenced to fifteen years in Windsor Prison. He served only seven before using a crudely fashioned rope ladder to escape.

After several years of aimless drifting, he made his back to New England, where—now going by the name Frank C. Almy—he found work on a farm in Hanover, New Hampshire. His employer, Andrew Warden, had five daughters, among them twenty-eight-year-old Christie, a bright, vivacious young woman with (as one contemporary account put it) "a fine rounded form." Before long, she was being wooed by the smitten Almy. A well-read man capable of quoting snippets of sentimental verse, Almy talked his way into her affections until—put off by his violent outbursts of temper and refusal to disclose anything about his past—she ended their relationship.

At the same time, Almy was let go by Christie's father. He worked for a few months in Massachusetts but was soon back in Hanover, where—his infatuation having turned into obsession—he holed up in one of the Wardens' hay barns for several weeks without detection. On the evening of July 17, Christie, her fifteen-year-old sister, Fannie, their mother, and a family friend were returning from a Grange meeting when they were waylaid by a pistol-wielding Almy, who dragged

George Abbott, aka Frank C. Almy, was the last man hanged in New Hampshire before capital punishment was repealed.

The Warden homestead

Christie into a meadow and started tearing off her clothes. Fannie ran for the sheriff.

As the two hurried to the rescue, they heard gunshots and found Christie dead from a bullet to the head. Far from putting as much distance as possible between himself and the crime scene, Almy returned to the barn where, remarkably, he managed to remain in hiding for the next month, emerging at night to forage for provisions and pay tearful visits to Christie's grave. He was finally captured when Mrs. Warden—after finding empty tin cans and beer bottles under a loose floorboard in the barn—notified authorities.

Taken into custody after a shootout that left him with a shattered left leg, Almy was tried, convicted, and hanged on May 16, 1893, before 150 invited witnesses.

THE BEAR BROOK MURDERS

Allenstown, New Hampshire
ca. 1980

His name was Terry Peder Rasmussen, though he would change identities so often during his sociopathic life that he would come to be known as the "Chameleon Killer." In the late 1970s, after a stint in the navy and years of drifting around from state to state, he moved from California to New Hampshire with his girlfriend Marlyse Honeychurch and her two young daughters, all three of whom would disappear within a few years.

In November 1985, two brothers out hunting in Bear Brook State Park in Allenstown came upon an overturned

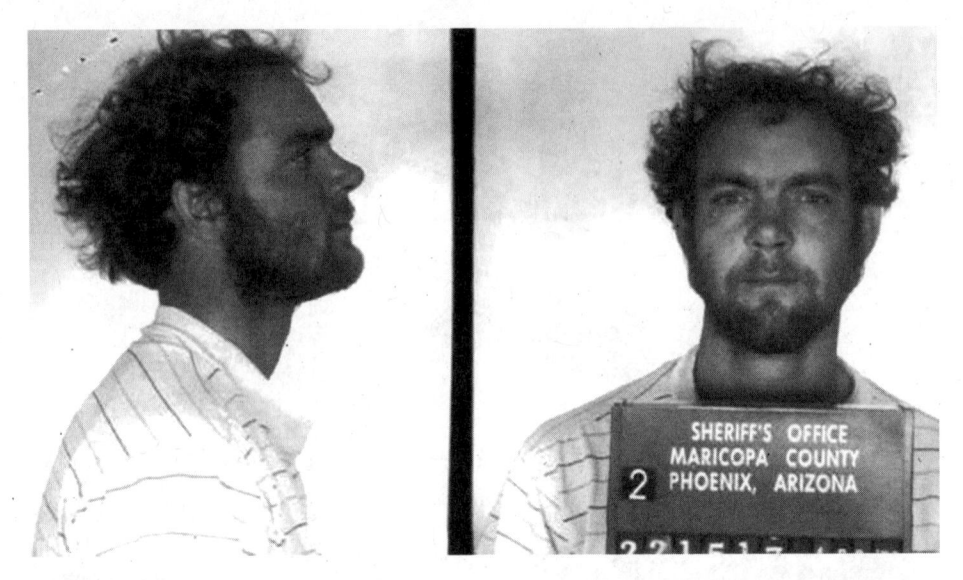

Terry Peder Rasmussen

fifty-five-gallon oil drum with a skeletal human foot sticking out of it. Inside were the remains of an adult woman and a prepubescent girl. Years passed before police, inspecting another nearby barrel, discovered the remains of two more children inside. All four had died of blunt force trauma.

Eventually, DNA testing revealed that three victims of the "Bear Brook Murders," as the case came to be known, were Honeychurch and her two daughters. The identity of the third little girl would never be determined, though genetic analysis proved that Rasmussen was her biological father. By the time the first barrel was discovered, the killer, going by the name Bob Evans, had returned to California with Denise Beaudin, single mother of an infant daughter. Beaudin, too, would vanish, almost certainly murdered by Rasmussen.

Over the next five years, Rasmussen, under the name Gordon Curtis Jensen, raised the little girl as his own daughter before abandoning her in 1986 in a California RV park. In 2001, living as Larry Vanner, he married a young chemist, Eunsoon Jun, whose dismembered body was found under a pile of cat litter in the basement of their home in June 2002. She, too, died of blunt force trauma to the skull. Arrested for the murder, Rasmussen pleaded guilty at his trial that November and was sentenced to fifteen years to life. He died of natural causes in prison eight years later.

What distinguishes Rasmussen from others of his homicidal breed was his choice of victims. Almost without exception, male serial killers—Ted Bundy, John Wayne Gacy, Jeffrey Dahmer, and so forth—target strangers. By contrast, Rasmussen murdered people with whom he had close relationships, a common characteristic of female serial murderers who prey on husbands, children, siblings, and friends.

STUDENT KILLERS IN ETNA

ETNA, NEW HAMPSHIRE
JANUARY 27, 2001

Invited to dinner at the home of her close friends and Dartmouth College colleagues Half and Susanne Zantop, Roxana Verona discovered the couple's blood-drenched bodies lying on the floor of the study. Both had been butchered, their heads and bodies hacked and slashed multiple times, their throats slit. Searching the crime scene, investigators found two foot-long, hard-plastic knife sheaths that had clearly held the murder weapons.

As the quiet college town reeled from the atrocity, theories about the perpetrator abounded. Rumors spread that the fifty-five-year-old Half was having an affair with a much younger woman, whose jealous husband or boyfriend had come to the house to exact revenge. Others speculated that Susanne was the primary target, marked for death by an unstable colleague enraged at her recent appointment to a powerful departmental committee.

Three weeks passed before investigators, having closely analyzed the two plastic sheaths, traced the knives to their purchasers: Robert Tulloch and James Parker, high schoolers from nearby Chelsea, Vermont, who were ultimately arrested at an Indiana truck stop while attempting to abscond to California. As part of a plea deal, Parker agreed to testify against his accomplice. A classic case of a folie à deux, the two teenagers, eager to "see the world," had decided to fund their travels by robbing homes and killing any witnesses. They had talked their way into the Zantop house by posing as students doing an environmental survey for class, and then slaughtered the couple when Tulloch flew into a rage at a perceived slight from Half.

For his part in the murders, Parker was sentenced to twenty-five years with the possibility of parole after sixteen. Tulloch received a life sentence with no possibility of parole.

Robert Tulloch (left) and James Parker (right), who was granted parole in 2024

NEW JERSEY

LIVINGSTON
A KILLER NURSE IN NEW JERSEY
171

NEW BRUNSWICK
A TELL-TALE HEART IN NEW BRUNSWICK
167

ELIZABETH
THE TORCH SLAYER STRIKES
168

HAMILTON TOWNSHIP
THE TRAGEDY BEHIND MEGAN'S LAW
170

TRENTON

CAMDEN
A MURDEROUS MINISTER
168

A TELL-TALE HEART IN NEW BRUNSWICK

NEW BRUNSWICK, NEW JERSEY • DECEMBER 3, 1840

On the morning of December 3, 1840, Abraham Suydam, a prominent banker from New Brunswick, New Jersey, set out from home to collect a debt from a carpenter, Peter Robinson, who had borrowed the money to purchase a lot and put up a house. Suydam never returned. Within twenty-four hours, news of the banker's mysterious disappearance had spread through the city. Suydam's wife posted a large reward for any information about her missing husband. Though certain rumor-mongers claimed he had absconded to Europe, the general consensus was that he had met with foul play. Suspicion fell on Robinson when he was seen sporting a gold pocket watch that had belonged to the missing banker.

Searching his house, deputies spotted a newly laid section of flooring in the basement. When they tore up the planks, they saw "a soft spot in the dirt," as if the ground had recently been turned up. With spades they began to dig and, within minutes, unearthed Suydam's decomposing corpse. Confronted with this overwhelming evidence of his guilt, Robinson proclaimed his innocence, claiming that a "mysterious stranger" had come to his house and done away with Suydam. He stuck to this preposterous story throughout his trial in March 1841, which culminated with his conviction. Shortly before his hanging the following month, he finally broke down and confessed.

Closely following the case in the newspapers, Edgar Allan Poe incorporated elements of it into his classic horror story "The Tell-Tale Heart," whose homicidal narrator, like Peter Robinson, conceals his victim's corpse beneath the floorboards of his home.

The guilt-ridden killer of Poe's "The Tell-Tale Heart" reveals the corpse beneath his floorboards.

THE TORCH SLAYER STRIKES

Elizabeth, New Jersey
February 23, 1929

On February 29, 1929, a woman's charred remains were found beside a highway in Cranford, New Jersey. She had been shot in the head before being doused with gasoline and set on fire. Though she was burned beyond recognition, investigators—by tracing her shoes to their maker, seller, and ultimate purchaser—were able to identify the victim as Mrs. Mildred Mowry, a fifty-year-old widow from Greenville, Pennsylvania.

Interviews with friends, along with letters found in her home, revealed that six months earlier she had wed a man she had met through a matrimonial agency: sixty-year-old Henry Colin Campbell. Besides the legitimate careers he had pursued at various times in his life—among them civil engineer, advertising man, and physician—he was a habitual criminal, having done time in prison on several occasions for forgery and grand larceny. He was also a confirmed bigamist, who had been married seven times and, at one point, had three wives at once. He was, in fact, married to another woman when he wed Mildred Mowry.

Under arrest, he admitted that, after bilking Mowry of her savings, he had decided "to rid himself of her" because he "knew he couldn't afford two wives." Dubbed the "Torch Slayer," Campbell was suspected of a strikingly similar slaying that had happened a year earlier, when the burnt corpse of Mrs. Margaret Brown was found by a New Jersey road stand, a bullet to her skull.

Though there was insufficient evidence to link him to the Brown murder, Campbell was convicted of killing Mildred Mowry and went to his death in the electric chair on April 17, 1930.

Henry Colin Campbell had many secrets, including a collection of dolls and teddy bears hidden behind a false wall in his home.

A MURDEROUS MINISTER

Camden, New Jersey
August 7, 1939

In April 1939, eighteen-year-old Wanda Dworecki was walking to the neighborhood drugstore when she was jumped by three men, dragged into their car, gagged, and beaten nearly to death before being dumped from the moving vehicle in a rural area south of Camden. She spent several weeks in the hospital recovering from a fractured skill. Upon her release, she confided to friends that she thought her father—who was constantly excoriating her for her supposedly promiscuous

Peter Shewchuk (left) was hired to murder Wanda Dworecki by her pastor father.

behavior—was behind the attempted murder. No one believed her.

Her dad, Walter Dworecki, was a respected man of the cloth and founder and pastor of the First Polish Baptist Church, where his forceful preaching style had earned him the nickname "Iron Mike." None of his admiring congregants were aware of his highly questionable past: his arrests for passing counterfeit $5 bills, torching his house to collect the insurance money, and assaulting a neighbor's son whose noisy street games so annoyed the reverend that he broke the boy's jaw with a broomstick. There was also the matter of his wife's suspiciously sudden death shortly after he insured her life for a hefty sum.

In August 1939, four months after Wanda's abduction, her body was found in a lover's lane not far from a high school. Her killer had put her in a headlock and strangled her with such force that her collarbone and breastbone were broken. Then he had dropped a heavy rock on her skull for good measure. It didn't take long for detectives to track down her murderer: twenty-one-year-old Peter Schewchuk, a former boarder in the Dworecki household who was known, in the terminology of the time, to be "feebleminded."

Under arrest, Schewchuk readily admitted that he had killed Wanda at the behest of her father, who had offered him $100, instructing him to "choke her, hit her with a rock, twist her neck. Make sure she's done." Taken into custody, Dworecki confirmed the story and confessed that he had plotted to kill his daughter for insurance money and had turned to Schewchuk after the men he had hired back in April botched the job.

Because of his mental disability, Schewchuk was spared the death penalty and sentenced to life. Reverend Dworecki went to the chair on March 28, 1940.

THE TRAGEDY BEHIND MEGAN'S LAW

HAMILTON TOWNSHIP, NEW JERSEY • JULY 29, 1994

In a particularly glaring understatement, official records describe Jesse Timmendequas's early family life as "dysfunctional." His mother was "a promiscuous alcoholic who had ten children by seven men," and Jesse's father, Skip, sexually abused the boy "several times a week for many years," once killed the boy's pet rabbit and forced him to eat it, and also raped a seven-year-old girl in his truck while eight-year-old Jesse looked on. It's little wonder that Timmendequas himself grew up to be a pedophiliac monster.

In 1979, at the age of eighteen, Timmendequas did nine months in jail after luring a five-year-old girl to a duck pond and attempting to rape her. Not long after his release, he assaulted a seven-year-old girl, strangling her nearly to death, and was imprisoned for six years. In 1992, he was sharing a house with two other paroled sex offenders in a middle-class suburban neighborhood and working as a landscaper. Living diagonally across the street was the family of seven-year-old Megan Kanka.

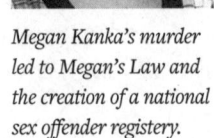

On the late afternoon of July 29, while Timmendequas was out in his yard working on his newly purchased boat, Megan wandered over. Asking if she wanted to see his new puppy, he brought her up to his bedroom, raped her vaginally and anally, strangled her with his belt, put two plastic bags over her head, then stuffed her body into a wooden toy chest he had converted to a toolbox, drove it to a park, and dumped it in the weeds. Arrested within twenty-four hours, he confessed to the murder and was eventually sentenced to death, though the sentence was commuted to life without the possibility of parole when New Jersey abolished the death penalty.

The high-profile case led to the passage of Megan's Law, designed to notify a community if a sex offender is living in their midst.

Megan Kanka's murder led to Megan's Law and the creation of a national sex offender registry.

Jesse Timmerdequas listens as the jury delivers their verdict.

A KILLER NURSE IN NEW JERSEY

LIVINGSTON, ET AL.,
NEW JERSEY
1987–2003

Exactly how many people Charles Cullen murdered in the course of his sixteen-year nursing career remains unknown. He confessed to forty victims, though estimates run as high as three hundred. His motives are also a mystery. Unlike other "Angels of Death" (as serial-killer nurses, most of them women, are known), it appears he did not derive sadistic gratification from inflicting death on his helpless victims. Nor did he administer lethal drugs so he could impress his fellow workers with his heroic efforts to save the dying patients.

Cullen was clearly unstable: He made twenty half-hearted suicide attempts, beginning at age nine. He also couldn't hold a job. Between 1987 and 2003, he was employed at nine hospitals in New Jersey and Pennsylvania but was fired from one after another when co-workers complained about his dangerously unprofessional behavior. Some became so alarmed by the number of patients who suddenly died after he visited their rooms that they reported their concerns to their supervisors. Hospital administrators, however—afraid of the lawsuits they would incur if the public learned of those suspicions—quietly terminated him for "poor performance," even supplying him with neutral references.

Because of the nursing shortage, however, Cullen had no problem getting quickly rehired by hospitals desperate for registered nurses willing to work the graveyard shift in intensive care units. He was finally arrested for killing a patient not under his care with a lethal dose of the heart medicine digoxin. Cullen claimed that he had done away with dozens of victims as an act of mercy—but many of them had been well on their way to recovery before he injected them with drug overdoses or tampered with their IV bags.

Pleading guilty to twenty-two murders at his New Jersey trial, he was sentenced to eleven consecutive life sentences, totaling 397 years in prison.

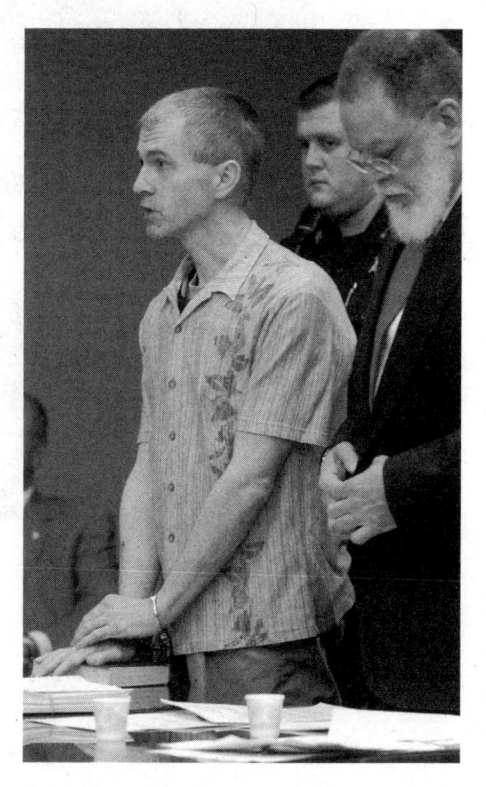

When asked about his motive, Charles Cullen claimed he thought he was "helping" patients.

NEW MEXICO

SANTA FE

TAOS
THE HEADLESS MAN OF TAOS
173

ALBUQUERQUE
ALIEN KILLERS IN ALBUQUERQUE?
174

ROSWELL
AN ABUSED TEEN SNAPS IN ROSWELL
175

THE HEADLESS MAN OF TAOS

Taos, New Mexico • July 1, 1929

Englishman Arthur Rochford Manby came to America at the age of twenty-three determined to make his fortune. Settling in Taos, New Mexico, he spent the following decades employing whatever unscrupulous means were necessary to fulfill his rapacious dreams, eventually acquiring a vast expanse of territory, a nineteen-room hacienda, and a multitude of enemies.

On July 3, 1929, US Deputy Marshal Jim Martinez showed up at Manby's home to serve the seventy-year-old land baron legal papers related to a recently reopened lawsuit. When no one responded to his repeated knocks, he peered through a window and spotted two large dogs prowling the hallway. He saw something else, too: a mass of green flies swarming a closed screen door. Martinez summoned the local sheriff, and the two men, along with some neighbors who had gathered at the scene, broke into the house, where they were instantly assaulted with the reek of death.

Inside the fly-infested room, a decapitated corpse lay on an army cot. The head—hardly more than a bare skull, its features mutilated beyond recognition—lay at the exact center of the carpeted room, about sixteen feet from the body. The coroner's jury concluded that the old man had died of natural causes two days earlier and that one of the dogs, having gone unfed for a couple of days, had gnawed off the head, chewed off the flesh, and dropped the skull on the floor.

Questions about this finding immediately arose. Many observers refused to

Last known photograph of Arthur Manby

believe that a loyal dog, even a hungry one, would behead its deceased master. When Manby's hastily buried body was exhumed and autopsied, doctors found that his head had been cleanly severed, not chewed, from his body. They also concluded that several holes in his side were made by buckshot, which had also shattered the skull's lower jaw. That the dead man had been murdered was no longer in doubt, though many of his townspeople—all too familiar with Manby's devious ways—suspected that the old con man had substituted a mutilated body for his own and absconded to escape his enemies.

The never-solved mystery of the "Headless Man of Taos," as it came to be known, would become an enduring part of northern New Mexico lore.

ALIEN KILLERS IN ALBUQUERQUE?

Albuquerque, New Mexico
September 9, 1999

For reasons known only to himself, the con man born Armand Chavez rechristened himself Diazien Hossencofft, a name so unpronounceable that friends just called him "D." Claiming at different times to be a CIA agent, a thoracic surgeon, a cutting-edge geneticist, and a ten-thousand-year-old shape-shifting alien, he made a handsome living selling a supposedly cancer-curing, anti-aging serum to wealthy, mostly female, clients unaware that they were being injected with nothing more potent than vitamin B_6.

In 1992, while visiting the SeaWorld theme park in San Diego, he met a vacationing Malaysian woman, twenty-nine-year-old Girly Chew. By 1993, they were married and living in Albuquerque, where Chew got a job as a bank teller while her husband pursued his ostensibly world-changing medical research. Four years later, Hossencofft returned from a prolonged business trip to Canada with an infant boy he claimed was a Mexican orphan and informed Chew that they would be adopting him.

It wasn't until 1998 that she discovered the baby was an illegitimate son he had fathered with a Japanese lover during his time in Canada. That year, after Chew confronted her husband about his infidelities, he attacked her so brutally that he was arrested for aggravated battery.

When he savagely assaulted her again one year later in January 1999, she moved out of the house, filed for divorce, got a restraining order, and enrolled in a karate class. Ignoring the restraining order, he made constant threatening phone calls to her at her workplace, promising that "she would be killed and her body never found."

In the summer of 1999, Hossencofft became involved with former model and fashion designer Linda Henning, a UFO conspiracy theorist who, under his influence, came to believe that the governments of the world were controlled by reptilian aliens in human form. Hossencofft himself, so he explained to Henning, was a benevolent alien from a place called the Gigaplanet, sent here to save the earth from the evil reptilians with the aid of Henning who, unknown to her, was actually a heroic "alien queen" trained in the arts of ninja combat.

When Chew disappeared on September 9, suspicion immediately lighted on the crackpot couple. Though Chew's body would never be found (as Hossencofft vowed), DNA and other forensic evidence proved sufficient to link him and Henning to her death. Under a plea deal, he confessed to the murder and was sentenced to life plus sixty-one years in prison. Tried separately, Henning—who claimed that she had cannibalized the victim—was likewise convicted of first-degree murder.

The first woman in New Mexico history to be faced with the death penalty, she was spared execution and sentenced to a term of seventy-three years.

AN ABUSED TEEN SNAPS IN ROSWELL

Roswell, New Mexico
July 4, 2004

On July 6, 2004, celebrity TV newsman Sam Donaldson—owner of the Chavez Canyon Ranch in Roswell, New Mexico—went to the main house to check on his foreman, Paul Posey, whom he hadn't seen or heard from in several days. As he approached the front porch, he saw "a large, reddish, dried swath" that he had no trouble identifying as blood. "I'd covered the war in Vietnam," he later explained, "and I'd seen a lot of it there." More blood was congealed on the kitchen and living room floors.

Quickly arriving at what was clearly a crime scene, police searched the property for victims. Following some backhoe tracks, they came upon a large manure pile. Inside the muck were three bodies: Paul Posey; his third wife, Tryone; and his thirteen-year-old stepdaughter, Mary Lee Schmid. All three, as autopsies determined, had been shot in the head with a .38-caliber pistol. Located at a friend's house, the fourth member of the family, Paul's fourteen-year-old son, Cody, was brought in for questioning and quickly confessed, relating a shocking tale of unrelenting physical and emotional abuse at the hands of his father, which had climaxed in a particularly grotesque incident on the eve of the murders.

According to Cody, he'd been summoned into his parents' bedroom where his father—who had become obsessed with online videos of incest porn—ordered him to have sex with his stepmother and then burned his arm with a welding tool when he refused. The next morning, the profoundly traumatized teen decided "to get [his father] off the planet cuz I'd be better off without him." He also dispatched his stepmother and sister, who had consistently abused and humiliated him since entering his life. He had loaded the corpses into the bucket of the backhoe and, finding the ground so hard that he couldn't dig a grave, buried them in the manure pile.

Eventually convicted of various charges—first-degree murder in the case of Schmid, second-degree murder in the case of Tryone, and manslaughter in the case of his father—he was sentenced as a juvenile offender in a youth psychiatric facility until he turned twenty-one.

Television footage of Chavez Canyon Ranch, site of the slayings.

NEW YORK

TROY
A CHILD JEKYLL AND HYDE IN TROY
179

ALBANY

BURLINGHAM
"THE FEMALE JACK THE RIPPER"
177

QUEENS
A *NEW YORK POST* HEADLINE SAYS IT ALL
183

AUBURN
A HISTORIC EXECUTION
178

NEW YORK CITY
THE PHANTOM MURDERER
181

NEW YORK CITY
A PARROT DROPS A DIME IN NEW YORK CITY
182

BROOKLYN
THE FIRST WOMAN IN THE ELECTRIC CHAIR
190

"THE FEMALE JACK THE RIPPER"

Burlingham, New York
May to September 1893

Irish immigrant Lizzie Halliday had been married five times before being hired as a housekeeper in 1889 by Paul Halliday, resident of the small village of Burlingham in upstate New York. A twice-widowed farmer just shy of his seventieth birthday, Paul soon proposed marriage, apparently as a way to avoid paying her wages. Lizzie, forty years his junior, accepted.

Not long after their wedding in May 1890, Lizzie eloped with a neighbor, stole a team of horses, and was soon arrested. Found not guilty by reason of insanity, she was sent to an asylum where she remained until May 1893. A few weeks after her discharge, having returned to the care of her husband, Paul's house burned down. His disabled son, home alone at the time, died in the conflagration.

Three months later, on the morning of Wednesday, August 30, 1893, Lizzie hitched her horse to an old buckboard and drove twenty-three miles to the home of a poor farmer named Thomas McQuillan, whose wife, Margaret, and nineteen-year-old daughter, Sarah Jane, hired themselves out as menials. Representing herself as a boardinghouse proprietor who required a live-in house cleaner, she proposed paying Margaret the "princely sum" of two dollars a day plus board for her services. Margaret jumped at the offer. Packing a few belongings, she accompanied Lizzie back to the Halliday farm.

That same night, after Margaret went to bed, Lizzie snuck into her room, chloroformed her, shot her through the heart with her husband's revolver, and hid her body in a pile of hay.

At some point during that evening, Lizzie shot her husband while he dozed on a couch, then crushed his skull with an axe. She then pulled the couch away from the wall, pried off a few floorboards, and dug a shallow grave. After rolling her husband's corpse into the hole, she replaced the planks, moved the blood-soaked couch back into place, and curled up to sleep on it.

Late the next morning, she drove back out to the McQuillan farm and persuaded Sarah to return with her on the pretext that Margaret had suffered an accident. That evening, while Sarah Jane slept, Lizzie shot her dead, dragged the body to the barn, and laid it beside her mother's corpse.

A few days later, on, September 4, neighbors, suspicious about Paul Halliday's whereabouts, searched the barn where they discovered the decomposing corpses of the two McQuillan women covered with hay. Two more days would pass before Paul's remains were unearthed from beneath the kitchen floorboards. Her case became a national sensation, the press branding her "The Female Jack the Ripper" and "The Worst Woman on Earth." Found guilty of murdering her husband, she was condemned to the electric chair, but the sentence was later commuted and she was sent back to her former institution, where she died of natural causes on June 18, 1918, at the age of fifty-eight.

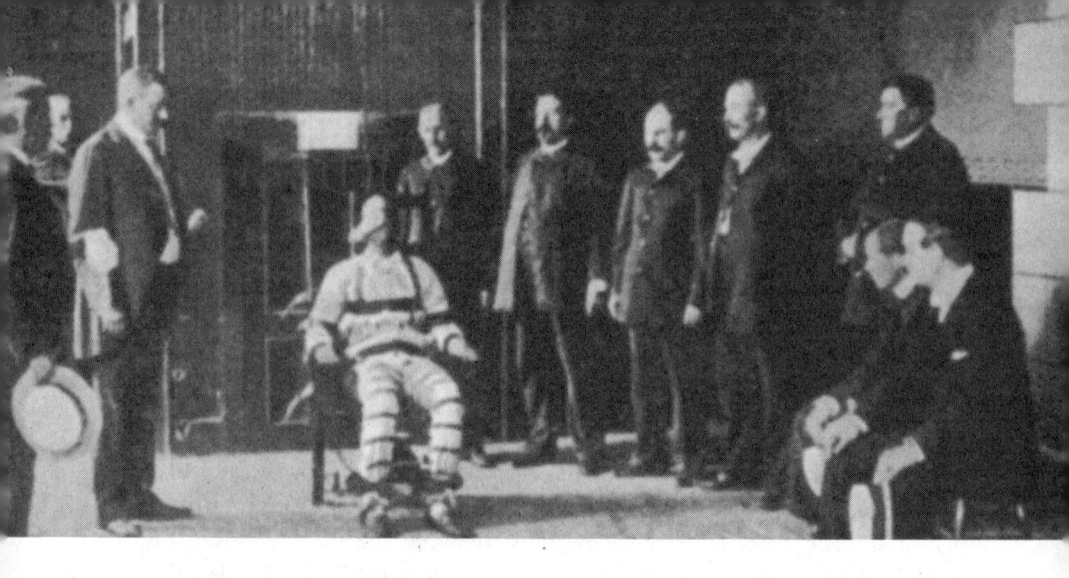

A HISTORIC EXECUTION

AUBURN, NEW YORK
MARCH 29, 1889

A denizen of the Buffalo, New York, slums, William Kemmler made a meager living as a fruit-and-vegetable peddler, spending much of his earnings on alcoholic binges. On the evening of March 29, 1889, he returned home drunk, got into a quarrel with his common-law wife, Tillie Ziegler, and attacked her with a hatchet, inflicting dozens of blows to her skull. She did not survive the night.

Though newspaper accounts of the brutal murder and succeeding trial kept the public riveted for months, it wasn't the crime that earned Kemmler a place in the history books but the manner of his death. On August 6, 1890, he became the first person ever killed in the electric chair.

Arguing that hanging was a holdover from a barbaric past, proponents of electrical execution persuaded the New York State legislature to pass a law replacing the gallows with the chair. On August 6, 1890, Kemmler walked calmly into the death chamber, where he was introduced to the twenty-six witnesses seated in a semicircle around the newly constructed apparatus. After a small hole was cut in the back of Kemmler's shirt and an electrode attached to his spine, he seated himself and was strapped in. Another electrode was affixed to his head.

Moments later, the executioner flipped the switch. Kemmler's body convulsed and grew rigid, straining against the straps. Seventeen seconds later, the electricity was turned off and he was declared dead. Even as the physicians were congratulating themselves on the efficacy of the new, more civilized means of execution, witnesses noticed that Kemmler was still breathing.

The electricity was ordered back on. As Kemmler's body sizzled and the stench of burning flesh filled the room, some witnesses fainted. After nearly four minutes, the current was turned off, and the doctors pronounced the execution a great success, assuring the sickened spectators that "the man never suffered a bit of pain."

The press took a different view, denouncing electrical execution as "a disgrace to humanity."

A cartoon of the toddler terror, Retta McCabe

A CHILD JEKYLL AND HYDE IN TROY

Troy, New York
September 1897

A decade after Robert Louis Stevenson dreamed up Dr. Jekyll and Mr. Hyde, the story seemed to come to life in upstate New York. Unlike the fictional character, the real one was not a grown man but, shockingly, a four-year-old girl. Her name was Retta McCabe. Described in the press as a "beautiful, blue-eyed, golden-haired child" with "laughing eyes and dancing dimples," she was known to transform in an instant into a being of "demonic malevolence."

One of her favorite pastimes was stuffing buttons and dry beans into the ears and nostrils of babies. In September 1897, she hurled her infant brother to the floor and stomped on him so viciously he died a week later in the hospital. When she asked her parents what had become of him and was told that he was "asleep to wake no more," she chuckled in delight.

Several weeks later, on Sunday, October 24, she made her way to the railroad station, several blocks from her home, and sat down on the tracks as a train approached. A policeman managed to save her at the last minute. As he carried her to the precinct house, she scratched and bit him so savagely that "he had to put her down more than once for fear that she would seriously disfigure his face." Placed in a cell, she flew into a violent rage, shrieking and tearing madly at her hair. All at once, "her blue eyes beamed with good nature, a sweet smile curved her red lips," and she turned into "a sunny little creature."

Too young to be consigned to the Syracuse Home for Feeble-Minded Children, Retta McCabe was returned to the care of her parents. What became of the "Child Jekyll and Hyde" (as she was called in newspapers around the country) is unknown.

THE FIRST WOMAN IN THE ELECTRIC CHAIR

BROOKLYN, NEW YORK
FEBRUARY 7, 1898

Born to a farmer in Millstone, New Jersey, Martha Garretson was fourteen when, according to her own recollections, she was "thrown from a sleigh upon an icy road," sustaining a head injury so severe that it permanently altered her personality, leaving her prone to fits of violent temper. Following one failed marriage that produced a son she gave up for adoption, she worked for a time as a seamstress before taking a job as live-in housekeeper for a widower named William W. Place, an insurance adjuster who resided in Brooklyn with his eleven-year-old daughter, Ida.

Within a year, William—motivated less by any romantic sentiments than by his wish to provide his child with a mother—took Martha as his wife. For reasons never fully explained, Martha soon developed a bitter antipathy toward Ida and resented the loving attentions her new husband lavished on her. On more than one occasion, she flew into such an unbridled rage that William ran from the house "to secure a physician to quiet her."

During one outburst in September 1896, she grew so frenzied that William had to summon the police. The situation climaxed in an outrage that would stun the nation. On February 7, 1898, during a violent quarrel with then-seventeen-year-old Ida, Martha threw a glassful of carbolic acid in the girl's face, then smothered her to death with a pillow. When William returned home from his Manhattan office later that day, she attacked him with an axe, delivering two near-fatal blows to his skull.

Convicted of the "fiendish butchery of her stepdaughter," she earned a place in the history books as the first woman to be executed in the electric chair—a pioneering feminist, as one newspaper editorial sardonically deemed her, who proved that, when it came to "moral depravity," a woman could be every bit the equal of a man.

Used to dealing with men, executioners were not sure how to protect Martha Place's modesty while attaching electrodes to her ankles.

THE PHANTOM MURDERER

NEW YORK CITY
JUNE 1930

Decades before the "Zodiac Killer" terrorized San Francisco, another serial murderer with a fondness for codes created a panic in New York City. His first victim was a grocer named James Mozynski. On the evening of June 11, 1930, Mozynski and his nineteen-year-old girlfriend, Catherine May, were parked on a lonely street in Queens when a man approached the car and shot Mozynski to death through the open driver's-side window. Then, in a bit of grotesque gallantry, he escorted May to a bus stop and handed her a sheet of paper.

Rubber-stamped in red ink on the page were Mozynski's name and the ciphers "3-X" and "3-X-097." Shortly afterward the New York Evening Journal received a bizarre letter from the killer who promised more murders to come and signed himself "3-X." Just six days later, in a chilling replay of the Mozynski slaying, twenty-five-year-old radio company employee Noel Sowley was killed with two shots to the left temple while parked with his sweetheart, Elizabeth Ring, on a Queens lover's lane. The gunman then handed Ring a paper identical to the one he had given Catherine May and shepherded her to a bus stop.

The following day, "3-X" (also dubbed the "Massacre Maniac" and the "Phantom Murderer" in the tabloids) sent another letter to the Evening Journal, boasting of his two murders and declaring that there were fourteen more people on his hit list, one of whom he planned to kill that very night in College Point, Queens. In what the New York Times called the "widest manhunt in the history of the New York Police Department," an army of "425 detectives, motorcycle, automobile, and gun squads, as well as 2,000 uniformed policemen" patrolled the Queens neighborhood all night, but the madman failed to show up.

The next morning, in another rambling letter, he apologized for not making good on his threat, explaining that his target had been spared because he had returned a secret document. At the same time, he warned that there were still seven people slated to die at his hands and listed their identities as "Z14, Z21, Y2, O6, X7, S1, V4." The only way they could avoid death, he added, was by following a message he delivered in code: "N.J.—O.G.K.—2—33—A.V.—3X—R.G.—4MLT—RP49—6."

The theory that the killer was a lunatic escaped from the Creedmore State Hospital for the Insane in Queens seemed bolstered when the Evening Journal received a final communication from "3-X" in which he claimed to be a secret agent for something called the "Russian Red Diamond Society," sent to the United States to assassinate former members who had betrayed the organization. His mission, he declared, was now complete, and he was set to fly back to Russia on a secretly chartered plane. "Three X is no more," he wrote. Though other shootings would be attributed to "3-X" in the coming months, none was definitively linked to him.

His identity and motives remain a mystery to this day.

A PARROT DROPS A DIME IN NEW YORK CITY

NEW YORK CITY • JULY 12, 1942

A popular tourist attraction in Harlem, the Green Parrot Bar and Grill was named for its presiding mascot, a foul-mouthed, eighty-year-old bird who perched by the cash register and told anyone who offered it a cracker to "stick it up your ass." He had also learned to greet regulars, squawking out their names and adding "You ugly bastard!"

On the evening of July 12, 1942, an inebriated man came into the restaurant. When the owner, Max Geller, refused to serve him, the drunk pulled out a gun and shot Geller in the throat. The bullet shattered his vocal cords and pierced his spine. He died three weeks later without regaining consciousness.

Questioned by detectives, the customers who had been at the bar that night were unable—or unwilling—to identify the killer. One of them, however, reported that he had heard the parrot screech "Robber! Robber!" as Geller slumped to the floor. Learning about the parrot's vocal habits, one detective speculated that the parrot had actually cried out "Robert," not "Robber." Assembling a list of Geller's regulars with that name, investigators eliminated each as a suspect except one: a taxi driver, Robert Butler, who had fled Manhattan right after the shooting. Butler was eventually traced to Baltimore and arrested. When he learned that he owed his capture to the parrot, he growled, "I never did like that bird."

Tried and convicted, he was sentenced to fifteen years in Sing Sing.

The Green Parrot Bar's crime-solving mascot

A *NEW YORK POST* HEADLINE SAYS IT ALL

QUEENS, NEW YORK • APRIL 14, 1983

After three hours of drinking, snorting cocaine, and acting increasingly unruly at a topless bar in Queens, twenty-three-year-old lowlife Charles Dingle was asked by the owner to leave. Dingle responded by drawing a pistol and shooting the barkeep in the head, then herding four women into the back room and raping a dancer.

Upon learning that one of his hostages was a mortician, he ordered her to remove the incriminating bullet from the victim's head with a kitchen knife. When she was unable to extract it, he had her decapitate the corpse. He then stuck the head in a cardboard carton, commandeered a cab, and drove around with the box beside him until he was arrested in Manhattan.

Convicted of second-degree murder, rape, and kidnapping, Dingle was sentenced to twenty-five years to life. Grotesque as it was, his crime may well have been forgotten had it not produced what is widely considered one of the most memorable headlines in tabloid history on page one of the April 15, 1983, issue of the *New York Post*: HEADLESS BODY IN TOPLESS BAR.

Perhaps the greatest newspaper headline of all time

NORTH CAROLINA

WINSTON-SALEM
A FAMILY ANNIHILATOR IN WINSTON-SALEM
186

RALEIGH

WINSTON-SALEM
THE LYNCH KILLINGS
187

CHARLOTTE
A WIDE RECEIVER TAKES A BAD ROUTE
189

ROBESON COUNTY
A SUPERSTAR'S FATHER IS KILLED
188

HYDE COUNTY
A REVEREND IN NAME ONLY
185

A REVEREND IN NAME ONLY

HYDE COUNTY,
NORTH CAROLINA
NOVEMBER 15, 1852

Known as a man of "violent temper and strong animal passions," Rev. George Washington Carawan led a remarkably impious life for a man of the cloth. Three weeks after his first wife's sudden death from an acute gastrointestinal illness that bore all the hallmarks of arsenic poisoning, he married his young housekeeper, whom he proceeded to beat regularly, often "knocking her down with a clenched fist." He also kept mistresses on the side, fathering a child with one of them, a transgression that got him temporarily dismissed from his church.

Sometime in early 1852, Carawan took in a boarder, a young schoolteacher named Clement Lassiter. Precisely what led to their eventual falling-out is unclear. According to one account, the preacher was busily thrashing his wife when Lassiter intervened. Flying into a rage, Carawan drove the young man from his home at gunpoint, claiming afterward that he had done so upon learning from his wife that Lassiter had forced himself on her. When Lassiter learned of this outrageous accusation, he sued the preacher for libel.

A few days after filing the suit, Lassiter disappeared as he was trekking to a town four miles away, where he hoped to find employment. His body, riddled with buckshot, was found in a shallow grave in the woods just off the main road. When news of the discovery

The trial of Reverend George W. Carawan went down as one of the most infamous in American history.

reached Carawan, he fled by train to Chattanooga, Tennessee, where he lived under an assumed name for four months before sneaking back home to dispose of some property and see his family. He was spotted entering his house by a young enslaved man named Seth, who had been forced into helping Carawan dispose of Lassiter's body.

Alerted by Seth, neighbors surrounded the house and took the preacher into custody. His trial for Lassiter's murder climaxed in a scene of high drama. No sooner had the jury read the verdict of guilty than Carawan pulled a single-barreled pistol from his coat and fired at the prosecuting attorney, striking him in the chest. As a deputy sprang at Carawan and began to grapple with him, he managed to pull himself free, draw a second pistol, and kill himself with a bullet to the head.

The Lawson family funeral

A FAMILY ANNIHILATOR IN WINSTON-SALEM

Winston-Salem, North Carolina
December 25, 1929

In December 1929, forty-three-year-old tobacco farmer Charlie Lawson took his wife, Fannie, and their seven children to Winston-Salem, bought them all handsome new outfits, then took them to the town photographer's studio for a family portrait. In the decades since, crime buffs have fruitlessly scrutinized Charlie's face in the picture for any sign of the madness that would erupt a week later in one of the most shocking cases of familicide in the country's history.

On Christmas morning Charlie and his son Arthur went out to hunt rabbits in the woods. When they returned, Charlie—fearing perhaps that the strapping sixteen-year-old might try to prevent him from carrying out his monstrous plan—sent the boy to town on an errand. With the teenager out of the way, Charlie then proceeded to slaughter the rest of his family.

First to die were his daughters Carrie and Maybell, twelve and seven, respectively. As they headed off by foot for a holiday visit to nearby relatives, their father emerged from behind the barn with his 12-gauge shotgun and shot Carrie in the head and Maybell in the back. After dragging their corpses into the barn, he made for the house.

Fannie had come onto the porch after hearing the gunfire. Her husband killed her with a shotgun blast to the chest, then stepped inside the house and did the same to his seventeen-year-old daughter, Marie. His supply of ammunition nearly exhausted, he used the butt of the 12-gauge to crush the skulls of his remaining children, James, Raymond, and Mary Lou, ages four, two, and four months. Then he walked into the woods and used his last remaining shell to kill himself.

Like the sites of so many sensational murders, the Lawson farm became a major tourist attraction, so much so that Charlie's brother, Marion, put up a fence around the property and charged twenty-five cents for admission. The motive for the massacre remains unclear. Some claimed that Charlie—previously regarded as a solid family man—had become erratic and evil-tempered after suffering a serious head injury while digging a trench with a mattock. Evidence would also come to light that he had raped his daughter Marie. When she became pregnant with his child and shared the shocking truth with her mother, so the theory goes, Charlie went insane and annihilated his family.

THE LYNCH KILLINGS

Winston-Salem,
North Carolina
May–June 1985

On Sunday, July 22, 1984, sixty-eight-year-old Delores Lynch was shot dead in the driveway of her Prospect, Kentucky, home, the top of her head blown off by a high-powered weapon. Her thirty-nine-year-old daughter, Janie, was slain by the same assassin, shot in the base of her skull inside the house. Because no valuables were taken, robbery was clearly not the motive. Mrs. Lynch's son, Tom, was brought in for questioning but quickly dismissed as a suspect.

A thirty-six-year-old dentist, Tom had left his wife, the former Susie Newsom, for his assistant and was embroiled in a bitter custody suit with his ex over their two young sons, John and Jim. At the time of the killings, Susie was living in Greensboro, North Carolina, with a new man, Fritz Klenner—a scandalous state of affairs in the view of some family members because she and Klenner were first cousins. A gun-obsessed sociopath who falsely claimed to be a licensed physician, former Green Beret, and CIA operative, Klenner had schooled himself in the production of both explosives and cyanide capsules.

In May 1985, ten months after the murders of Delores and Janie Lynch, Susie's father, mother, and grandmother were slaughtered at their home in Winston-Salem. It soon became clear to investigators that, besides the shared modus operandi, the two crimes had a common denominator: All the victims were related, either by blood or marriage, to Susie Newsom Lynch.

Three of them had made known their intentions to testify on her ex-husband's behalf in an upcoming visitation hearing. Because it seemed unthinkable that Susie herself had carried out the slaughter, her incestuous lover immediately became the prime suspect. On June 3, 1985, knowing that the police were on their way, Klenner and Susie loaded her sons into his Chevy Blazer and took off with the law right behind. Over the next twenty-five minutes, Klenner periodically slowed down or stopped his car to spray his pursuers with automatic fire from an Uzi.

The chase came to an end when Klenner detonated an explosive device planted under the passenger seat, blowing up the vehicle and all four occupants. An autopsy later revealed that the two little boys had been killed in the moments before the blast, having been given cyanide capsules, then shot in the head, almost certainly by their mother.

A SUPERSTAR'S FATHER IS KILLED

ROBESON COUNTY, NORTH CAROLINA • JULY 23, 1993

On August 3, 1993, a fisherman came upon a man's body snagged on a submerged tree limb in a South Carolina creek. An autopsy revealed that he had died from a single gunshot to the chest. Because of its advanced state of decomposition, the corpse was promptly cremated, though the jaw and hands were preserved in the hopes that the victim might later be identified by dental work or fingerprints.

Two days after the body was discovered, a vandalized Lexus sports car was found abandoned in a wooded area near Fayetteville, North Carolina. Tracing the vehicle to a dealership outside Chicago, investigators learned that it had been sold to basketball superstar Michael Jordan, who had bought it as a gift for his father, James. Dental records soon confirmed that the murder victim was fifty-seven-year-old James Jordan. Owing to the perpetrators' brainless behavior—one of them used the stolen car's cellular phone to call his drug dealer, the other made a rap music video of himself wearing an NBA championship ring given to the elder Jordan by his son—they were soon under arrest.

Best friends since third grade, Larry Demery and Daniel Green, eighteen and nineteen, respectively, already had criminal records for armed robbery. On the night of the murder, the pair had robbed two couples leaving a motel and held up a country store before spotting the cherry-red Lexus parked near a Quality Inn alongside an interstate highway. There was a man dozing in the front seat: James

A proud James Jordan (left) with wife, Deloris, and their superstar son, Michael

Jordan, getting some sleep on his long drive home from a friend's funeral.

The plan, as Demery later confessed, was to tie the man up, rob him, then "drive him down the road, just put him out, [and] drive off with his stuff." As they stood there peering through the partially rolled-down driver-side window, however, Jordan stirred and Green, who was carrying a stolen pistol, shot him once in the chest. Shoving the body onto the passenger side, Green got behind the wheel and drove off, Demery following in his own car.

Once they had put enough distance between themselves and the crime scene, they pulled over next to a cornfield. It wasn't until they started going through Jordan's belongings that they realized who he was. Driving the corpse to a spot on the borderline between North and South Carolina, they dumped it over a bridge into Gum Swamp Creek, where it was found eleven days later.

Tried in early 1996, the two were convicted of first-degree murder and sentenced to life imprisonment.

A WIDE RECEIVER TAKES A BAD ROUTE

CHARLOTTE, NORTH CAROLINA
NOVEMBER 16, 1999

On the night of November 15, 1999, Rae Carruth—an NFL wide receiver for the Carolina Panthers—took his eight-months pregnant girlfriend, Cherica Adams, to the movies. Afterward, they went back to his house, where she picked up her car, a black BMW. The two then headed for Adams's apartment in their separate vehicles, with Carruth leading the way in his SUV.

They were driving through a suburban neighborhood shortly after midnight when Carruth put on his brakes, bringing Adams to a stop. Just then, a car that had been trailing them pulled up alongside her, and a passenger in the back seat stuck his hand out the window and fired five shots at Adams, hitting her four times in the neck and back. As Carruth's SUV and the shooter's rental car sped off in different directions, Adams managed to pull into a residential driveway and call 911 on her cell phone.

After undergoing emergency surgery at the hospital, she was able to provide a detailed statement, describing how Carruth had blocked her car before the gunman opened fire. She held on for a month before succumbing to multiple organ system failure. Delivered by emergency Caesarean, her baby survived, though with permanent brain damage as a result of his mother's traumatic injuries.

In the days immediately following the shooting, investigators, digging into Carruth's phone and bank records, were led to a man named Van Brett Watkins, a "habitual criminal" (as newspapers described him) who confessed that the football star—already paying child support to a previous girlfriend—had hired him to kill the mother-to-be and their unborn baby. Charged with first-degree murder, conspiracy to commit murder, and the "use of an instrument to kill an unborn child," Carruth fled but was discovered within twenty-four hours hiding in the trunk of a car outside a Tennessee motel.

Convicted of second-degree murder and conspiracy, he spent nineteen years in prison before being paroled in 2018.

Charlotte native Cherica Adams was just starting a career in real estate when she was murdered.

NORTH DAKOTA

NIAGARA
A MURDERING "ECCENTRIC" IN NIAGARA
191

TURTLE LAKE
A CATTLE DISPUTE TURNS MURDEROUS IN TURTLE LAKE
192

GRAND FORKS
A CLOWN, A HUNTER, AND A LION WALK INTO A BAR
193

BISMARCK

A MURDERING "ECCENTRIC" IN NIAGARA

Niagara, North Dakota
ca. 1900–1906

Migrating to North Dakota from his Buffalo, New York, birthplace in 1882, Eugene Butler acquired a 480-acre spread in the tiny town of Niagara and turned it into a thriving farm. Apart from the young itinerant workers he hired at harvest time, he lived alone for most of the year and was viewed by his neighbors as a harmless, if eccentric, recluse. As the years progressed, however, his peculiarities became more pronounced.

He refused to have his photograph taken for fear that the camera would "suck out his soul," became convinced that every "old maid" in the county was trying to trap him into marriage, and insisted that he was being pursued by "invisible people." When he took to galloping around the countryside in the dead of night, awakening his neighbors with his clamorous shouts, he was finally committed to a mental asylum, where he lived out the remainder of his days, dying in 1911 at the age of sixty-two. His estate passed into the hands of relatives.

Four years later, workmen were sent to the farmhouse to do renovations. Digging in the cellar, one of them made a horrifying discovery: six human skeletons, all with their skulls crushed, two with broken legs. As the subsequent investigation showed, one had been dumped into the cellar through a "cleverly constructed trap door," and the others had been dropped through a downward sloping hole dug under the foundation from outside the house. There was no trace of any clothing; all the victims had been stripped naked after their violent deaths.

With no means of identifying the bodies, various theories were put forth. Some speculated that the decomposed skeletons were from a single family, slaughtered at the same time. Others believed that they were the remains of Butler's hired hands, murdered over a period of years. No positive identification or definitive motive has ever been established.

Rather than give the bones a proper burial, the sheriff had them placed in a box and transported to his office, where many were later stolen as macabre souvenirs.

The coffins of the slaughtered Wolf family and their young farmhand laid out before burial

A CATTLE DISPUTE TURNS MURDEROUS IN TURTLE LAKE

Turtle Lake, North Dakota • April 22, 1920

On the morning of Thursday, April 22, 1920, Jacob Wolf, a married father of six young girls, showed up at the home of his nearest neighbor, Joseph Kraft, asking to borrow a piece of farming equipment. When Kraft assented, Wolf said he would return for it at noon. He never showed up. It wasn't until Saturday, a full forty-eight hours later, that a puzzled Kraft stopped off to investigate while driving into town with his wife.

Inside the house, he found the Wolfs' infant daughter, Emma, in her crib, wailing from hunger and cold. After carrying the baby out to the car and handing her to his wife, he went to the cowshed, drawn by the grunts of rooting hogs. Unfed for two days, they were feasting on the face and arms of Jacob Wolf's corpse. A double-barrel shotgun blast from behind had blown away most of the right side of his body. Two of his daughters, Maria and Edna, ages ten and eight, respectively, lay on the floor, partially covered with hay. Both had been shot in the back of the head.

The other four members of his family, along with thirteen-year-old chore boy Jacob Hofer, had been dumped into the farmhouse cellar through a trapdoor in the kitchen. Except for Wolf's three-year-old daughter, Martha, killed with a hatchet blow to the skull, the others—his wife, Beatta, and daughters Lydia and Bertha—had been shot at close range in the face, head, or back.

Three weeks would pass before the perpetrator, a neighbor named Henry C. Layer, was arrested. According to his subsequent confession, one of his cows had been attacked and badly injured by Wolf's dog. On the morning of the massacre, he had

192 • 50 STATES OF MURDER

gone over to the Wolfs' house to demand damages. A heated argument ensued. When Wolf produced a shotgun and ordered Layer to leave, the two men got into a struggle, in the course of which both barrels of the gun discharged, killing Mrs. Wolf and the chore boy, who were both standing nearby.

Layer wrested control of the gun and shot Wolf in the back as he fled for the barn, then did away with all the children, except for the baby. Sentenced to life at hard labor, Layer died five years later during an appendicitis operation in the prison hospital.

A CLOWN, A HUNTER, AND A LION WALK INTO A BAR

Grand Forks, North Dakota • October 27, 2007

Bar fights that turn fatal are a depressingly familiar part of the news. Before the 2007 beating death of Joel Lovelien, however, none involved a cowboy, a clown, a hunter, and a lion. On October 27, 2007—the Saturday before Halloween—thirty-eight-year-old Lovelien, costumed as a player for his favorite hockey team, was at the Broken Drum Bar and Grill with his fiancée, Heather Eastling. Parked outside was a bus chartered by a group of Halloween revelers barhopping across the city.

At about 11:30 p.m., Lovelien stepped outside to answer a cell phone call. He returned a short time later, telling Heather that someone had been left behind by the departing bus and he was going back out to "check on him." Within minutes, a man came running into the bar, shouting "Call 911!" Hurrying outside, Heather and other patrons found Lovelien lying in a spreading pool of blood in the parking lot. He was rushed to the emergency room, but was dead by the time he got there. He had choked on his own blood from a beating so brutal that the bones in his face were shattered.

Questioned by police, patrons recalled seeing a number of the costumed partiers standing near Lovelien as they boarded their ride for their next destination, including a clown, a cowboy, a rapper, and a construction worker. Searching the parking lot, police also found a blood-speckled piece of yellow cloth that vaguely resembled an animal's paw. Witness statements led detectives to twenty-three-year-old Travis Stay, who had been wearing a lion's costume crudely fashioned from a yellow hoodie.

After getting into a drunken fight with another passenger, Travis was denied entrance back onto the bus. He was left behind in the parking lot, where he was seen talking to Lovelien. Police found Stay's bloody lion costume—missing one of its "paws"—discarded in the trash. When the blood proved a match for Lovelien's, Stay was arrested for the murder.

He was ultimately acquitted on all charges, leaving the case officially unsolved.

OHIO

BROOKFIELD
A BUTCHER IN BROOKFIELD
199

COLUMBUS
THE OLYMPIAN KILLER
196

BATH TOWNSHIP
A NOTORIOUS KILLER AND HIS FIRST VICTIM
198

CINCINNATI
THE INWOOD PARK HORROR
197

CINCINNATI
THE TANYARD MURDER
195

Newspaper illustration showing the scene of Herman Schilling's murder and cremation

THE TANYARD MURDER

CINCINNATI, OHIO
NOVEMBER 7, 1874

Sometime in the spring of 1874, Cincinnati saloonkeeper Andrea Egner discovered his fifteen-year-old daughter, Julia, in bed with a twenty-five-year-old tannery worker named Herman Schilling. When Julia became pregnant, she was banished from home and died before giving birth. Swearing vengeance on the man he held responsible for his daughter's disgrace and death, Andrea, along with his son, Frederick, found Schilling at the tannery one morning and beat him with barrel staves and fists.

They were arrested and convicted on assault charges and fined $50 plus court costs. Shortly afterward, on the night of November 7, 1874, an adolescent boy who lived close to the tannery was awakened by desperate cries of "Help! Murder!" Searching the premises the following morning, police discovered a bloody pitchfork and, in the boiler-room furnace, Schilling's nearly incinerated skeletal remains.

The two Egners were promptly arrested again, as was a third suspect, George Rufer, a recently laid-off tannery worker who blamed Schilling for his firing. The three men professed innocence until, under relentless interrogation, young Frederick broke down and confessed. According to his story, the three men had conspired to murder Schilling. At the appointed hour, they had snuck into the tannery and hidden themselves until they saw Schilling enter. Sneaking up behind him, Rufer struck him repeatedly on the back of the head with a heavy wooden club, knocking him to the ground. When the powerful Schilling leaped back up and began to grapple with his assailant, the elder Egner ran him through with a five-pronged pitchfork.

Carrying the body to the boiler room, the three men shoved it into the furnace. Asked by his interrogators "whether Schilling was still alive when they forced him into the furnace," Frederick replied, "I don't know."

As the perpetrators of what became known as the "Tanyard Murder," Andrea Egner and George Rufer were convicted of murder and sentenced to life in prison. Charged as an accessory, Frederick was set free after two years in jail.

THE OLYMPIAN KILLER

COLUMBUS, OHIO • JUNE 16, 1929

James Snook had distinguished himself in two very different fields. A champion marksman, he won two gold medals as a member of the US Pistol Shooting Team at the 1920 Antwerp Olympics. As a professor at Ohio State University's College of Veterinary Medicine, he gained renown as the inventor of the "Snook hook," a surgical instrument for spaying female cats and dogs still in use today. At forty-nine years old, the balding, bespectacled husband and father was the very picture of Midwestern middle-class respectability.

It wasn't until mid-June 1929—when two high school boys came upon the body of twenty-five-year-old medical student Theora Hix—that a very different side of the esteemed professor would be revealed to a shocked and titillated world. Though she favored a prim, conservative look, Theora was as sexually adventurous as any Jazz Age flapper and conducted a torrid three-year affair with Snooks, meeting him for regular trysts in a "love nest" he had rented.

Though newspapers would paint Snook as a vile seducer of an innocent young woman, it appears that Hix had very much the upper hand in their relationship, initiating him into the then-forbidden pleasures of oral sex and pressuring him into performing a vasectomy on himself. On the night of June 16, the two drove out to Snook's local shooting range, where Hix ended up dead, her throat slit, her skull shattered with hammer blows.

Under a grueling interrogation, Snook admitted to the murder, claiming that, after informing her that he was going off for a few days to visit his mother, the pathologically possessive Hix threatened him with a pistol he had bought her for self-defense. Grabbing the ball-peen hammer he kept in his car, Snook smashed her repeatedly in the head. Then, realizing that he had fractured

The testimony from Snook's trial for the murder of Theora Hix was deemed too salacious for most newspapers to publish at the time.

her skull, he cut her throat "to relieve her suffering."

At his sensational trial, Snook offered a different account, one so salacious that no newspaper could print it. In this version, after awkwardly attempting intercourse in the cramped car, Hix had gotten down on her knees and started performing fellatio on him. All at once, she began biting down on his penis and "pulling hard" on his scrotum. When she refused to stop, he had bludgeoned her with the hammer, then severed her jugular vein "to make her death easy." The jury took less than thirty minutes to convict him.

He went to the chair on February 28, 1930—the only Olympic gold medalist ever executed for murder.

THE INWOOD PARK HORROR

CINCINNATI, OHIO
MARCH 2, 1937

During the hot summer months, Inwood Park provided a range of recreation for Cincinnatians: wading pools, playgrounds, and kite-flying contests for children, band concerts for their parents, and nightly dancing for young couples at the pavilion. On winter nights, however, the park was deserted.

Sometime around 2:00 a.m., March 2, 1937, cabbie Edgar Bradley picked up an obviously intoxicated couple outside a bar and dropped them at a park entrance. The next morning, the woman's corpse was discovered inside the dance pavilion. She was sprawled in a large pool of blood, her clothes pulled up to her neck, her legs splayed, her face so grotesquely mutilated that it was unrecognizable. Her killer, as the coroner later determined, had stomped on her chin, crushing her jaw and tearing it away from the skull, then ground his heel into her throat so viciously that an artery ruptured, causing her to drown in her own blood.

The "inhuman lust slayer" (as the press called him) then ravaged her body with his teeth, leaving bite wounds all over her abdomen and genital area. Comparing the victim's fingerprints with those on file, detectives came up with a match. She was Edith Caudill Hirl, a twenty-nine-year-old with a checkered past who had been arrested for petty larceny the previous October and had recently been kicked out by her husband of two weeks when he came home from work and found her with another man.

Thanks in large part to Bradley, who came forward as a witness, police were able to identify the man last seen with Hirl: Charles "Teddy" Hines, a twenty-five-year-old whose long police record included several arrests for beating women. Proceeding to his home, detectives learned that he had left town on the morning of the murder. It was not until March 24 that Hines was located in Evansville, Indiana, where he was working as a restaurant dishwasher.

Returned to Cincinnati, he was convicted of the "Inwood Park Horror" (as it came to be known) and electrocuted on January 17, 1938.

Notorious cannibal serial killer Jeffrey Dahmer committed his first murder at his childhood home in Ohio.

A NOTORIOUS KILLER AND HIS FIRST VICTIM

BATH TOWNSHIP, OHIO • JUNE 18, 1978

On Sunday, June 18, 1978, radio stations WCUE and WKDD hosted their second annual Ohio Music Festival at Chippewa Lake Park, featuring a lineup of rock bands popular in the Midwest. Among the attendees was Steven Hicks, a recent high school graduate just shy of his nineteenth birthday who had thumbed a ride to the concert. He was hitchhiking back home later that day when he was picked up by a man around his age named Jeff, who was living alone in his family house—his soon-to-be-divorced father had moved out and his mother was off visiting relatives.

When Jeff invited him back for a few beers, Hicks agreed. Exactly what went on between them is unclear, though any physical contact would likely have been limited to a few drunken kisses because Hicks was straight and Jeff was still conflicted about being gay. What is certain is that when Hicks announced he was ready to leave, Jeff—whose terror of abandonment would be a factor in his future atrocities—smashed the other boy's head with a dumbbell, then strangled him to death. Dragging the body to the basement, he dismembered it with a kitchen knife, stuffed the parts into plastic garbage bags,

198 • 50 STATES OF MURDER

and buried them in a shallow grave in the woods behind the house.

Several weeks later—fearful that the grave might be discovered—he dug up the bags, stripped the decomposing flesh from the bones, dissolved the flesh in acid, and flushed the ghastly sludge down the toilet. He then pulverized the bones with a sledgehammer and scattered the fragments around the woods.

Thirteen years would pass before the many unspeakable crimes of Hicks's killer came to light, and his distraught parents learned that their missing son had been Jeffrey Dahmer's first victim.

A BUTCHER IN BROOKFIELD

BROOKFIELD TOWNSHIP, OHIO
FEBRUARY 8, 1991

After leaving her bartending job early on the night of February 7, 1991, twenty-two-year-old Tami Engstrom joined her uncle, Daniel Hivner, at his favorite watering hole, a dive called the Nickelodeon Lounge, where she proceeded to get so inebriated that she fell off her barstool. At closing time, Hivner agreed to let one of his drinking companions, a thirty-two-year-old asphalt laborer named Kenneth Biros, drive Engstrom to a diner and sober her up with some coffee before bringing her back to the tavern, where her uncle would be waiting to drive her home. Biros never returned.

Confronted the next day by Engstrom's husband, Biros claimed that, while on the way to the diner, Engstrom had fallen asleep. When he had shaken her by the shoulder to wake her up, she had "freaked out," leapt from the car, and run off. He stuck to the story for the next couple of days until, under questioning by police, he confessed that he had done something "very bad."

According to his revised account, he had driven her out to some railroad tracks and made a sexual advance, running a hand up her leg. Pushing him away, Engstrom had jumped from the still-moving car, stumbled, and struck her head so violently on the steel rail that she died. After consulting with an attorney, Biros agreed to lead detectives to the young woman's remains, which turned out to be scattered in several different locations across the border in Pennsylvania.

Far from having died accidentally, Engstrom, as an autopsy determined, had been strangled to death, savagely beaten, and stabbed dozens of times. She had then been dismembered, her head and right breast severed from her torso, her right leg amputated above the knee, her viscera scooped out of her abdominal cavity, and her rectum and vulva cut out (and never recovered).

Biros made international headlines when on December 8, 2009, he became to first person in US history to be put to death with the injection of a single lethal drug—sodium thiopental—slower acting but said to be far less painful than the customary three-drug cocktail.

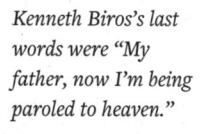

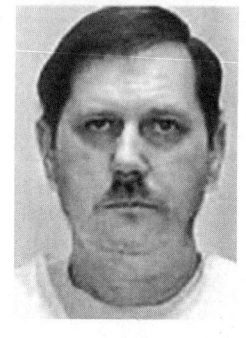

Kenneth Biros's last words were "My father, now I'm being paroled to heaven."

OKLAHOMA

SAPULPA
A SHOOTOUT IN SAPULPA
201

LOCUST GROVE
THE OKLAHOMA GIRL SCOUT MURDERS
202

EDMOND
GOING POSTAL IN EDMOND
205

OKLAHOMA CITY
SIRLOIN STOCKADE MASSACRE
204

MCALESTER
"FRENCH FRIES!" IN McALESTER
201

A SHOOTOUT IN SAPULPA

SAPULPA, OKLAHOMA • FEBRUARY 3, 1934

A crack minor league shortstop who failed to make it to the majors, Austin "Aussie" Elliott turned to bank robbery when he was just eighteen. Captured, convicted, and sentenced to the Oklahoma State Penitentiary in 1932, he promptly escaped and joined Charles Arthur "Pretty Boy" Floyd's gang as a getaway driver. After participating in a few heists, he was arrested and imprisoned again. In October 1933, five months into his fifty-year sentence, he pulled off another escape. Six months later, having eluded a massive manhunt, he took refuge in a farmhouse just outside the town of Sapulpa, Oklahoma, along with a pair of fellow fugitives, Raymond Moore and Eldon Wilson.

On February 3, 1934, acting on a tip that the trio was hiding out at the farm, a party of five lawmen—Sapulpa police chief Tom Brumley, officers Floyd Sellers and C. B. Lloyd, Sheriff Willis Strange and his deputy, Wesley Gage—headed out to the farm. They split up as they approached the house. While Brumley went around to the rear, Strange stood at the front door and ordered everyone to come out with their hands up. At that moment, on the opposite side of the house, Raymond Moore emerged from the back door with a semiautomatic pistol and killed Brumley with a bullet to the head. Hearing the shot, the officers out front opened fire, and a raging gun battle erupted that left Elliott dead and Wilson mortally wounded.

In the meantime, Moore had fled into the woods and hid in a gully. Officer Lloyd went after him and the two exchanged gunfire. Lloyd fell dead, though not before blowing Moore's head off with a shotgun. Clinging to life, Wilson—every bit the "tough desperado" described by newspapers—was locked in the county jail and attended by a local physician, while a company of National Guardsmen rushed there from Tulsa kept a howling lynch mob at bay.

"FRENCH FRIES!" IN McALESTER

McALESTER, OKLAHOMA OCTOBER 27, 1961

Described by one newspaper interviewer as the "most genial psychotic that I have ever known," James French was a bright, articulate man who, during one stint in a federal prison, completed high school and two years of college and wrote a book about the compulsion to commit violent crimes. It was a subject he knew a good deal about.

In early December 1958, while hitchhiking in Amarillo, Texas, he was given a lift by twenty-four-year-old West Virginia welder Frank Boone. Late that night, French got behind the wheel to give Boone some rest. While the latter grabbed some sleep in the passenger

James Donald French, who went to the chair with a macabre quip

seat, French shot him in the head with a .32 pistol, relieved him of $1,000 in cash, dumped his body in Stroud, Oklahoma, and took off in the stolen car. He was arrested the following day after stopping at an Arkansas service station to wash the blood from the vehicle.

Asked about his motives, French told one reporter, "I repaid his kindness with a bullet, I didn't have to kill him to take his money. But there are violent impulses in violent men. I'm one of them." He was sentenced to life in the Oklahoma State Penitentiary in McAlester. Three years later, he decided that his cell mate, Eddie Lee Shelton, "deserved to die" because he was "too stupid to live." Believing that, in accordance with custom, Shelton should enjoy a last meal, French treated him to a steak sandwich from the prison canteen before strangling him to death with a towel and shoelaces.

French not only took full responsibility for the murder but insisted that he receive the death penalty. "Because of what I did, I deserve to die," he declared. "The rules are clear: To take a life is to forfeit your own." After three trials ending in convictions—the first two verdicts overturned on technicalities—he got his wish, becoming the last man to be executed before the US Supreme Court ruled capital punishment unconstitutional in 1972.

Before going to the electric chair, he provided a reporter with the perfect headline for a news story on his execution: "FRENCH FRIES!"

THE OKLAHOMA GIRL SCOUT MURDERS

LOCUST GROVE, OKLAHOMA
JUNE 13, 1977

Horror stories about psycho-killers who slaughter young victims at summer camps are a staple of American folklore. That nightmarish fantasy came to terrifying life in June 1977. On the twelfth of that month, 140 Girl Scouts arrived by bus for a two-week camping adventure in the woods. Among them were Lori Lee Farmer, Michelle Heather Guse, and Doris Denise Milner—ages eight, nine, and ten, respectively—who were assigned to the same tent, one of eight fanned around the counselors' tent. The following morning, their bodies were found on a trail 150 yards away.

Farmer and Guse, who had been bludgeoned to death, were zipped up in their

The tent of the four young victims

sleeping bags. The partially nude body of Milner lay atop them. An autopsy would reveal that she had been sexually molested and strangled with a rope. A suspect was quickly identified: Gene Leroy Hart, a convicted kidnapper and rapist sentenced to 308 years behind bars who had escaped from prison in 1973 and eluded recapture ever since.

After one of the largest manhunts in Oklahoma history, he was finally arrested ten months after the appalling triple murder but then acquitted at his March 1979 trial. Returned to the state penitentiary to serve out his previous term, he dropped dead of a heart attack three months later.

Although DNA tests conducted three decades later pointed to Hart as the likely culprit, the "Oklahoma Girl Scout Murders" (as they came to be known) remain officially unsolved.

Gene Leroy Hart, captured

OKLAHOMA • 203

SIRLOIN STOCKADE MASSACRE

Oklahoma City, Oklahoma
July 17, 1978

In June 1978, Melvin Lorenz and his wife, Linda—both US Air Force sergeants—were driving through a small Oklahoma town with their twelve-year-old son, Richard, when they were flagged down by a lone woman whose seemingly disabled car was parked on the shoulder. When the family pulled over to help, they were ambushed, robbed, and shot to death by the woman's two male accomplices.

A few weeks later, the murderous trio decided to knock over an all-you-can-eat chain restaurant—the Sirloin Stockade—in an Oklahoma City shopping center. Waiting in their parked car until all the customers had left, they entered the restaurant, herded six employees into the freezer, gunned them down, and made off with $1,300 from the cash register.

Six months passed before police tracked down the female member of the gang, a drifter named Verna Stafford, who fingered her husband, Roger, and his brother, Harold, as the shooters. Either by accident or suicide, Harold had died in a motorcycle crash a week after the "Sirloin Stockade Massacre." The sociopathic Roger—who had also shot and killed a young McDonald's employee during a robbery four years earlier—was tried and sentenced to death.

Despite his confident prediction that he would never be executed—"I'm too good-looking," he proclaimed—he went to his much-deserved end by lethal injection on July 1, 1995.

Roger Dale Stafford, Oklahoma's first mass murderer

GOING POSTAL IN EDMOND

Edmond, Oklahoma
August 20, 1986

The origin of the phrase "going postal"—referring to a disgruntled employee who snaps and commits a mass shooting at their workplace—is a matter of debate. Many crime specialists, however, trace it to a horrendous incident that occurred at the Edmond, Oklahoma, post office in the summer of 1986.

Following a two-year stint in the marines, Patrick Sherrill worked at a variety of jobs before enlisting in the Oklahoma National Guard where—owing largely to the sharpshooting skills he had honed in the Marine Corps—he became a firearms instructor. In the spring of 1985, after several failed attempts to find work with the postal service, the forty-four-year-old Sherrill was hired as a mail carrier.

Deeply antisocial, with a gruff, irritable personality, he seemed ill-suited to the job, incurring numerous suspensions and formal complaints for infractions ranging from repeated misdelivery of mail to pepper-spraying a pet dog that barked at him from behind a chain-link fence.

Sherrill himself laid the blame for his work troubles not on his own shortcomings but on the malice of his supervisors, who were supposedly out to get him. He would, so he muttered to more than one acquaintance, "get even with them."

On the morning of August 20, a day after receiving yet another reprimand for his substandard job performance, Sherrill placed three handguns in his mailbag and drove to work. Over the course of fifteen terrifying minutes, he methodically shot and killed fourteen of his fellow workers, beginning with a supervisor he believed was harassing him. Six other employees were badly wounded.

His rampage—the deadliest workplace shooting in US history—came to an end when he seated himself at a supervisor's desk, put the barrel of one of his guns to his right temple, and pulled the trigger.

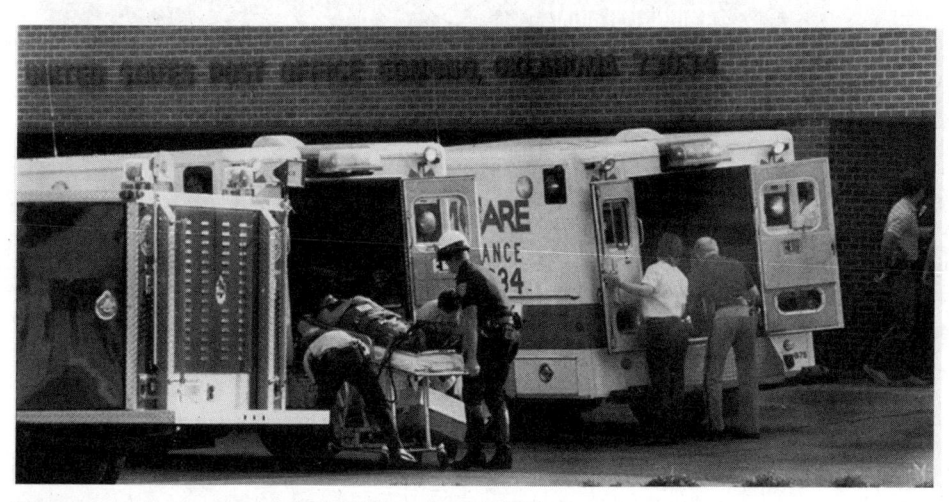

Emergency workers tend to victims of the Edmond postal shooting.

OREGON

PORTLAND
THE VIOLENT LIFE OF MICHELE DEE GATES
207

PORTLAND
A MYSTERY WRITER DOESN'T GET AWAY WITH MURDER
209

★ SALEM

SPRINGFIELD
A MONSTER MOM IN SPRINGFIELD
208

THE VIOLENT LIFE OF MICHELE DEE GATES

PORTLAND, OREGON
JANUARY 4, 1980

When four-year-old Ruth Anne O'Neil failed to return home after going to the corner candy store in January 1980, her mother notified the police. The girl's body was found that afternoon, dumped on a rubbish heap in a nearby backyard. Two days later, the public was stunned when the identity of the killer was revealed in the press: O'Neil's thirteen-year-old babysitter, Michele Dee Gates, who admitted to having drowned the child in her family's pool before disposing of the body in her next-door neighbor's yard.

Even more shocking, Gates—soon to be diagnosed as a "narcissistic sociopath"—confessed that, during an outing to the zoo two years earlier with three-year-old cousin, Natyah Ottino, she had pushed the little boy into a duck pond and watched as he drowned. Psychiatric examiners concluded that the roots of her psychopathology could be traced to her profoundly unstable background. When her young parents separated, Gates was left in the care of her grandmother and her step-grandfather.

Charged as a juvenile with Ruth O'Neil's murder, Gates was sent for several years to a school for disturbed children in Maine. While byzantine legal proceedings dragged on, she returned to Portland, where she lived on her own and—in a development whose dark irony never fails to be noted by historians of the case—volunteered as a swimming

Michele Dee Gates's case spurred lawmakers to reform Oregon's juvenile justice system.

instructor at the local YMCA. In 1985, at the age of nineteen, she was convicted as a juvenile for the murder of Ruth O'Neil but was freed from the state's custody two years later when she turned twenty-one. Her criminal impulses, however, didn't remain dormant for long.

In 1992, now engaged to a man named Joe Shorthouse, Gates hired an ex-boyfriend to kill Shorthouse's ex-wife and burn down her house. After the FBI helped uncover the plot, Gates was tried, convicted, and sentenced to fifteen years in prison. Released in 2005, she married a man named Mark Leland. Thirteen years later, during a Christmastime visit to the home of her estranged father, James Gates, the old man shot Leland to death with a .357 Magnum.

A MONSTER MOM IN SPRINGFIELD

SPRINGFIELD, OREGON
MAY 19, 1983

Sexually molested by her strict, fundamentalist father when she was twelve, Diane Downs grew up to have a deeply troubled relationship with men. Sent off to a Baptist Bible college, she was, in her own words, "kicked out of school for promiscuity" after two semesters. At eighteen she began living with her high school boyfriend, Steve, who—after being threatened by her shotgun-wielding father—agreed to marry her. The tumultuous marriage was replete with infidelities on both sides from the start.

Despite their constant battles, some involving physical violence, the couple quickly had two babies, Christie and Cheryl. A few years later, when Downs gave birth to a boy fathered by another man, Steve accepted the infant—baptized Stephen Daniel—as his own. From the start, Diane proved to be a neglectful, at times abusive mother. It struck more than one observer as ironic that in 1981, now divorced and working as a postal employee, she decided to supplement her income by becoming a surrogate mother.

Her unbridled sexual behavior at work was such that she seemed intent on taking every one of her male co-workers to bed. In 1982, she became obsessed with one of her married lovers and convinced herself that the only thing keeping him from leaving his wife for her was his determination never to be a father.

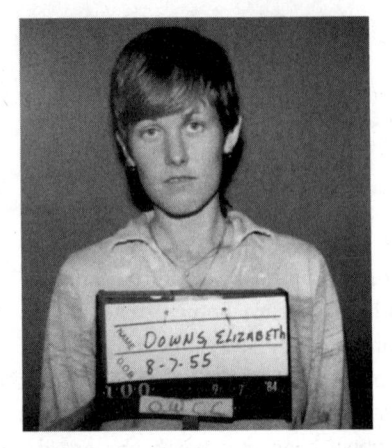

Diane Downs shot three of her children and gave birth to a fourth child in jail.

On the night of May 19, 1983, she drove her sleeping children to a remote wooded area and shot all three with a .22-caliber handgun. Seven-year-old Cheryl was killed outright. The other two children survived, though three-year-old Danny was paralyzed from the waist down and eight-year-old Christie suffered a stroke that left her permanently disabled.

Downs's story—that she had been flagged down in the woods by a "bushy-haired stranger" who shot the children during an attempted carjacking—was met with official skepticism from the start. Arrested and tried in May 1984, she was convicted partly through the testimony of Christie, whose heartbreaking words on the witness stand reduced the courtroom to tears.

Sentenced to life plus fifty years, the "Monster Mom" managed to escape from the Oregon Women's Correctional Center in July 1987 and remained at large for ten days before her recapture and transfer to a maximum-security prison.

A MYSTERY WRITER DOESN'T GET AWAY WITH MURDER

PORTLAND, OREGON • JUNE 2, 2018

In 2011, writer Nancy Brophy posted an online essay entitled "How to Murder Your Husband." As a novelist whose plots often involved mystery and suspense, she explained, "I spend a lot of time thinking about murder." She went on to enumerate the leading motives for such a crime, beginning with the "biggest" one of all: financial ("Divorce is expensive, and do you really want to split your possessions?"). After considering the pros and cons of various methods, from guns and garrotes to hiring a hitman, she acknowledged that "it's easier to wish people dead than to actually kill them. But the thing I know about murder," she added, "is that every one of us has it in him/her when pushed far enough."

Her own husband, Daniel, an instructor at the Oregon Culinary Institute, was, by all accounts, a devoted spouse, often going out for Starbucks coffee and bringing it to her in bed, where she spent her mornings writing her self-published fiction. Early on the morning of June 2, 2018, students arriving at the culinary school discovered sixty-three-year-old Daniel lying dead on the floor of a back kitchen, shot in the back and chest with what forensic scientists later determined was a Glock pistol.

Although Nancy insisted she had still been in bed when her husband was killed, security camera footage showed her arriving at the school in her Toyota minivan at the time of the murder. Investigators soon discovered that she was in possession of a "ghost gun"—a firearm assembled at home from untraceable parts bought online, one of which, in Nancy's case, was a Glock barrel she had purchased on eBay. As for a motive, it turned out to be the number one reason she had named in her 2011 essay: financial. Her husband's life was insured for $1.4 million, which she moved to collect in the immediate aftermath of his death.

Tried in April 2022, she was convicted of second-degree murder and sentenced to life imprisonment.

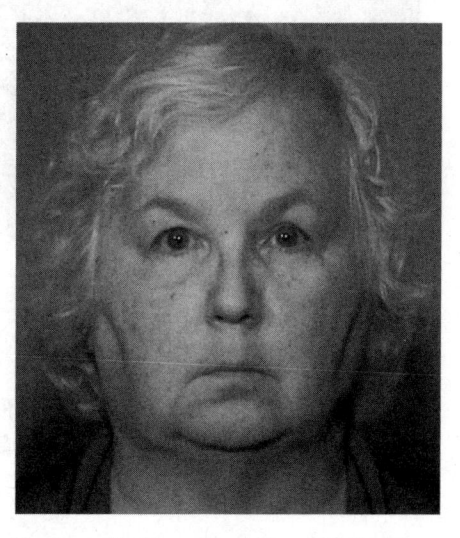

Mystery writer Nancy Brophy turned fiction into reality.

PENNSYLVANIA

PHILADELPHIA
THE POISON RING
213

YORK
THE "GIRL TORTURER" OF YORK
211

CRAWFORD COUNTY
AN AMISH MAN UNHINGED
215

HARRISBURG

PINE GROVE FURNACE STATE PARK
THE "BABES IN THE WOODS" TRAGEDY
214

YORK
THE YORK WITCHCRAFT MURDER
212

The Philadelphia House of Refuge

THE "GIRL TORTURER" OF YORK

York, Pennsylvania
February 22, 1906

Raised by a stereotypically cruel stepmother, a thirteen-year-old girl named Lillian Thornman left her Philadelphia home and made her way to York, where she found work as a servant. A victim of harsh corporal punishment, she had developed a sadistic streak of her own. In the spring of 1905, annoyed at the antics of three-year-old Esther Louis Harris, Thornman sat the little girl on a heated stove and held her there until the shrieking child admitted that "she was the devil."

Several months later, Thornman threw a panful of boiling grease at a little boy named Leon Johnston. She would later admit that the "first thing she thought of when she became angry at little children was of burning them." Her "mania for burning" (as the newspapers described it) reached its lethal pitch in February 1906 while she was doing light housework in the flat of Mr. and Mrs. Robert Dorsey. When their three-year-old daughter, Helena Dorsey, began teasing her, Thornman drew a rocking chair close to the stove, where a large pot of water was boiling. She then lifted the little girl onto the chair and tilted it, throwing Dorsey onto the red-hot surface and overturning the pot, which spilled its scalding contents onto the child.

Hearing Helena's screams, a neighbor rushed into the apartment and grabbed Dorsey, whose skin peeled from her body as she was lifted from the stove. She died soon afterward. Under arrest, the "Girl Torturer" was asked by reporters why she had committed such a horrifying crime. "I don't know why but I just can't help it," she replied. "The devil made me do it."

Pleading guilty to manslaughter at her April trial, Thornman was incarcerated in the Philadelphia House of Refuge for delinquent children.

THE YORK WITCHCRAFT MURDER

YORK, PENNSYLVANIA
NOVEMBER 27, 1928

A holdover from the early days of German immigration to the area, hex magic continued to be practiced in parts of Pennsylvania into the first decades of the twentieth century. Its practitioners, known as "powwowers," typically relied on a book of spells, charms, prayers, and remedies known as *The Long Lost Friend*. One of these folk healers was a man named John Blymire. After suffering various reversals of fortune—including a divorce and the deaths of both his children in infancy—Blymire became convinced that he had been hexed by another powwower.

While working at a cigar factory in 1928, he met two other hard-luck cases who shared his belief: John Curry, a fourteen-year-old whose abusive stepfather was making his homelife unbearable, and forty-year-old Milton Hess, a formerly prosperous farmer who had fallen on hard times when his crops failed, his cows stopped giving milk, thieves stole his chickens, and several family members fell ill. Consulting a local witch named Nellie Noll, Blymire was told that he, Curry, and Hess had all been cursed by a powwower named Nelson Rehmeyer. The only way to break the spell, she advised, was to bury a lock of Rehmeyer's hair six feet underground in a spot behind his barn and take his copy of *The Long Lost Friend*.

On the evening of November 27, Blymire and two accomplices—Curry and Hess's eighteen-year-old son, Wilbert—went out to Rehmeyer's place. When the latter opened his door, the trio stepped inside and set upon him, ultimately braining him with a chair. Dousing the body with kerosene and setting it on fire, they fled the scene without either the book or the hair, believing that his death was sufficient to lift the spell. They were quickly arrested and put on trial for what newspapers across the nation dubbed the "York Witchcraft Murder."

All three defendants were convicted of first-degree murder, sentenced to life in prison, and eventually paroled.

Home of "powwower" and murder victim, Nelson Rehmeyer

Mugshots of Poison Ring conspirators (clockwise from top left): Herman Petrillo, Paul Petrillo, Morris Bolber, and Carina Favato

THE POISON RING

Philadelphia, Pennsylvania • 1932–1938

During the height of the Great Depression, Philadelphia became the site of what has been termed the "largest mass murder plot in US history." At its center were Herman Petrillo, a spaghetti salesman and counterfeiter; his cousin, Paul, a tailor who turned to insurance fraud when the economy catered; a "witch" named Carina Favato who trafficked in magic charms; and a self-styled spiritualist, Morris Bolber, aka the "Rabbi," who originally conceived of the diabolical scheme.

Catering primarily to unhappily married immigrant women, the "Poison Ring" (as it came to be known) arranged to have their husbands' lives insured, then either provided a client with enough arsenic to do away with her unwanted, often unemployed mate or—should she prove too squeamish—arranged for a professional assassin to do the job. With its own network of insurance agents, doctors, and undertakers, the elaborately organized gang claimed as many as seventy-five victims in the six years of its operation, bringing its ringleaders more than $100,000 in insurance claims.

Their crimes were exposed in 1938 when, tipped off by an informant, investigators discovered lethal amounts of arsenic in the corpse of Ferdinand Alfonsi, a poor day laborer whose wife, Stella, was having an affair with Herman Petrillo and whose life had been heavily insured without his knowledge immediately prior to his agonizing death. In the end, two dozen members of the ring were arrested, tried, and convicted. In exchange for their cooperation with authorities, Bolber and Favato were spared the death penalty and spent the rest of their lives behind bars.

Both Petrillos went to the chair, Paul with hopeless resignation, Herman struggling so desperately that he had to be forced down onto the seat.

THE "BABES IN THE WOODS" TRAGEDY

Pine Grove Furnace State Park, Pennsylvania
November 1934

Early on Saturday morning, November 24, 1934, two men out gathering firewood in a state park came upon a green blanket stretched over an oddly shaped mound. Curious, they lifted the covering and were stunned to discover the bodies of three little girls, clothed in nice outfits and lying together on their sides as if snuggling in their sleep. From their close facial resemblance, authorities speculated that they were sisters, a fact confirmed by a hair analysis conducted by a college biology professor. An autopsy revealed that they had been either strangled or suffocated to death.

Taken to the local funeral home, they were put on display in the hope that someone might recognize them. In spite of the hordes that showed up to view them, however—a reported 10,000 people within the first twenty-four hours—they remained unidentified. Photographs distributed to newspapers throughout the country produced no better results. The case of the "Babes in the Woods," as it was called, became a nationwide sensation—"the biggest crime mystery since the Lindbergh baby kidnapping." A solution came after the bodies of a man and a young woman were found in a derelict train station about one hundred miles away.

In an apparent murder-suicide, the man had shot his companion in the heart and head with a .22-caliber rifle before putting a bullet in his own brain. When their abandoned car was discovered shortly afterward, authorities were able to identify them as thirty-eight-year-old Elmo Noakes of Roseville, California, and his eighteen-year-old niece, Winifred Pierce. Evidence gathered from an intensive police investigation revealed that two of the murdered girls were Noakes's daughters, ages eight and ten, the third his thirteen-year-old stepdaughter. The full details of the tragedy would never be definitively established.

According to the prevailing theory, Noakes, a widower, had fallen in love with his teenaged niece, who had come to work as his housekeeper after his wife died of blood poisoning following a self-induced abortion. When Pierce's family raised "bitter objections" to his improper attentions to their daughter, the pair fled California with Noakes's daughters. For whatever reason—possibly, as one newspaper speculated, "because he was desperately broke and wanted to spare his children a life of poverty and starvation"—he choked them to death, tenderly laid out their bodies, then killed himself and his incestuous lover a few days later.

AN AMISH MAN UNHINGED

Crawford County, Pennsylvania • March 18, 1993

Growing up in an Old Order Amish community whose members drive horse-and-buggies, live without electricity, and send their children to one-room schoolhouses for an education that ends in eighth grade, Edward Gingerich was a natural-born mechanic fascinated with modern technology. He felt so deeply conflicted about his faith that he gave serious thought to joining the world of the "English" (as the Amish call outsiders).

Pressured into marriage with a devout young woman named Katie who soon bore him three children, he grew progressively unhappy with his traditional way of life. Before long, Edward's depression had spiraled into such a serious breakdown that he did several stints in a mental hospital. Diagnosed as a paranoid schizophrenic, he was put on powerful antipsychotic drugs, which he stopped taking upon his release because "they made him feel like a zombie."

He was soon back in the grip of his nightmarish delusions, hearing voices that warned him his wife was the devil. On March 18, 1993, Edward came into the kitchen where Katie was washing the dishes, knocked her to the floor with a savage blow to her face, then—in full view of two of their children—stomped on her head until her brains spilled from her shattered skull and disemboweled her with a steak knife. Found "guilty of involuntary manslaughter but mentally ill," Edward Gingerich—the only Amish man ever to be convicted of homicide—did five years in prison before his release in March 1998.

In January 2011, he hanged himself in his barn, leaving a message that read, "Forgive me please."

Edward Gingerich was the first Amish person to be found guilty of homicide.

RHODE ISLAND

WOONSOCKET
A SEX WORKER SERIAL KILLER IN WOONSOCKET
219

PROVIDENCE

WARWICK
THE WARWICK SLASHER
219

TIVERTON
A MINISTER GOES FREE IN TIVERTON
217

SOUTH KINGSTON
A MURDER FANTASY MADE REAL
218

A MINISTER GOES FREE IN TIVERTON

Tiverton, Rhode Island • December 21, 1832

Reported in newspapers throughout the country, the 1833 murder trial of Ephraim K. Avery in Tiverton, Rhode Island, was the greatest criminal sensation of its time. What made the case so riveting to the public was not only the lurid murder Avery was accused of, but Avery's standing as one of the leading figures in the American Methodist movement, a respected minister and seemingly devoted family man.

The story broke in late December 1832 when the body of a woman was found hanging from the pole of a fenced-in hayrick. The victim was quickly identified as Sarah Cornell, a thirty-year-old who had been repeatedly expelled from various congregations for her "loose behavior." When a cursory postmortem exam revealed that the unwed woman was pregnant, her death was ruled a suicide. A subsequent autopsy, however, turned up evidence that she had been strangled, not hanged. Severe bruises to her lower body and legs also suggested that she had been raped, then dragged to the spot where her corpse was discovered.

Notes and letters found among her possessions quickly pointed to Avery as the likeliest suspect. From Cornell's physician, Dr. Thomas Wilbur, authorities learned that Avery had urged the desperate woman to induce an abortion by taking thirty drops of oil of tansy—a fatal dose, as the miscreant minister was evidently aware. Witnesses also came forward who placed Avery in the vicinity at the time of the murder.

A coroner's jury concluded that Avery had impregnated Cornell, then—when his plot to have her poison herself failed—resorted to murder "to conceal a deed so disreputable to a man of the cloth." At his twenty-seven-day trial in the spring of 1833, the longest in American history up to that time, the defense devoted most of its time to attacking the victim, describing her as "a girl whose character was so utterly repulsive" that she had finally chosen to "rid herself of an existence which she no longer valued." Despite the overwhelming circumstantial evidence of Avery's guilt produced by the state, Avery was acquitted. Outraged citizens hanged him in effigy and he barely escaped a lynch mob during a trip to Boston. He eventually left the ministry and retreated to farm in Ohio.

A flock of demons look on as Ephraim Avery murders his pregnant mistress.

RHODE ISLAND • 217

A MURDER FANTASY MADE REAL

South Kingston, Rhode Island
May 18, 1975

On Sunday afternoon, May 18, 1975, five-year-old Jason Foreman, who'd been out playing with some friends in the neighborhood woods, headed back home and was never seen again. A massive search over the following week—involving hundreds of police officers, navy and marine reservists, FBI agents, two helicopters, state police dogs, and as many as seven hundred civilian volunteers—failed to find any trace of the missing boy.

Seven years later, twenty-three-year-old Michael Woodmansee, a loner who lived with his father up the street from the Foremans, lured a fourteen-year-old newspaper delivery boy, Dale Sherman, into his home, plied him with alcohol, then attempted to strangle him. Breaking free, the teenager fled back to his house and informed his father, who reported the incident to the police. When Woodmansee was taken into custody, his interrogators—sensing that there might be a connection between the attack on the paperboy and the still unexplained disappearance of the five-year-old nearly a decade earlier—began questioning him about the Foreman child.

After initially protesting his ignorance, Woodmansee broke down and confessed his guilt. He had been fantasizing about murder for some time, he explained, thinking that "it would be easy to get away with and some form of fun." After he lured the little boy into his home, he had stabbed him once in the chest and temporarily stored his body in a trunk before removing it, defleshing the skeleton, shellacking the skull and about one-third of the bones, and keeping them in a dresser drawer.

A police search of Woodmansee's room turned up not only his ghastly souvenirs but a journal in which he spoke of cannibalizing his five-year-old victim. Sentenced to forty years for second-degree murder on a plea bargain, Woodmansee—much to the outrage of the public—was paroled in May 2011 after twenty-eight years. Perhaps fearing for his own safety—particularly after Jason's father announced during a radio interview that, should his son's murderer be "released anywhere in my vicinity," he fully intended to track him down and kill him—Woodmansee voluntarily committed himself to a psychiatric hospital upon his release.

Michael Woodmansee's journal contained details "so horrific that even Stephen King couldn't come up with it," according to Raven Aubin, sister of Woodmansee's victim.

THE WARWICK SLASHER

WARWICK, RHODE ISLAND
SEPTEMBER 1, 1989

America's youngest known serial killer, Craig Price was just thirteen when he committed his first outrage, sneaking into the home of his neighbor, twenty-seven-year-old Rebecca Spencer, and butchering her with a carving knife. Two years passed before the compulsion to kill overtook him again.

On September 1, 1989, high on LSD and marijuana, Price crept into another neighboring house and slaughtered thirty-nine-year-old Joan Heaton and her two daughters, ten-year-old Jennifer and seven-year-old Melissa.

With a homicidal maniac on the loose in their community and its citizens gripped by fear, investigators consulted FBI profiler Gregg McCrary, who suggested that, in his frenzied stabbing, the killer may well have cut himself and advised them to keep an eye out for suspects with bandaged hands or arms. A few days later, Price, one finger wrapped in gauze, was spotted by a sharp-eyed policeman. Asked how he injured himself, he gave two conflicting stories, neither of which checked out. When a search of his family's backyard shed turned up a plastic trash bag full of blood-soaked evidence, Price was arrested and promptly confessed, relating the horrific details of his atrocities with utter nonchalance.

Convicted of first-degree murder, he was sentenced to the state's maximum penalty for a juvenile offender at the time: incarceration in a youth correction center until he turned twenty-one. The notion that the remorseless young psycho-killer would go free in five years provoked such widespread outrage that the state legislature swiftly passed a law toughening sentences for teenage offenders. Ultimately, his own actions guaranteed that he would remain behind bars for decades.

In April 2017, he savagely attacked a fellow innate with a five-inch shiv and was sentenced to an additional twenty years.

A SEX WORKER SERIAL KILLER IN WOONSOCKET

WOONSOCKET, RHODE ISLAND
FEBRUARY 2003–JULY 2004

Visitors to Jeffrey Mailhot's apartment were invariably struck by the extreme neatness of the place, the way everything was arranged with compulsive precision. Some, however—streetwalkers he picked up in his neighborhood and brought back home—were unlucky enough to glimpse a very different side of the man: a wildly uncontrolled sexual rage that climaxed in homicidal violence.

Bringing a sex worker back to his apartment, he would come up behind her and put her in a stranglehold. A number of the women managed to escape. Three ended up dead, dismembered in his bathtub, stuffed into trash bags, and deposited in dumpsters around the city. Working on tips from several survivors of his attacks, police arrested Mailhot, who finally confessed to the three murders. Asked by detectives if he would continue killing if he weren't in custody, Mailhot admitted that he "couldn't stop. It was a compulsion."

Pleading guilty, he was sentenced to three life terms.

SOUTH CAROLINA

CLOVER
THE EYEDROP KILLER
223

LEXINGTON AND
RICHLAND COUNTIES
LAST WILLS AND TESTAMENTS
222

COLUMBIA

CHARLESTON
**THE LAST HANGING
IN CHARLESTON**
221

THE LAST HANGING IN CHARLESTON

Charleston, South Carolina • June 28, 1910

On the morning of Tuesday, July 21, 1910, tailor Max Lubelsky, a member of Charleston's thriving Jewish community, was discovered on the floor of his clothing store, blood pouring from his head. The money drawer had been emptied and a man's suit stolen. Rushed to the hospital, Max died thirty minutes later from a half dozen skull fractures and a hemorrhage of the brain.

Neighborhood witnesses reported seeing a "round-faced Negro . . . clean shaven and [wearing] a blue serge suit" loitering outside the shop earlier that morning. Over the following days, a number of suspects were taken into custody, subjected to brutal interrogation, and ultimately released. Two weeks after Max Lubelsky's murder, his widow, Rose, now running the store, was waiting on a young Black customer. When she finished wrapping his purchase and extended a hand for the $8 payment, he clubbed her on the head with a two-foot-long piece of stove wood and fled.

Blood streaming down her face, Mrs. Lubelsky staggered out the door and screamed for help. Several men came running. Seeing a young Black man walking down the street away from the store, they gave chase and grabbed him. By then a large crowd had gathered. Only the timely intervention of the police saved the young man—twenty-two-year-old Daniel Duncan—from a lynching. Though he would protest his innocence to the end, he was convicted on circumstantial evidence and not entirely reliable witness testimony.

Duncan's hanging on July 7, 1911, was a gruesome affair. Instead of climbing the scaffold and being dropped through a trap, condemned men in Charleston stood on the ground with the noose end of the rope around their necks and the other end attached to a five-hundred-pound weight suspended over a hole. When a lever was pulled, the weight dropped, and the prisoner was jerked into the air. Theoretically, his neck would snap when the weight of his body yanked him back down. In some cases, however, the violent plunge would fail to kill him, and he would slowly strangle to death. Duncan swung in the air for nearly forty minutes before he was declared dead.

He would enter the history books as the last man to be executed by hanging in South Carolina before the state switched to the electric chair the following year.

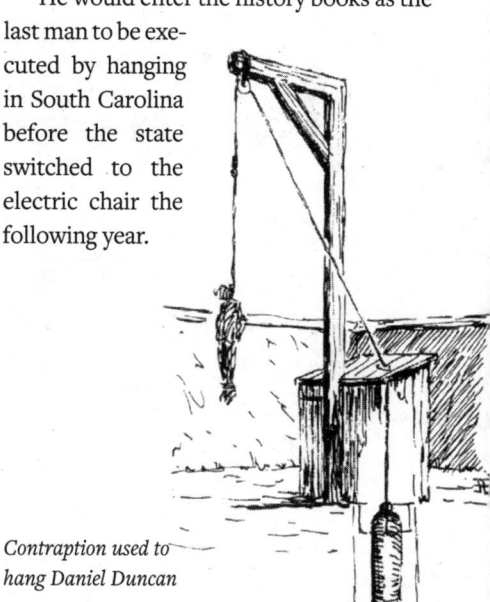

Contraption used to hang Daniel Duncan

LAST WILLS AND TESTAMENTS

Lexington and Richland Counties, South Carolina
June 1985

Returning home from an end-of-the-school-year pool party on the afternoon of May 31, 1985, seventeen-year-old Shari Faye Smith stopped at the roadside mailbox at the end of her driveway. Then she disappeared. From the evidence at the scene—her car still running, the driver's door open, Smith's purse on the front seat, scattered letters on the ground—it seemed clear that she had been snatched as she picked up the mail.

Two days later, a man speaking in an electronically distorted voice made the first of what would be a series of sadistic phone calls, informing Smith's parents to expect a letter from their daughter the following day. The sheer heartbreaking pathos of the document left no doubt that the teenager had fallen into the hands of a particularly malevolent being. Dated June 1, 1985, at 3:30 a.m. and written in Shari's hand, it was titled "Last Will & Testament."

Declaring her love for her family, boyfriend, and "all the other friends and relatives," she urged them not to worry because she would soon be with her heavenly father. "Please don't let this ruin your lives," she wrote. "Keep living one day at a time for Jesus. Some good will come out of this." Most devasting was a request she included in the middle of the letter: "casket closed."

On June 5, directed to the spot by another phone call from the kidnapper, police found Smith's body behind an old Masonic Lodge less than twenty miles away from her home. An autopsy revealed that she had been dead for four days, evidently killed shortly after being forced to write her will. From residue on her face, forensic experts concluded that her killer had strapped duct tape around her nose and mouth, asphyxiating her.

It was Smith's last will and testament, written on yellow legal pad paper, that finally led to the madman's arrest. From impressions on the paper made by the writing on the torn-off top sheet, FBI forensic analysts were able to lift a partial phone number that pointed to Larry Gene Bell, a thirty-six-year-old sexual psychopath with a long history of assaults on women, one of which had landed him in prison.

Sentenced to death, he went to the chair on October 4, 1996, proclaiming that he was Jesus Christ.

Shari Faye Smith's heartbreaking "Last Will & Testament"

Chemical structure of deadly eye-drop ingredient, tetrahydrozoline

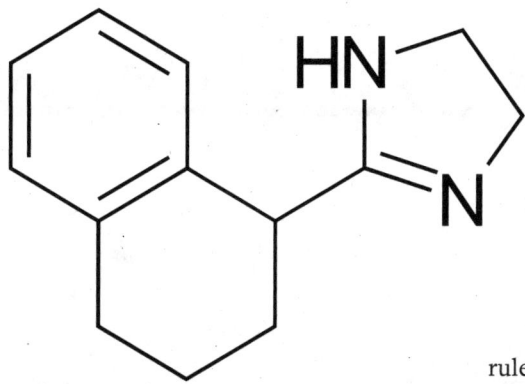

THE EYEDROP KILLER

CLOVER, SOUTH CAROLINA
JULY 21, 2018

Founder of a national chain of physical therapy clinics that made him a wealthy man, Steven Clayton had divorced six wives before marrying again in 2013 at the age of fifty-nine. The seventh Mrs. Clayton was the former Lana Sue Walsh, a onetime Veteran Affairs nurse twelve years his junior. Three years after the nuptials, on May 30, 2016, Lana showed up at the local sheriff's office to report that she had inadvertently shot her sleeping husband in the back of the head with a crossbow arrow while playing around with the weapon in their bedroom.

Improbable as the story seemed, Clayton confirmed it. Bleeding but alive when the cops showed up at his million-dollar lakefront home, he announced that he was fine and speculated that his wife may have inadvertently shot him during one of her regular spells of sleepwalking. The shooting was ruled accidental, though subsequent events would cast it in a very different light.

Two years later, on July 21, 2018, police summoned to the house found Steven dead at the foot of the grand staircase. According to Lana, he had been bedridden with vertigo for the past two days but refused to see a doctor. Evidently, he had gotten up while she was outside mowing the lawn and taken a fatal tumble while attempting to come downstairs.

An autopsy revealed a very different cause of death: His body contained "poisonous levels" of tetrahydrozoline, an ingredient in over-the-counter eyedrops that, if ingested in sufficient quantities, can cause death in less than thirty minutes. Lana, who claimed to be the victim of "mental abuse," would ultimately confess that she had spiked Clayton's drinking water with Visine for three days, though she claimed she only wanted to "make him suffer," not kill him. To avoid the risk of the death penalty, Lana pleaded guilty to first-degree manslaughter at her January 2020 trial.

"This one takes the cake as far as being bizarre," the judge said of the case before sentencing the "Eyedrop Killer" to twenty-five years in prison.

SOUTH DAKOTA

STANLEY COUNTY
THE HUMAN MONSTER
226

SIOUX FALLS
THE DUCT TAPE KILLER OF SIOUX FALLS
228

PIERRE

SPEARFISH
A RECIDIVIST MEETS HIS END IN SPEARFISH
227

SIOUX FALLS
A UNION DISINTEGRATES IN SIOUX FALLS
225

A UNION DISINTEGRATES IN SIOUX FALLS

SIOUX FALLS, SOUTH DAKOTA
OCTOBER 22, 1893

A young lawyer with a taste for fancy clothes and a reported "mania for gambling," Harry Lacey married Clara Bunker in October 1873, a union so opposed by her wealthy father, William, that, soon after the wedding, he walked into the Mississippi River and drowned himself. His widow, Lydia, soon moved in with her daughter and Harry, who proceeded to squander much of her fortune in bad real estate investments.

The atmosphere in the household became so poisoned that, during an argument over money in December 1891, an enraged Harry ordered his mother-in-law from the house, then, when Clara came to her mother's defense, he struck her and brandished a revolver, threatening to shoot her and kill himself. Harry was arrested, fined $50, and moved out of the house. Shortly afterward Clara filed for divorce on the grounds of "extreme cruelty and violent threats." The suit was dropped after the three agreed on a new living arrangement: Lydia moved into her own house; Harry and Clara lived a short distance away.

The separation did little to ease the antagonism between Lydia and Harry. Perceiving that Clara always took her mother's side in these disputes, Harry seethed with resentment toward his wife. On the late afternoon of Sunday, October 22, 1893, Harry entered his house, nodded to his wife, sat down at the kitchen table, and picked up the newspaper. Without saying a word, Clara rose from the table and headed for her mother's house.

A few minutes later, Harry followed her. Kicking in the locked back door, he shot Lydia behind the left ear, killing her instantly. When Clara tried to grapple the gun away from him, he wrenched it from her and shot her in the back of the head. He then walked outside, sat down on a wheelbarrow, pressed the muzzle of the revolver to his right ear, and pulled the trigger—the bloody climax to what newspapers called the "most awful tragedy" ever to occur in the city.

THE HUMAN MONSTER

Stanley County, South Dakota • March 1903

German immigrant William Kunnecke—the "Human Monster," as he came to be called in the press—married a mail-order bride and took up sheep ranching in Idaho, reportedly supplementing his herd with rustled livestock. Around 1896, his wife's nephew, a youth named Koeninger, came to work for him as a farmhand. Two years later, Koeninger—who was owed $800 in back wages—mysteriously vanished. His body was never found, having been incinerated—so investigators later surmised—in a mountain shack owned by Kunnecke that went up in flames at the time of the young man's disappearance.

Not long afterward, in the spring of 1900, a sheepman named Litzman—known to carry large sums of money because of his distrust of banks—paid a visit to the Kunnecke ranch, where he stayed for a meal. His body was found the next day on the trail leading back to his farmstead, his pockets empty of cash. Authorities would later conclude that he had been poisoned. By then, however, Kunnecke and his wife had absconded to South Dakota and were running a sheep ranch in Stanley County.

In 1903, an eighteen-year-old named Billy Rohrbecker showed up at the ranch, inquiring about his older brother, Charlie, another of Kunnecke's farmhands who had disappeared without a trace before collecting his back wages. After persuading Billy that Charlie had quit and left for parts unknown, Kunnecke offered the boy a job assisting his sheepherder, Andy Demler. In a matter of weeks, Demler, too,

The South Dakota State Penitentiary could not hold William Kunnecke for long.

When William Kunnecke did not want to pay his farmhands, he buried them on the plains of western South Dakota.

disappeared—gone east for better prospects, according to Kunnecke.

Billy was puzzled by the older man's abrupt departure but did not become seriously alarmed until several days later. Riding out to the sheep camp a few miles away, he discovered both Demler's sheepskin coat in the bunkhouse and his faithful dog sniffing at what was clearly a frozen pool of blood. Convinced that Demler had met with foul play and that he himself was likely to be the next victim, the boy made his escape and notified authorities. Eventually, Demler's hacked-up body parts were found on the prairie. Evidence indicated that he had been shot in the back of the head with a pistol, then finished off with a shotgun blast to his mouth.

Convicted of murder and sentenced to life in the South Dakota State Penitentiary, Kunnecke managed to escape in 1919 at the age of sixty-nine and was never seen again.

A RECIDIVIST MEETS HIS END IN SPEARFISH

SPEARFISH, SOUTH DAKOTA
JANUARY 24, 1946

The only person in South Dakota to be executed in the electric chair, George Sitts had his first run-in with the law at the age of nineteen, when he spent ninety days in an Iowa jail for carrying a concealed weapon and receiving stolen property. Three years later, he was given ten years in a Minnesota prison for burglary. He was released in 1941, halfway through his sentence, but was back behind bars a year later for violating parole. He was thirty-two years old when he was set free in 1944.

After working for a time in Portland, Oregon, he traveled to Minneapolis in late 1945 to visit a girlfriend, only to find that she had decamped to Texas. Lacking sufficient funds to follow her, he held up a liquor store at gunpoint. The clerk, Erik Johannson, grabbed his own revolver and the two men exchanged shots. Sitts was hit in the shoulder, and Johannson dropped to his knees, two bullet wounds in his chest. Sitts then stepped toward the clerk, delivered the coup de grâce to his head, and sped off into the night.

Sitts remained at large for less than twenty-four hours before being picked up by police. Pleading guilty to second-degree murder, he was sentenced to life and placed in the county jail while awaiting transfer to the state penitentiary. Somehow managing to get hold of a hacksaw blade, he escaped three weeks later after sawing through two bars of his

George Sitts (center) escorted by South Dakotan lawmen

cell window. Making for the Black Hills of South Dakota in stolen cars, he was stopped at a roadblock near Spearfish by a pair of lawmen, and he shot both of them dead as he emerged from his car. He managed to evade a massive manhunt for another eleven days before being arrested in Beulah, Wyoming. Returned to South Dakota, he was quickly tried, convicted, and sentenced to the electric chair.

He went to his death on April 8, 1947, with a quip on his lips: "This is the first time authorities helped me escape prison."

THE DUCT TAPE KILLER OF SIOUX FALLS

SIOUX FALLS, SOUTH DAKOTA
AUGUST 27, 1994, AND JULY 29, 1996

According to one longtime friend, Robert Leroy Anderson had begun fantasizing about abducting and killing women as far back as high school. He first acted out his sick obsession in August 1994 when, with the aid of an accomplice, he snatched twenty-nine-year-old Larisa Dumansky from a factory parking lot as she left work for the night. Driving her out to the countryside, he repeatedly raped her, then wrapped duct tape around her throat and mouth and watched her slowly suffocate to death before burying her remains in a shallow grave.

Two years later—with Dumansky's disappearance still a mystery—he set his sadistic sights on twenty-eight-year-old Piper Streyle who, with her husband, Vance, ran a summertime children's Bible camp. On the morning of July 26, 1996, believing that her husband had gone off to work, Anderson showed up at the Streyles' trailer only to find that Vance was still home. Caught off guard, he stammered something about enrolling his kids in the camp and left his name and phone number.

Three mornings later, he returned. This time, Piper was alone with her two young children. In full view of the traumatized kids, he overpowered their mother, dragged her to his waiting Ford Bronco, and drove her to a remote spot, where—after gagging her with duct tape and cutting off her T-shirt—he tortured, raped, and killed her. Her body was dumped into the Big Sioux River, never to be found.

When Vance Streyle told police of the chubby, balding stranger who had come to his home a few days earlier, they quickly tracked down Anderson. Searching his trailer and vehicle, they turned up a number of incriminating items, including blood- and semen-stained jeans,

Robert LeRoy Anderson in custody

handcuff keys, a toolbox filled with torture devices and duct tape, and a plywood bondage platform designed to accommodate ankle and wrist restraints. With the aid of a botanist who identified bits of vegetation found in the toolbox, police searched the area where the plants were known to grow and turned up the sliced halves of the kidnapped woman's T-shirt and several strips of duct tape with strands of her hair stuck to them.

Shortly after Anderson was tried and convicted of kidnapping Piper Streyle, his accomplice in the abduction of Dumansky confessed to that crime and led police to her skeletal remains. Tried and found guilty of the murders of both women, the "Duct Tape Killer" (as he was nicknamed) was sentenced to die by lethal injection.

Four years later, in March 2003, he hanged himself in his prison cell, an outcome that offered grim satisfaction to Vance Streyle, who told reporters: "This is what we were after anyway. It just saved time and effort."

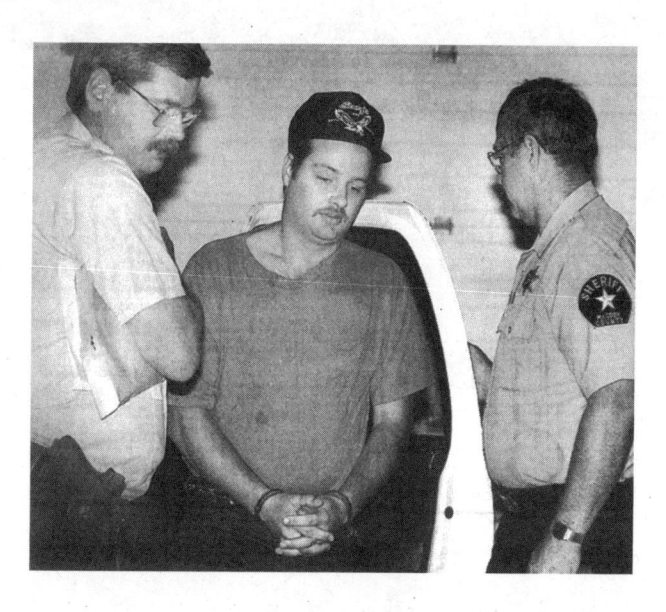

TENNESSEE

GOODLETTSVILLE
STRINGBEAN SHOT DEAD IN GOODLETTSVILLE
232

EAST TENNESSEE
THE NIGHT MARAUDER
231

NASHVILLE ★

ANTIOCH
THE SOUL SUCKER
232

THE NIGHT MARAUDER

East Tennessee
1919–1924

When a serial murderer is on the loose, the press typically comes up a lurid nickname for the phantom-like killer, such as the "Sunset Slayer," the "Skid Row Slasher," or the "Gainesville Ripper." So it was in the case of the homicidal sex fiend dubbed the "Night Marauder" who terrorized East Tennessee in the early 1920s.

His rape-and-murder spree began in August 1919, when Mrs. Bertie Lindsay of North Knoxville was awakened in the middle of the night by a flashlight shining in her face. A burly man armed with a pistol loomed over her bed. When she let out a scream, leaped up, and made for the window, the intruder shot her in the heart before making his escape. Over the next five years in the neighboring counties of Knox and Blount, forty-three nearly identical home invasions would be attributed to the Night Marauder.

In every case but one, he chose houses that were unequipped with electricity and lit only by kerosene lamps, making it impossible for anyone to flip a switch and get a good look at him. His victims were married or single women who—after being warned at gunpoint not to move or make a sound—were assaulted in their beds. Seven people died at his hands: Four women were shot while resisting the attacks and three men were killed while trying to protect their wives or daughters.

Over the years, a number of suspects were tried for the crimes, and one—an innocent Black man named Maurice Mays—was tragically sent to the chair. An apparent breakthrough came when the Blount County sheriff received a taunting letter from the Night Marauder, which was traced to William Sheffey, an employee of the Aluminum Company of America factory in the acronymic town of Alcoa. Though Sheffey insisted on his innocence, neighbors testified that he "had a habit of going out at night after 11 and not returning before dawn."

Far more damning was the discovery that, a decade earlier while working as a schoolteacher in Sevier County, he had been arrested and tried for a crime strikingly similar to the Night Marauder murders: the slaying of twenty-two-year-old Dora Davis, shot to death by an intruder who attacked her after climbing through her bedroom window. Exonerated of that crime, Sheffey then spent time in the army before making his way to Alcoa, where he held the valued position of storeroom

William Sheffey was tried but never convicted for the Night Marauder crimes.

manager. Sheffey was tried three times for the murder of Luther Wells, fatally shot when he came to his wife Ada's defense in December 1923. After two mistrials, he was acquitted in August 1926.

Two weeks later, he married his third wife. Soon afterward, the newlyweds headed for California, leaving the Night Marauder case forever unsolved.

STRINGBEAN SHOT DEAD IN GOODLETTSVILLE

GOODLETTSVILLE, TENNESSEE • NOVEMBER 10, 1973

A beloved fixture of the Grand Ole Opry, comic-musician David Akeman endeared himself to fans as the banjo-playing "Stringbean," a sweet-tempered bumpkin dressed in an extra-long shirt tucked into pants so tiny they were belted just above his knees. As a regular on the TV show *Hee Haw*, he appeared as a scarecrow dispensing corny jokes and playing novelty tunes like "I'm My Own Grandpa."

Despite his fame and wealth, Akeman embraced a simple rustic life, sharing a small cabin thirty miles north of Nashville with his wife, Estelle. A child of the Great Depression, he distrusted banks and was known to carry a large roll of cash in the breast pocket of his overalls. Rumor had it that he kept a small fortune stashed in his home. On Sunday, November 11, 1973, his friend and fellow musician Louis "Grandpa" Jones, drove to Stringbean's cabin to fetch him for a grouse-hunting trip, only to discover both Akemans had been shot dead.

The ensuing investigation led to the arrest of two cousins, John and Marvin Brown, who had broken into the cabin

David Akeman as his beloved alter ego, "Stringbean"

and ransacked it the night before while Stringbean was giving what turned out to be his last performance at the Opry. After plundering the house and failing to turn up the rumored fortune, they had waited for the Akemans' return. When Stringbean, who had spotted something that aroused his suspicions, entered the cabin with his pistol drawn, he was shot dead by one of the burglars. Estelle was chased down and executed as she tried to flee.

Each of the cousins was convicted and sentenced to two consecutive ninety-nine-year terms. Marvin Brown died of natural causes in 2003, while—to the outrage of many in the country music world—John Brown was granted parole in 2014 after forty-one years behind bars.

THE SOUL SUCKER

Antioch, Tennessee
July 2005

Introduced as a child to crystal meth and alcohol by his mother, who worked as a topless dancer, Garland Milam began his criminal career the way that many future serial murderers do: by torturing and killing small animals. At ten years old, he was breaking the necks of kittens and smothering puppies. A few years later, having embarked on his life as a homeless drifter, he worked for a time on a goat farm where, after being informed that he was being laid off, he vented his anger by tying plastic bags over the heads of baby goats and watching them suffocate.

Bumming around the country while numbing his homicidal urges with liquor and drugs, he ended up in Antioch, Tennessee, just outside Nashville, in the summer of 2005, where he set up camp in the woods behind a strip mall. When he and another homeless man, Tim McCoy, got into an argument over beer money on July 24, Milam strangled McCoy with a belt. After the struggling man "quit moving," Milam said later, "his soul rode his last breath out of his body and I inhaled it. It was better than crystal meth." Milam then set McCoy's corpse on fire.

The next day—now "addicted to sucking the souls out of the people I was killing"—he told another vagrant, Johnny Paul Davis, about the murder. When Davis wondered why Milam was confiding in him, the latter said, "Because now I have to kill you." He then gave Davis a head start, chased him down, and strangled him with a dog leash.

Turning himself in a short time later, the "Soul Sucker," as he was nicknamed, pleaded guilty, waived a trial, and was sentenced to two consecutive fifty-one-year terms in prison.

Garland Ray Milam gave one of his victims a five-minute head start before he chased him down.

TEXAS

TEXARKANA
THE TEXARKANA MOONLIGHT MURDERS
236

DALLAS
THE EYEBALL KILLER
240

KILLEEN
A MISOGYNIST TURNS MURDEROUS IN KILLEEN
239

DEER PARK
THE CANDY MAN OF DEER PARK
238

AUSTIN ★

HOUSTON
THE NOT-BEATNIK KILLERS
237

ELMENDORF
ALLIGATOR JOE OF ELMENDORF
235

Joe Ball's pet gators

ALLIGATOR JOE OF ELMENDORF

ELMENDORF, TEXAS • 1936–1938

With the repeal of Prohibition, bootlegger Joe Ball opened a rowdy roadside tavern on the outskirts of his Texas hometown. For entertainment purposes, he installed a concrete pool out back and stocked it with five fully gown alligators, amusing his customers on Saturday nights by tossing live animals—puppies, kittens, possums, raccoons—to the frenzied reptiles. The unfortunate creatures weren't the only victims of Ball's cruelty.

Between 1936 and 1938, several of his barmaids abruptly disappeared. On Saturday, September 24, 1938—tipped off that a fifty-five-gallon iron barrel recently purchased by Joe contained a human body—police drove to his roadhouse to bring him in for questioning. Before they could lead him away, Joe calmly walked behind the bar, pulled a handgun from the cash register, and killed himself with a bullet to the heart.

It didn't take long for police to discover that two of Ball's mistresses had died at his hands, and that he had stored one of them in the barrel before dismembering and burying her remains. Referring to Ball as the "Bluebeard of South Texas," newspapers reported that he had killed "at least a half-dozen women." What earned Ball his lasting notoriety, however, wasn't the number of his alleged victims but the horrifying method by which he had ostensibly disposed of some of them.

According to one unidentified source, Ball "had chopped up the bodies of his victims and fed them to his pet alligators." Though the allegation was laughed off by everyone closely involved in the case, the tale of "Alligator Joe," widely reported in the press, achieved legendary status and became an enduring part of serial killer folklore.

THE TEXARKANA MOONLIGHT MURDERS

TEXARKANA, TEXAS
AND ARKANSAS
FEBRUARY–MAY 1946

Following a double date on the night of Saturday, February 22, 1946, twenty-five-year-old Jimmy Hollis drove his girlfriend, Mary Jeanne Larey, six years his junior, to a rural lovers' lane. They'd been parked there for only ten minutes when a figure, hooded in a white pillowcase with eyeholes scissored out and wielding a handgun, materialized out of the darkness. Ordering the couple out of the car, he demanded that Hollis take off his pants, then nearly clubbed him to death with the pistol, fracturing his skull in three places.

After telling Larey to run, he chased her down and raped her with the barrel of his gun before fleeing. The following month, on Saturday, March 23, twenty-nine-year-old Richard Griffith and his teenaged girlfriend, Polly Ann Moore, drove to a deserted lovers' lane after a midnight movie and a late-night snack. Their bodies were found in the car the next morning. Griffith's trousers were pulled down to his ankles, and both he and Moore had been shot in the back of the head.

When another young couple—teenagers Paul Martin and Betty Jo Booker—were slain in a lovers' lane three weeks later, residents of the area were thrown into a panic, a state of affairs captured in the title of a 1976 exploitation movie inspired by the crimes: *The Town That Dreaded Sundown*. The "Phantom Slayer," as he was dubbed, claimed his last victim on May 3, when he fired through the porch window of thirty-seven-year-old Virgil Starks, hitting the farmer in the back of the head as he relaxed in his living room armchair.

Although many students of the case believe the perpetrator was a career criminal named Youell Swinney—whose wife claimed to have watched him slay Martin and Booker—the case of the "Texarkana Moonlight Murders" remains officially unsolved.

The Texarkana serial murders inspired this low-budget 1976 cult classic.

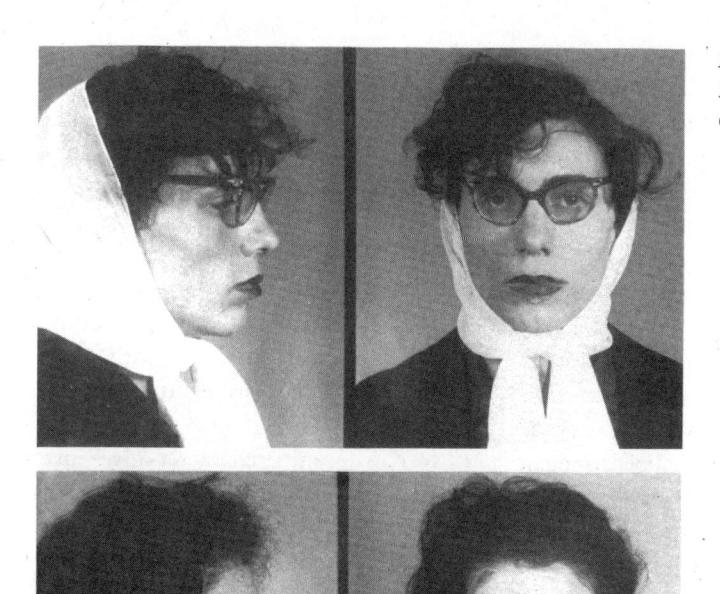

Mug shots of Leslie Douglas Ashley (top) and Carolyn Lima (bottom)

THE NOT-BEATNIK KILLERS

HOUSTON, TEXAS • FEBRUARY 6, 1961

During the late Eisenhower era, the word "beatnik"—originally coined to describe the type of nonconformist hipster protesting against the stultifying materialism of the time—came to be applied to any young person pursuing a life that deviated from the social norm. So it was in the case of Leslie Douglas Ashley and Carolyn Lima, a couple so far out of the cultural mainstream that despite having nothing to do with the attitudes or mannerisms of the so-called Beat Generation, they were branded the "Beatnik Killers."

A transgender youth, Ashley began working the streets while in her teens. She was twenty-two when she met Lima, a beauty school dropout five years her junior, at a lesbian bar. Shortly afterward,

TEXAS • 237

she moved in with Ashley and became her partner in sex work. Sometime in December 1960, Lima was picked up by Fred A. Tones. A small-time real estate agent whose respectable image as a churchgoing family man concealed his sordid secret life, he became one of Lima's regulars. Before long, Ashley made it a threesome.

Exactly what transpired on the night of February 6, 1961, remains ambiguous, but during a sex party in his office, Tones was shot to death with the .22-caliber handgun that Lima carried for protection. She and Ashley then lugged his corpse to their car and drove it to a vacant lot, where they doused it with gasoline and set it ablaze. Going on the run, they made their way to New Orleans for Mardi Gras, then headed to New York City, where the FBI tracked them down and arrested them three weeks later.

Back in Houston, they were tried, convicted, and sentenced to death, though neither would be executed or spend much time in jail. After a successful appeal, Lima did only five years and enjoyed her fleeting fifteen minutes of celebrity as the subject of a Z-grade exploitation film *Burn Baby Burn: The Carolyn Lima Story*. Declared insane at her retrial and consigned to a psychiatric hospital, Ashley promptly escaped, made her way to Florida, and found work in a traveling carnival as "Bobo the Clown." Elevated to the FBI's "Ten Most Wanted List," she was arrested six months later and sentenced to fifteen years.

Released after five years, Ashley underwent gender-affirming surgery and adopted the name Leslie Elaine Perez. She became active in Houston politics and a leading figure in the local ACT UP campaign.

THE CANDY MAN OF DEER PARK

DEER PARK, TEXAS
OCTOBER 31, 1974

In 1972, singer Sammy Davis Jr. scored his only number one hit with "The Candy Man," a saccharine ditty (from the 1971 movie *Willy Wonka & the Chocolate Factory*) whose title character mixes love into his confections, making "the world taste sweet." Two years later, the name became attached to an infinitely more sinister figure: a man who murdered his own son with a poison-laced Halloween treat.

To dig himself out of a mountain of debt, thirty-year-old optician and father of two, Ronald Clark O'Bryan came up with a diabolical plan. After insuring the life of his eight-year-old son, Timothy, for $40,000, he purchased a pack of giant-sized Pixy Stix—long plastic straws filled with sugary powder—and doctored them with potassium cyanide. Accompanying Timothy on his trick-or-treat rounds, he contrived to pass off one of the deadly sweets to his son. When Timothy asked if he could eat a piece of candy before going to bed, his father offered him the tainted goody, helping him to remove the clumped-up powder from the tube. Almost at once, the boy began vomiting and convulsing. He died less than an hour later en route to a hospital.

News of Timothy's death ignited a panic among local parents, who assumed—as O'Bryan had intended—that the homicide was the work of a sadistic madman handing out poisoned Halloween

A MISOGYNIST TURNS MURDEROUS IN KILLEEN

KILLEEN, TEXAS
OCTOBER 16, 1991

Exactly why George Hennard harbored such a hatred of women is unclear, though he made little secret of it. During his years as a merchant seaman, as one shipmate recalled, he would go off on misogynistic rants, declaring that all "women were snakes." Later, two sisters living a few blocks away from him in Belton, Texas, complained to the police after he sent them a rambling five-page letter, railing at the "treacherous female vipers . . . who tried to destroy me and my family."

While watching the Clarence Thomas confirmation hearings at a local grill on the evening of his thirty-fifth birthday, he exploded during Anita Hill's testimony, screaming, "You bitch! You bastards have opened the door for all the women!" The following morning, after polishing off his usual convenience store breakfast, he drove seventeen miles from Belton to Killeen. One hundred fifty people were enjoying lunch at the popular Luby's cafeteria when Hennard crashed his pickup truck through the plate-glass front window and stepped out of the cab armed with a pair of semiautomatic pistols.

As the terrified restaurant patrons ducked under tables and chairs, he moved around the restaurant, methodically executing people while shouting, "All women of Killeen and Belton are vipers! See what you've done to me and my family!" By the time police arrived ten

Ronald Clark O'Bryan and his murdered son, Timothy

treats to children at random. It wasn't long, however, before investigators, digging into O'Bryan's history, learned of his crushing debts, the life insurance policy he had recently taken out on his son, and his efforts to purchase potassium cyanide in the weeks leading up to Halloween.

Convicted of first-degree murder, the "Candy Man," as his prison-mates nicknamed him, was executed by lethal injection on March 31, 1984.

Mass shooter George Hennard crashed his pickup into a packed cafeteria before killing nearly two dozen patrons.

minutes later, twenty-three people, most of them women, were dead and another twenty-seven were wounded. Exchanging gunfire with two officers, Hennard was shot four times before retreating to an alcove near the restrooms and dying by suicide with a bullet to the head.

At the time of his homicidal spree, the Luby massacre was the deadliest mass shooting in US history. Hennard maintained this dubious distinction until the Virginia Tech shootings in April 2007 claimed the lives of 32 people.

THE EYEBALL KILLER

DALLAS, TEXAS
DECEMBER 1990 – MARCH 1991

Encouraged by his fiercely demanding adoptive mother, Charles Albright took up taxidermy at the age of eleven, developing a fascination with the realistic fake eyes sold at a local hobby shop. Two years later, he fell afoul of the law when, after being caught shoplifting, he laid into the store owner and was charged with petty larceny and aggravated assault. Albright was put on juvenile probation on that occasion but did a year in jail not long after, when he and some college friends were arrested for burglarizing a string of stores.

Upon his release, he enrolled in Arkansas State Teachers College, where he gained a reputation as both a brilliant student and an inveterate prankster who once cut the eyes out of photographs of his roommate's ex-girlfriend and glued the defaced pictures to various places in the dorm, including just above the men's room urinal. Kicked out of college for stealing school property, Albright eventually got a job as a high school science teacher by using a forged transcript showing that he had received both his bachelor's and master's degrees. When the scam was discovered, he was fired, charged with fraud, and once again put on probation.

Now a husband and father, he worked a random assortment of jobs: illustrator, carpenter, bullfighter, hair stylist. Albright supplemented his earnings with occasional felonies, one of which—stealing a saw and other merchandise from a hardware store—earned him a two-year prison sentence. Paroled after six months, he converted to Catholicism and became a much-admired member of an East Dallas church. His newfound piety, however, did not prevent the now fifty-one-year-old Albright from sexually molesting the nine-year-old daughter of some friends, a crime that earned him a probated sentence of ten years after he pleaded guilty to "knowingly and intentionally engaging in deviant sexual intercourse" with a girl younger than the age of fourteen. But that outrage was just a prelude to the atrocities that began in December 1990.

Within a three-month period, three Dallas sex workers met similar, brutal deaths, their killer beating them, shooting them in the head, then cutting out their eyes with an X-ACTO knife and making off with the ghastly trophies. Several other streetwalkers had managed to escape murderous attacks by the same middle-aged john. From their descriptions of the attacker, police were able to track down and arrest Albright.

Despite his protestations of innocence, the "Eyeball Killer," as Albright was dubbed, was convicted of murder and sentenced to life.

Other than murdering sex workers and cutting out their eyeballs, Charles Albright was a star college football player, popular high school science teacher, and devoted boyfriend to Dixie Austin.

UTAH

OGDEN
THE OGDEN HORROR
245

BINGHAM
A CRACK SHOT IN BINGHAM
243

SALT LAKE CITY
A FORGER-TURNED-BOMBER IN SALT LAKE
246

SALINA
A SOLDIER SNAPS IN SALINA
244

SAN JUAN COUNTY
A KILLER'S LAST LAUGH
245

Bingham, Utah, circa 1913

A CRACK SHOT IN BINGHAM

BINGHAM, UTAH
NOVEMBER 21, 1913

Target of the largest manhunt in Utah history, Mexican-born Rafael "Red" Lopez was known as an expert marksman, so skilled with a rifle that he reportedly performed as a sharpshooter in Buffalo Bill Cody's traveling Wild West show. At the time of the murder that set him off on his outlaw career, he was working as a miner in Bingham, Utah.

His victim was an old acquaintance and fellow miner, Juan Valdez. Exactly why Lopez killed him is uncertain. Some say it was revenge for Valdez's part in the death of Lopez's brother, others that it sprang from a dispute over a woman. Whatever the case, a four-man posse was soon on Lopez's trail. Taking refuge at a ranch about forty miles away, Lopez ambushed the approaching lawmen, killing three with long-range shots from his Winchester. When word of the triple murder spread, volunteers from across the state, both law officers and civilians, hurried to the scene, forming themselves into posses that numbered roughly two hundred men.

Rafael "Red" Lopez escaped a manhunt in Utah and went on to participate in the Mexican Revolution, likely fighting with the forces of Pancho Villa.

UTAH • 243

By then, Lopez had made his way back to Bingham and holed up in a mine. When a group of deputies tried smoking him out, Lopez shot two of them dead. Subsequent efforts to starve him out were met with no better success. In early January, lawmen finally entered and searched the cave, but Lopez was long gone and would never be seen in Utah again.

Fleeing to Texas, he formed a gang of outlaws that included former members of Butch Cassidy's "Wild Bunch" and was eventually killed in 1921 by the legendary Texas Ranger Frank Hamer, the man who, thirteen years later, would take down Bonnie and Clyde.

A SOLDIER SNAPS IN SALINA

SALINA, UTAH
JULY 8, 1945

Following the Normandy invasion and the rapid advance of Allied forces across western Europe, thousands of captured German soldiers were shipped to POW camps around the United States. One of these was located in the Utah town of Salina. During the day, the 250 prisoners were sent to work in the fields, helping local farmers harvest their produce. At night, they slept in forty-three wood-floored tents, overlooked by three guard towers.

Among the guards was Clarence V. Bertucci. A twenty-three-year-old from Louisiana who had enlisted at eighteen, Bertucci had never advanced beyond the rank of private owing to repeated infractions, three of which had landed him in the stockade. Deemed unfit for combat duty, he told others that he felt "cheated" of his chance to kill Germans and vowed that he would one day "get my turn."

Shortly after midnight on July 8, 1945, after having a few beers in town, Bertucci showed up for his shift. Once the previous watch was settled in their quarters, he climbed one of the towers, threaded a 250-round belt of .30-caliber cartridges into his Browning machine gun, and opened fire on the tents below, hitting thirty of them as he methodically swept his weapon back and forth. By the time he ran out of bullets a half minute later, he had killed eight German prisoners and wounded twenty others, one of them mortally.

Taken into custody for "the worst massacre at a POW camp in US history," Bertucci displayed not a trace of remorse. He was ultimately declared insane and committed to a mental institution. As for his motives, his commanding officer could come up with only one explanation: "He just didn't like Germans."

PFC Clarence Vincent Bertucci "didn't like Germans."

A KILLER'S LAST LAUGH

SAN JUAN COUNTY, UTAH
JUNE 19, 1957

A thirty-seven-year-old native of Lubbock, Texas, who had spent more than half his life in various prisons, mostly for armed robbery, James W. Rodgers arrived in Utah in 1957, where he found work as a security guard at the Rattlesnake Pit uranium mine forty miles northeast of Monticello. On June 19, while power shovel operator Charles Merrifield was seated at the controls, Rodgers walked up to him and shot him four times at point-blank range.

"I can't tell you why I did it," he said afterward. "He'd been getting on my nerves for some time." Driving off in a pickup truck, he was arrested three hours later in Cortez, Colorado. Convicted and sentenced to death, he opted for execution by firing squad.

When asked if he had any last requests on the day of his execution, he replied, "A bulletproof vest."

THE OGDEN HORROR

OGDEN, UTAH
APRIL 22, 1974

Stanley Walker and Michelle Ansley, twenty and eighteen years old, respectively, were closing up their home audio store when a pair of gun-wielding men entered, herded the two young clerks into the basement, and bound them hand and foot. When sixteen-year-old Cortney Naisbitt, a relative of the owner, entered a short time later to thank Walker for a favor, he, too, was taken captive.

The intruders—Dale Selby Pierre and William Andrews, both enlisted US Air Force airmen—then set about loading stereo equipment into their van. While they were at it, Stan's forty-three-year-old father, Orren Walker, and fifty-two-year-old Carol Naisbitt, Cortney's mother, came by to see why their sons hadn't returned home and also ended up bound and gagged in the basement. What followed was a crime justifiably regarded as one of the most horrific in Utah history.

Left to right: Stanley Walker, Michelle Ansley, and Carol Naisbitt, three of the victims of the Hi-Fi massacre

Inspired by a sadistic scene from the 1973 Clint Eastwood film *Magnum Force*—in which a vengeful pimp murders a sex worker by pouring liquid drain cleaner down her throat—the robbers forced the five hostages to drink cupfuls of Drano. The three males and Carol Naisbitt were then shot in the head. Ansley was dragged into a corner and repeatedly raped before being killed. When Orren Walker showed signs of life, one of the men shoved a ballpoint pen into his ear and stomped on it until it exited through his throat. Miraculously, he survived, as did Cortney Naisbitt, though both suffered permanent, life-altering injuries.

William Andrews (left) and Dale S. Pierre (right) became known as the "Hi-Fi Murderers."

Working on a tip from an anonymous informant—an air force employee to whom Andrews had confided his plans to rob the store—police soon had the perpetrators under arrest. Such was the appalling nature of the crime that much of the public hailed their eventual executions as justice served.

A FORGER-TURNED-BOMBER IN SALT LAKE

SALT LAKE CITY, UTAH • OCTOBER 15, 1985

By the age of fourteen, Mark Hofmann had acquired the two skills that would eventually make him one of the most notorious figures in Utah criminal history. A passionate coin collector and amateur chemist, he used his electroplate set to forge a rare mint mark on an ordinary dime and successfully passed it off as genuine to the American Numismatic Society. And while still in elementary school, he learned how to make black powder and used it to construct a few simple pipe bombs that he set off in a park.

Though he enrolled in college as a premed major, Hofmann's life took a fateful turn when he began acquiring rare books and documents and selling them for handsome profits. Though he dealt in various pieces of Americana—papers

Latter-Day Saints leaders examine a supposedly rare Mormon document forged by Mark Hofmann (far left).

signed by George Washington, Daniel Boone, Paul Revere, Mark Twain, and many others—he specialized in ephemera related to the early history of the LDS church. Because some of these documents cast doubt on the legitimacy of the church's founder, Joseph Smith, church leaders were eager to acquire them and hide them from public view.

Though some raised their eyebrows at the ease with which Hofmann was able to locate these exceptional finds, no one suspected the truth: that they were all forgeries, so skillfully done that even the most eminent experts vouched for their authenticity.

When one of his loyal clients, Steve Christensen, began pressuring him to produce a long-promised collection of rare documents, Hofmann—by then deeply in debt from his lavish lifestyle—left a package with a homemade pipe bomb at the former's office door that killed him when he picked it up. To divert attention from himself, Hofmann then left another bomb at the home of Christensen's former employer, J. Gary Sheets, whose investment firm was embroiled in a financial scandal. Though intended for Sheets, it was his wife, Kathy, who found the package lying in front of the house, picked it up, and was blown to pieces. Hofmann himself was badly injured the following day when a third bomb—whose intended target remains a mystery—detonated as he was removing it from his car.

Arrested and charged with first-degree murder among other crimes, Hofmann, in a deal brokered by his lawyers, pleaded guilty to second-degree murder and was given the then-maximum sentence in Utah: five years to life.

VERMONT

WILLISTON
MOTHER-IN-LAW MURDERED IN WILLISTON
249

MONTPELIER

DUXBURY
THE MONSTER FROM DUXBURY
250

NEWBURY
THE MEANEST MAN IN A PRETTY TOWN
252

WEST DOVER
AN INNOCENT MAN GOES FREE IN WEST DOVER
253

MOTHER-IN-LAW MURDERED IN WILLISTON

WILLISTON, VERMONT
AUGUST 27, 1865

Sixty-one-year-old Sally Griswold owned one of the finest properties in town, a handsome brick house on 140 acres of prime farmland that she shared with her adopted daughter, Adelia Potter, and Adelia's husband, Charles. There was no love lost between Griswold and her son-in-law, who—knowing that his wife would inherit the estate—couldn't wait to get the old lady out of the way.

Pro hitman John Ward

VERMONT • 249

On August 27, 1865, the Potters set off by buggy for a trip to Canada. The following Sunday, Griswold's body was discovered in a calf pen near the barn. Her skull had been fractured and her throat cut, and there were wounds on her hands, arms, and face, which, as the *New York Times* reported, "tended to show that the murdered woman must have had a violent struggle for her life." It wasn't long before a man named John Ward, known to have left Williston in a hurry the morning after the murder, was identified as the prime suspect.

Investigators soon learned that the gentlemanly and well-educated twenty-seven-year-old was in fact a professional hitman. Tracked to New York City by a deputy US marshal, Ward was tailed and arrested when he returned to Vermont to collect his blood money from the man who had hired him, Charles Potter. He and Potter were tried the following April. Potter was acquitted on a legal technicality. Ward was found guilty and sentenced to death. While awaiting his execution, he confessed to having participated in the murder, but claimed that an accomplice had cut Griswold's throat while he himself held her down.

Ward was hanged on March 20, 1868, ending what has been called "the most famous murder case in the state's early history."

THE MONSTER FROM DUXBURY

DUXBURY, VERMONT
APRIL 23, 1880

After her husband's death in 1873, Mary Meaker—unable to provide for her two small children, Alice and Henry—turned them over to the town poor farm (the rural equivalent of a Victorian workhouse). Six years later, their much older half-brother Horace—offered $50 by town officials to assume care of the children—agreed to take them into his household.

The arrangement did not please Horace's forty-year-old wife, Emeline, a "coarse, brutal, domineering woman" whose hardscrabble life had left her deeply embittered and seething with suppressed rage that she would vent against her helpless eight-year-old sister-in-law. The abuse started shortly after Alice came to live with the Meakers. The frail, timid child was treated like enslaved person and savagely beaten at the slightest provocation.

Within a year, Emeline's pathological hatred of "the little bitch" (as she called Alice) had grown so intense that she decided to do away with her. At his mother's bidding, her slow-witted, eighteen-year-old son, Almon, purchased fifteen grains of strychnine at a local drugstore, ostensibly as rat poison.

Back home, he and his mother stole into the sleeping girl's bedroom, slipped a sack over her head, bundled her into a hired buggy, and drove to a remote hilltop, where—after mixing the poison with some sugar-sweetened water—they forced the girl to drink the lethal potion. As Alice convulsed and cried out, Emeline clamped a hand over her mouth to muffle the noise. When the child stopped breathing, Almon drove the buggy to a spot outside Stowe, where he buried her in a swampy thicket.

Within days, neighbors noticed that Alice was missing and conveyed their concerns to town officials. Under questioning by the sheriff, the weak-willed Almon spilled out the awful truth. Found guilty of what newspapers branded "one of the most diabolical and revolting murders known in history or fiction," he and Emeline were both given the death penalty, though Almon—deemed to be "mentally deficient" and in thrall to his mother—had his sentence commuted to life in prison.

Emeline was hanged on March 30, 1883, making her the first woman to be legally executed in Vermont.

Emeline Meaker (bottom) enlisted her submissive son Almon (top) to commit one of nineteenth-century Vermont's most notorious crimes.

THE MEANEST MAN IN A PRETTY TOWN

NEWBURY, VERMONT • DECEMBER 31, 1957

Much about the 1957 abduction and murder of Vermont dairy farmer Orville Gibson remains shrouded in mystery. Even his standing among his neighbors is a matter of debate. Some accounts describe him as "a retiring but generous man . . . always willing to help out when help [was] needed." Others paint him as an inveterate bully, "the meanest man in one of the prettiest towns in New England," who got what was coming to him. Questions also surround the incident that led to his demise.

Around Christmas 1957, Gibson's hired hand, Eri Martin, inebriated at the time, spilled two forty-gallon cans of milk while attempting to roll them down a ramp in a wheelbarrow. That much is beyond dispute. Gibson would claim that Martin injured himself when he lost control of the wheelbarrow and its handles cracked him in the ribs. Martin, however, told a different story: When Gibson declared that he would deduct the cost of the spilled milk from Martin's wages, the two got into a heated quarrel that ended when an enraged Gibson subjected the smaller man to a vicious beating, leaving Martin with broken ribs and an injured kidney.

Over the following days, Martin's version spread through town, inciting such outrage that there was talk of "tarring and feathering" Gibson. Early on December 31, Gibson went into his barn to milk the cows and disappeared. Eighty-five days would pass before his bloated, hog-tied corpse was found floating in the Connecticut River. An autopsy revealed that he had been asphyxiated before being dumped in the water. Because community animosity against Gibson had run so high following his alleged attack on Martin, his murder was widely seen as an act of vigilante justice. Newspaper editorials decried the killing as "a Yankee lynching" that would remain "an everlasting blot on Vermont's name."

Two men would eventually be tried for and acquitted of the crime, making it one of the state's most famous unsolved cases.

The story of Orville Gibson became part of Newbury's lore.

AN INNOCENT MAN GOES FREE IN WEST DOVER

West Dover, Vermont
September 12, 1994

On Monday night, September 12, 1994, police responding to a 911 call from the Timber Creek condominiums found thirty-one-year-old Christine Grega lying naked and soaked on the bathroom floor. According to her husband, John—a Long Island, New York, businessman there on a family vacation—he had returned from a playground outing with his toddler son and found his unconscious, badly bruised wife half in and half out of the bathtub. Assuming she had slipped and struck her head, he had pulled her onto the floor and administered CPR before running to a neighbor's unit to phone the police.

An autopsy revealed that Christine's death was no accident. She had been beaten, strangled, and anally raped so brutally that she had suffered "traumatic injury to her rectum." It didn't take investigators long to learn that, owing largely to John's drinking and drug use, the Gregas' marriage was coming apart. Christine, on the brink of leaving him, had been withholding sex for months. Detectives also discovered that John had recently taken out a life insurance policy on his wife that paid him $350,000 in the event of her accidental death.

Arrested in December, Grega stoutly maintained his innocence and pointed a finger at a pair of housepainters who

John Grega spent nearly two decades in prison for a crime he didn't commit.

worked at the complex at the time of his wife's murder, one of whom had a "substantial violent police record." Tried in July 1995, Grega was convicted and sentenced to life in prison. After nearly eighteen years behind bars—during which he continued to fight for a retrial—he was vindicated when DNA evidence ruled him out as the perpetrator. His conviction was vacated, and he was released in August 2012. His hard-won freedom, however, was short lived.

On January 23, 2015, he lost control of his Chevrolet van a few blocks from his Long Island home, hit a tree, and was killed.

VIRGINIA

HAMPTON ROADS
THE HAMPTON ROADS KILLER
259

RICHMOND
A WIFE KILLER FROM RICHMOND
255

CARROLL COUNTY
THE VIRGINIA COURT MASSACRE
256

NORFOLK
LIFE IMITATES ART IN NORFOLK
258

Henry Clay Beattie Jr.

A WIFE KILLER FROM RICHMOND

Richmond, Virginia
July 18, 1911

The profligate scion of a prominent Southern family, twenty-two-year-old Henry Clay Beattie Jr. began sleeping with Beulah Binford—variously described as "wild" and "of questionable reputation"— when the girl was only thirteen. When Binford became pregnant two years later, Beattie shipped her off to Washington, DC, where she gave birth to a boy who was given up for adoption and died in infancy.

One month after the child's funeral, Beattie married a young woman selected for him by his father: a cultured twenty-year-old, Louisa Owen, from a highly respectable family. Nine months almost to the day after the wedding, she bore him a son. By then, Beulah Binford, now seventeen, had returned to Richmond and resumed her affair with Beattie. Shortly after the birth of his child, Beattie acquired a secondhand, single-barreled shotgun, procured at his request by his cousin Paul.

Three days later, he took Louisa on a late-night automobile drive on the Midlothian Turnpike. Within an hour, he had shown up at the home of his wife's uncle, her corpse beside him in the car, a shotgun hole in her face, her hair clotted with blood, brain matter running from one ear. According to his story, she had been killed during an attempted robbery by a "bearded highwayman" who ran off into the woods following the aborted holdup. Local newspapers reported the crime as "one of the most horrible and atrocious murders known in the history of the state."

The evidence,, however, quickly cast doubts on Beattie's tale. Bloodhounds brought to the scene could not pick up any trail of the purported killer. A puddle of dried blood on the road undercut Beattie's claim that Louisa had been shot while seated in the car. Beattie also maintained that the robber had been standing close to the vehicle when he fired his gun. The absence of any powder marks on the victim's face, however, indicated otherwise. Beattie's fate was sealed when police traced the purchase of the shotgun to his cousin and his ongoing relationship with Beulah came to light.

His two-week trial in late summer 1911—covered by newspapers across the nation—climaxed with his conviction. Just before going to the electric chair on November 24, he issued a brief confession, stating that he was "truly sorry" for murdering his wife and—expecting to "soon pass into His presence"—was now "at peace with God."

THE VIRGINIA COURT MASSACRE

CARROLL COUNTY, VIRGINIA • MARCH 14, 1912

Head of a clannish mountain family in the backwoods community of Carroll County, Virginia, Floyd Allen—a prosperous landowner, storekeeper, and occasional officeholder—was known for a hair-trigger temper that might explode into violence at the slightest provocation. A "stalwart figure with beetling brows and bushy, reddish whiskers" (as the *New York Times* described him), he proudly bore the scars of thirteen bullet wounds, "five inflicted in quarrels with his own family." In one not-atypical incident, he shot his brother Jack in the head when the two got into a dispute involving the ownership of a barrel of brandy.

In December 1910, two of Allen's nephews were charged with disorderly conduct after getting into a fracas with a group of other young men outside a schoolhouse where a church service was in progress. Fleeing across the border to North Carolina, they were arrested and turned over to a Carroll County deputy sheriff, who tethered them to his buggy—one by handcuffs, the other by rope—before driving them back to face trial.

Along the way, they were intercepted by Allen, who released his nephews after beating the deputy unconscious with his pistol butt. Arrested for assault, Floyd was tried in the local courthouse and found guilty. No sooner had the judge pronounced the sentence—one year in prison—than Floyd stood up and proclaimed, "Gentleman, I ain't a-going."

256 • 50 STATES OF MURDER

Floyd Allen (top row, second from left) and his "gang"

Wytheville Courthouse, site of the Virginia Court Massacre

VIRGINIA • 257

At that moment, a blazing gun battle erupted in the packed courthouse. Exactly who fired the first shot remains a mystery. Some say it was Floyd or one of his relatives, others that it was one of the lawmen present. What is known is that in less than a minute, two hundred shots had been fired and—in what came to be known as the "Virginia Court Massacre"—five people were killed or mortally wounded: the judge, the town sheriff, an attorney, a juror, and one witness.

Shot in the leg, Floyd Allen slipped off his horse while trying to escape and was arrested the next day. Along with his youngest son, Claude, he was convicted of first-degree murder. In what the *New York Times* called "the first double execution of a white person in the history of the penitentiary," the two went to the electric chair on March 28, 1913.

LIFE IMITATES ART IN NORFOLK

NORFOLK, VIRGINIA
MAY 13, 1976

According to his mother, David McRae Jr. "always wanted to be a policeman." During high school, he spent time as a cadet in a police community relations program and, after dropping out and joining the army, became a military policeman. His mental instability first manifested itself while he was stationed in Germany, where he attempted suicide by swallowing an overdose of barbiturates. When he returned to the United States, he spent three months at Walter Reed Hospital before receiving an honorable disability discharge.

Back home in Norfolk, he lived with his parents and worked as a deliveryman for a wholesale pharmaceutical firm. In his increasingly paranoid fantasies, he began to identify with Travis Bickle, the protagonist of his favorite movie, *Taxi Driver*, who comes to see his city as a cesspool and resolves to rid it of its "filth and scum."

McRae started to haunt Norfolk's vice district and stake out a seedy bar, Club 54, keeping a small spiral notebook recording his surveillance of "the dope peddlers and pimps and queers" who frequented the place. On the night of May 13, 1976, he strode into the crowded tavern and opened fire with a .45-caliber Colt semiautomatic, killing four men—all, like himself, were Black—with lengthy rap sheets for crimes ranging from assault and larceny to "soliciting for immoral purposes" and "impersonating a woman." Three others were wounded. "He acted like he had a job to do," one witness said. "He was going about it in a very methodical way."

At the climax of Bickle's killing spree in *Taxi Driver*, he tries to die by suicide, but his gun has run out of bullets. McRae, who had paused to reload during his rampage, had no such luck. He put his gun to his head and killed himself.

THE HAMPTON ROADS KILLER

HAMPTON ROADS, VIRGINIA
JULY 1987–JULY 1996

Over a nine-year span beginning in July 1987, the bodies of eleven men, all but one of them naked, were found dumped in an area of southeastern Virginia called Hampton Roads. Nine had been strangled; the others were too decomposed to determine the manner of death. All were described in the press as "drifters, transients, or hustlers" who had last been seen in or near gay bars in Norfolk or Portsmouth. With the gay community up in arms over the perceived public indifference to the crimes, a serial killer task force was set up to hunt down the predator.

It wasn't until he claimed his twelfth victim, however, that the "Hampton Roads Killer" was finally caught. On the morning of July 22, 1996, the nude body of thirty-eight-year-old Andrew D. Smith was found on a roadside not far from an interstate highway in Chesapeake. An autopsy determined that the cause of death was ligature strangulation and that the murder had occurred within the last forty-eight hours.

Interviews with Smith's acquaintances led police to Elton Manning Jackson, a forty-one-year-old man, who—after initially telling police that he didn't know Smith—admitted that the pair had engaged in "consensual sex" two nights before Smith's body was discovered. Other men who'd had sexual encounters with Jackson reported that they had barely managed to escape after he attempted to choke them with a leather strap. Obtaining warrants to search Jackson's house, investigators found, among other evidence, blood stains on his mattress that matched Smith's DNA.

Tried for Smith's murder in August 1998, Jackson—who continued to maintain his innocence—was convicted and sentenced to life, ending the Hampton Roads Killer's nearly decade-long reign of terror.

Experts at the time were puzzled that Jackson has killed both Black and white victims, due to the popular notion that serial killers seek out a single "type" of victim.

WASHINGTON

SEATTLE
THE WAH MEE MASSACRE
263

OLALLA
THE FASTING FIEND OF STARVATION HEIGHTS
261

OLYMPIA

BELLEVUE
THE BELLEVUE THRILL KILLERS
265

PUYALLUP
A MIDLIFE OBSESSION ENDS BADLY IN PUYALLUP
262

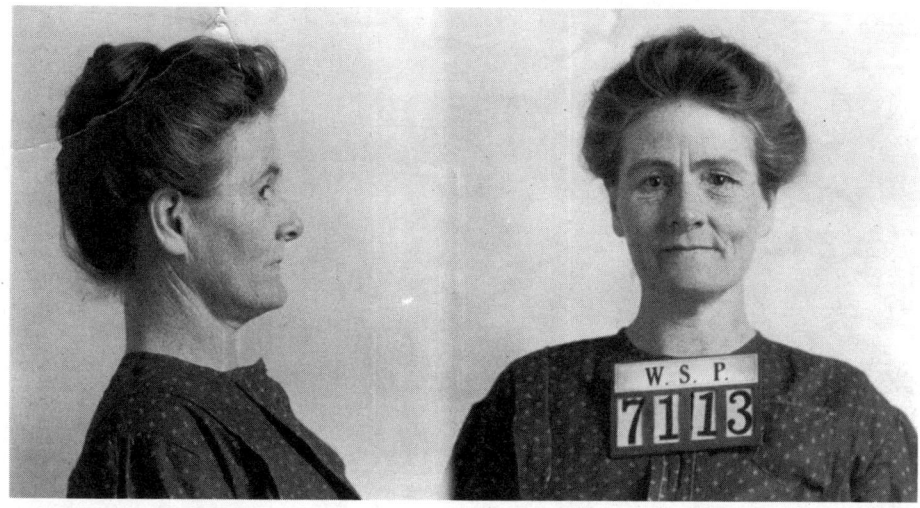

Linda Hazzard was known for her contrversial medical practices and beliefs.

THE FASTING FIEND OF STARVATION HEIGHTS

OLALLA, WASHINGTON
FEBRUARY–MAY 1911

In 1911, a pair of wealthy English travelers, Claire and Dora Williamson, came under the care of a medical quack, Linda Burfield Hazzard, who preached the supposedly miraculous health benefits of extreme fasting. Believing that all physical and mental ailments were the result of overeating, Hazzard devised a treatment consisting of prolonged food deprivation combined with daily, hours-long enemas and "osteopathic massages" that took the form of painful beatings.

Her sanitorium—located in Olalla, Washington, a small village west of Seattle across Puget Sound—had the highfalutin name of Hazzard's Institute of Natural Therapeutics. Locals called it Starvation Heights. Arriving in Olalla in February 1911, the Williamson sisters were immediately put on a bizarre and meager diet.

Over the next two months, as they grew increasingly debilitated, Hazzard managed to get her hands on their cash and jewelry and persuade them to make her the executor of their considerable estate. By mid-May, the sisters had been reduced to barely living skeletons. When Claire finally succumbed to starvation—her weight having plunged from 115 to 50 pounds—Hazzard was arrested and put on trial for first-degree murder.

Investigation into Hazzard's practice revealed that as many as fifteen other patients had died while enduring her "cure." Dubbed the "Fasting Fiend" in the press, she was convicted of manslaughter and sentenced to two to twenty years at hard labor, though she walked free in 1915 after the governor—for unknown reasons—pardoned her.

When she fell ill at the age of seventy in 1938, she attempted to restore her health by fasting. She died shortly thereafter.

A MIDLIFE OBSESSION ENDS BADLY IN PUYALLUP

Puyallup, Washington • September 29, 1978

Even after he divorced following thirty years of marriage and moved to Alaska, Joe Tarricone kept in close touch with his ex-wife and children in New Mexico. Devoted to the kids, he never failed to send money for their monthly expenses. So, when he suddenly ceased communicating with them in the fall of 1978, they feared that something terrible had befallen him.

Their suspicions focused on Renee Curtiss, a strikingly pretty onetime escort thirty years younger than Tarricone, who worked at his Anchorage meat supply company and had become the object of his romantic, midlife obsession. In mid-1978, partly to escape his unwanted attentions, Renee moved with her mother to a rental house in Puyallup, Washington. Undeterred by her rejections, Tarricone showed up for a birthday barbecue hosted by Renee in September of that year. Also in attendance was Renee's adopted brother, Nick, who, at her request, had flown down from Fairbanks.

Joseph Tarricone suffered from a fatal obsession with a woman.

262 • 50 STATES OF MURDER

Two photographs of Wai Chiu Ng from his FBI wanted poster

A hulking, dim-witted thirty-year-old with a criminal record for child molestation, Nick would shortly be convicted of manslaughter for the shooting death of his second wife, a murder he committed only days before arriving at his sister's home. A week after the barbecue, under the pretext of helping with a malfunctioning washing machine, Nick lured Tarricone into the basement, shot him in the head, then, with the help of his mother and sister, dismembered the corpse with a chainsaw. The parts were placed in black plastic trash bags and buried in the yard where they would remain undiscovered for nearly thirty years, until a construction crew, at work on the property, dug them up in July 2007.

Nick, who had been paroled in January 1986 after eight years behind bars for his wife's death, would be found guilty of first-degree murder and sent back to prison for life. Renee, likewise convicted, would receive the same sentence.

THE WAH MEE MASSACRE

SEATTLE, WASHINGTON
FEBRUARY 19, 1983

Located in the basement of a tenement hotel in Seattle's Chinatown, the Wah Mee Club had operated for decades as an illegal high-stakes gambling den for an exclusively Chinese clientele. On February 19, 1983, it became the site of the deadliest mass murder in Washington State history, known as the "Wah Mee Massacre."

Its instigator was twenty-two-year-old Kwan Fai "Willie" Mak, a high school dropout with a serious gambling habit who had racked up major debts and decided to solve his money worries by knocking over the Wah Mee. His accomplices were twenty-year-old Keung Ki "Benjamin" Ng, a fellow dropout with a history of violent crimes, and Wai Chiu "Tony" Ng, a comparative straight arrow who had borrowed a large sum from Mak and agreed to participate as a way to settle the debt.

On the evening of February 19, 1983, Mak and Tony, frequent patrons of the club, were buzzed inside by a security

Wah Mee Club patrons, c. 1950

guard. They hung around for half an hour until they were joined by Benjamin, who carried a brown paper bag stuffed with precut nylon cords. They ordered the club's ten patrons and staff to lie on the floor and then hogtied and robbed them. Four more customers entered while the heist was in progress and received the same treatment. Once the cash register was emptied, Tony was instructed to take the loot and wait outside.

His two cohorts then methodically shot the victims in the head at point-blank range, killing thirteen. Miraculously, there was a survivor who was able to identify Mak and Benjamin. The pair was arrested within hours. Tony fled to Canada, where he was ultimately tracked down and extradited to Seattle. Found guilty of robbery and assault, he received a thirty-year sentence. Paroled in 2014, he was deported to his native Hong Kong.

Mak received a death sentence that was commuted to life in prison without parole, the same punishment meted out to Benjamin.

Benjamin Ng in court, 1983

T̶̶̶
THRI̶̶

BELLEVUE, WA̶
JANUARY 4, ̶

On January 5, 1997, the body of ̶-year-old Kimberly Wilson was ̶-ered in a park not far from her hom̶ rope tightly wound around her neck. A̶ autopsy revealed that before being strangled to death, she had been subjected to a savage beating and stomping.

When police went to her family home, they made a gruesome discovery: three slaughtered corpses—Kimberly's mother and father, Rose and Bill Wilson, and her seventeen-year-old sister, Julia—lying in their blood-drenched bedrooms. The skulls of the parents had been crushed with a blunt object, their heads and necks stabbed multiple times. Julia, who had apparently tried to fend off her attackers, had sustained massive wounds to her face and head and a gash to her throat that severed her trachea and jugular vein.

h̶
to t̶
Barany̶
was dead, ̶
where they m̶
a week after the̶
graphic confession,̶
an accomplice but refu̶
person he was in thrall t̶
however, soon gathered eno̶
to take Anderson into custody.

Tried the following fall, the tw̶ aged thrill killers were convicted and ̶-tenced to four consecutive life terms wit̶ no possibility of parole.

The slaughtered Wilson family, left to right: Kimberly, her parents Bill and Rose, and sister Julia

THE BELLEVUE
~~L~~ KILLERS

Interviewing Kimberly's ~~friends~~, police learned that she had recently broken up with her boyfriend, David Anderson. A misfit crew of teenage goths, police seventeen-year-old sociopath who—in a classic case of a folie à deux—had forged a pernicious bond with a worshipful minion, Alex Baranyi, Anderson had long dreamed of, and even spoken to others about, committing a murder for the sheer thrill of it.

Targeting Kimberly after she rebuffed ~~hi~~s sexual advances, Anderson lured her ~~to t~~he park where, by prearrangement, ~~Baranyi~~ was lying in wait. After Kimberly ~~was dead, t~~he pair proceeded to her home, ~~where they m~~assacred the family. Arrested ~~for the~~ slayings, Baranyi made a ~~confession,~~ admitting that he had ~~killed Kimberly, refu~~sing to "rat out" the ~~mastermind of the crime.~~ Investigators, ~~however, had eno~~ugh evidence

CHARLESTON ★ • GREENBRIER

TESTIMONY FROM THE BEYOND

267

Erasmus Shue and his wife, Zona

TESTIMONY FROM THE BEYOND

GREENBRIER, WEST VIRGINIA • JANUARY 23, 1897

In the years before Erasmus Shue drifted into Greenbrier County, he had done a two-year stretch in the penitentiary for horse theft and been twice married to women who had died under peculiar circumstances, the first from a broken neck allegedly sustained when she fell from a haystack, the second when he accidentally dropped a brick on her head while repairing the roof of their house.

None of this was known to twenty-one-year-old Zona Heaster, who fell in love with and married the handsome blacksmith not long after making his acquaintance. Three months after the wedding, Zona's body was found at the foot of the stairs leading to the second floor of their log house. When town physician George W. Knapp arrived on the scene, he found a sobbing Shue seated cross-legged on the floor, cradling his wife's lifeless body and clutching her head to his chest.

Prevented by the seemingly overwrought husband from making anything more than a cursory examination, Knapp gave the cause of death as heart failure—or, as he termed it, "everlasting faint." When it came time to prepare the body for burial, it was Shue who clothed the corpse, taking care to place a high collar around her neck and a large veil over her head, which he tied under her chin in a bow.

From the first, Zona's mother, Mary—who had never taken to her rough-hewn son-in-law—questioned Dr. Knapp's conclusion. Several weeks later, Mary showed up at the office of local prosecutor John Alfred Preston with an uncanny tale. For four nights running, she told Preston, her daughter's ghost had appeared before her and revealed that her husband had flown into a rage and broken her neck when he returned from work that day and found she had not prepared meat for his supper. To illustrate the savagery of the act, the ghost had swiveled her head 180 degrees until it was facing backward. Though justifiably skeptical of this story, Preston paid a visit to Dr. Knapp, who explained that Shue had kept him from making a thorough examination.

On February 22, 1897, a month after her death, Zona's corpse was exhumed. The autopsy revealed the true cause of death: a broken neck and crushed windpipe. At Shue's trial, his mother-in-law took the stand to testify about the visits from her daughter's spirit. Though Shue's attorney did his best to discredit Mary as a hysterical mother, the jury was moved by her story. Shue was found guilty and sentenced to life, barely escaping a lynch mob before being moved to the West Virginia State Penitentiary, where he died three years later during a prison epidemic.

A roadside marker in Greenbrier County commemorates the incident as "the only known case in which testimony from a ghost helped convict a murderer."

AN UNEXPLAINED FAMILICIDE

Wheeling, West Virginia
March 6, 1997

Experiencing debilitating anxiety attacks, Mark Storm—a thirty-year-old riverboat pilot for a barge transfer company—voluntarily admitted himself to a Wheeling psychiatric center on Sunday, March 2, 1997. Four days later, after being prescribed three different medications, he checked himself out, his attending physician having deemed that "the patient was ready to be discharged." Walking a short distance to the city's business district, he was picked up by a friend who later reported that Mark "seemed a little bit disoriented."

During heated phone conversations that afternoon with his older brother, Benjamin, and mother, Roberta, Mark seemed so agitated that the pair discussed committing him to a mental hospital. At about 7:00 p.m., along with his wife, Betty, and two young daughters, he attended the birthday party of a next-door neighbor's child, where, as the host later testified, he seemed "stressed out and quiet" as the festivities went on around him. Back home after forty minutes, he had another tense phone conversation with Benjamin that ended with Mark hanging up on his brother.

Slightly more than an hour later, at about 9:00 p.m., Mark took his licensed 9mm semiautomatic pistol, went into the living room and shot his wife, then executed his daughters, eight-year-old Jessica and her three-year-old sister, Megan, as they lay in their bunkbeds. He then drove to the house Benjamin shared with their mother and knocked on the door. When Benjamin came to the door with his fiancée, Sylvia Sacco, and saw the gun in Storm's hand, he tried to wrestle it away but was overpowered and shot in the head.

Telling Sacco to leave, Mark strode upstairs and killed his invalid mother in her bed before going out the back door to the river behind the house and shooting himself in the head. No precise motive for the rampage that left five of his family members dead was ever determined. A malpractice suit filed against the physician who had discharged him from the psychiatric clinic after four days was eventually settled for $5.7 million.

A FOLIE À DEUX IN STAR CITY

STAR CITY, WEST VIRGINIA
JULY 6, 2012

Growing up in nearby towns in West Virginia, Skylar Neese and Shelia Eddy became fast friends in second grade. That relationship began to change in high school when a third girl, Rachel Shoaf, forged a close and apparently sexual bond with Eddy. For a while all three—pretty, popular honor students—made an inseparable trio. Increasingly, however, tensions grew between Neese and the other two girls, who, as events would prove, had become entwined in a classic folie à deux: a toxic intimacy between a dominant psychopathic personality (in this case Eddy) and a pliable partner in the latter's thrall.

By the fall of 2012, Eddy and Shoaf had begun to think of ways of killing Neese and disposing of her body, possibly by dissolving it in acid or feeding it to pigs. Their reason? As Shoaf later explained, "We didn't want to be friends with her anymore."

At about midnight on July 6, 2012, having agreed to accompany her two frenemies on a nighttime joyride, Neese climbed out of her bedroom window and into Shoaf's sedan. They drove to a remote spot where her two former best friends set upon her with kitchen knives, stabbed her to death, and—the ground being too rocky for the shovel they brought along—covered her body with dead branches. Her whereabouts would remain a mystery until the following January, when Shoaf—who had a nervous breakdown in the interim—confessed to the murder and led them to Neese's remains.

In exchange for her cooperation, Shoaf was allowed to plead guilty to second-degree murder and was sentenced to thirty years in prison. Eddy was tried, convicted, and given a life sentence.

No Amber Alert was issued for Skylar Neese when she went missing.

WISCONSIN

PINE GROVE
THE WISCONSIN GHOUL
272

BROOKFIELD
A CONGREGANT SNAPS IN BROOKFIELD
273

MADISON

SPRING GREEN
MASSACRE AT THE "BUNGALOW OF LOVE"
271

KENOSHA
AN INFAMOUS HANGING IN KENOSHA
271

AN INFAMOUS HANGING IN KENOSHA

KENOSHA, WISCONSIN
JULY 23, 1850

At about midnight on July 23, 1850, in the newly incorporated city of Kenosha, Wisconsin, neighbors of Irish American farmer John McCaffary and his wife, Bridget, were awakened by the piteous shrieks of a woman crying, "Oh, John, spare me!" Rushing to the scene, they saw John, soaked and muddy, emerging from a hogshead barrel sunk into the ground as a well. When asked about his wife, he replied that "there was someone in the well."

That someone turned out to be Bridget, who had been dragged across the muddy yard and pressed down under the water until she drowned. Tried in May 1851, John McCaffary was found guilty of "willful murder" and sentenced to death. An estimated two to three thousand people showed up to witness his execution in front of Kenosha's newly constructed courthouse and jail.

His hanging, performed on a contraption that "hoisted him into the air" rather than dropping him through a trap, proved to be a ghastly spectacle. Slowly strangling as he dangled from the rope, John took twenty minutes to die. Owing primarily to the efforts of one crusading newspaper editor who viewed the "dreadful" execution as little more than state-sanctioned murder—Wisconsin abolished the death penalty in 1853, a landmark event commemorated in August 2001 when the Wisconsin State Historical Society erected a marker at John McCaffary's gravesite.

MASSACRE AT THE "BUNGALOW OF LOVE"

SPRING GREEN, WISCONSIN
AUGUST 15, 1914

In 1909, America's most celebrated modern architect, Frank Lloyd Wright, created a public scandal when he abandoned his wife and six children and ran off to Europe with his mistress, Mamah Borthwick, the wife of one of his clients. Upon his return to America, he began to construct a home for the two of them in rural Wisconsin. He named this "bungalow of love" (as the morally outraged locals called it) Taliesin in tribute to a renowned Welsh poet.

In the summer of 1914, it became the site of "the most horrific single mass murder in Wisconsin history." Among the employees at Taliesin was a recent hire, Julian Carlton, who served a variety of functions from handyman to butler. Carlton's affable facade masked a profoundly unstable personality.

On one sunny mid-August afternoon, while Wright was away on business, Carlton hacked Borthwick and her two visiting children to death with a hatchet as they lunched on the porch. He then bolted the door to the dining room where a crew of workmen were eating, set the room on fire with gasoline-soaked rugs, and attacked the burning men as they desperately broke through the door or climbed out a broken window.

In the end, his rampage claimed the lives of seven victims. Carlton himself did not survive for long. Swallowing acid in a suicide attempt, he failed to kill himself but burned his esophagus so badly that he was unable to eat and died of starvation a month later.

Ed Gein's "House of Horrors"

THE WISCONSIN GHOUL

PINE GROVE, WISCONSIN • DECEMBER 8, 1954

With its concrete walls and semi-cylindrical roof of corrugated metal, Mary Hogan's tavern looked less like a roadside watering hole than a warehouse topped with a Blatz Beer sign. Its proprietor's past was shrouded in mystery. A formidable fifty-five-year-old woman who weighed nearly two hundred pounds and spoke with a heavy German accent, the thrice-divorced Hogan was rumored to have connections with the Chicago mob. Some whispered that she had once been a big-city madam.

At about 5:30 p.m. on Wednesday, December 8, 1954, a local farmer named Seymour Lester came to the tavern to buy a pint of ice cream for his fourteen-year-old daughter, who was sick with the flu. Stepping inside, he was immediately struck by how silent and empty the place seemed. Then he spotted an overturned chair by a table near the jukebox and a bloody trail leading to the front door. Hurrying to the nearest farmhouse, he notified the local authorities, who were soon on the scene.

From the evidence—a spent .32-caliber cartridge beside the chair, a spilled coffee cup, and a paperback novel on the tabletop—lawmen concluded that Hogan had been relaxing with her book when someone entered, shot her dead, then dragged her body out to the parking lot where, judging from the tire tracks, she had been loaded into a pickup truck and driven away.

Despite an intensive investigation, no trace of her could be found. For the next two years, the local paper would mark the anniversary of her disappearance with stories headlined: "WHAT HAPPENED TO MARY HOGAN?" The appalling answer came in November 1957 when, after the similar disappearance of another middle-aged woman, Plainfield hardware store owner Bernice Worden, lawmen searched the decaying farmhouse of psycho-killer Edward Gein, soon to gain international infamy as the "Wisconsin Ghoul."

There, amid the other unspeakable artifacts found in his "House of Horrors"—chairs upholstered in human skin, a belt made of female nipples, soup bowls fashioned from sawed-off skull tops, and much more—they came upon Hogan's flayed-off face in a paper bag.

A CONGREGANT SNAPS IN BROOKFIELD

Brookfield, Wisconsin
March 12, 2005

Founded in 1933 by ad man turned radio evangelist Herbert W. Armstrong, the Worldwide Church of God (WCG) followed doctrines and practices at odds with mainstream Christianity, among them the observation of Jewish holy days, dietary restrictions, and the belief that Anglo-Saxon people are the descendants of the Ten Lost Tribes of Israel.

Upon his death in 1986, other groups splintered off from the WCG, including the Living Church of God, a denomination of roughly seven thousand believers who strictly adhere to Armstrong's teachings. Believing that a church is not a building but a community of worshippers, parishioners meet in hotels or other public spaces where they are served by itinerant pastors.

On Saturday, February 26, 2005, one church member, forty-four-year-old Terry Ratzmann, stalked out of the Brookfield, Wisconsin, Sheraton Hotel conference room where his congregation conducted its Sabbath services, apparently upset by something in the sermon. A computer programmer whose position had recently been terminated, Ratzmann was a loner who lived at home with his mother and sister and devoted his free time to gardening. Neighbors regarded him as a "normal Joe," so averse to violence that when rabbits pillaged his garden, he caught them in "humane traps" and drove them twenty miles to release them in the wild rather than shooting them. He was a devout churchgoer who once refused to attend his next-door neighbor's wedding because it took place on the Sabbath.

Two Saturdays after abruptly leaving the February 26 service, Ratzmann showed up at the conference room while the worship was in progress, pulled a newly purchased 9mm Beretta semiautomatic pistol from his briefcase, and began shooting, killing the pastor, his seventeen-year-old son, and five congregants before turning the gun on himself. No motive was ever established.

Mass shooter Terry Ratzmann

WYOMING

PARK COUNTY
TARZAN OF THE TETONS
277

IRON MOUNTAIN
WYOMING'S DEATH RIDER
276

RAWLINS
GOVERNOR SKIN SHOES?
275

CHEYENNE
A COMEUPPANCE IN CHEYENNE
278

"Big Nose" George (left) and John Eugene Osborne (right)

GOVERNOR SKIN SHOES?

Rawlins, Wyoming • March 22, 1881

Nicknamed "Big Nose George" for his most prominent facial feature, George Parrott was a member of an outlaw gang operating in Wyoming in the late 1870s. His enduring notoriety stems less from his criminal exploits than from the manner of his death and the disposition of his body. Found guilty of murder for the slaying of two lawmen following a botched train robbery, Parrott was dragged from his cell in the Rawlins jail by a 200-man lynch mob. Flinging a noose over the crossarm beam of a telegraph pole, they ordered him to stand on a box and jump. When he refused, they put a ladder against the pole, forced him to climb to the top, then yanked the ladder away. Wrapping his arms and legs around the pole, Parrott hung on until his strength gave out and he dangled to his death. His body was then autopsied by town physician Dr. John Eugene Osborne who, among other desecrations, peeled the skin from the corpse's chest and thighs and sent it to a tannery where it was made into various items, including a pair of two-tone shoes that Osborne wore to his inaugural ball in January 1893 after his election as the first Democratic governor of Wyoming.

WYOMING'S DEATH RIDER

Iron Mountain, Wyoming • July 18, 1901

After a colorful early life as a cowhand, silver miner, stagecoach driver, cavalry scout, frontier lawman, and Pinkerton detective, legendary Western gunman Tom Horn switched to the more lucrative profession of hired killer. As an employee of various cattle companies, he did away with an indeterminate number of actual or suspected rustlers, earning quite a reputation as a deadly scourge of "beef-stealing thieves." In the Johnson County War of the early 1890s—a bloody conflict between Wyoming livestock barons and homesteaders over prime grazing land—Horn worked as a paid assassin on behalf of the wealthy ranchers.

On July 18, 1901, a fourteen-year-old boy named Willie Nickell—son of a pugnacious sheep rancher who had long been a thorn in the side of a prominent local cattleman—was shot to death not far from his home. Questioned as a suspect, Horn, a prized employee of the cattleman, boasted that he had killed the boy with his Winchester rifle from about three hundred yards away—"the best shot I ever made." He was tried in October of that year, found guilty, and hanged in Cheyenne the following November.

Historians still debate his guilt, in part because Horn was drunk at the time he made his confession. Moreover, the victim's family had been engaged in a long-running feud with a neighbor that had already involved several violent confrontations. Still, though possibly innocent of the murder for which he was hanged, "Wyoming's Death Rider" (as one historian dubbed him) was responsible for as many as seventeen other killings.

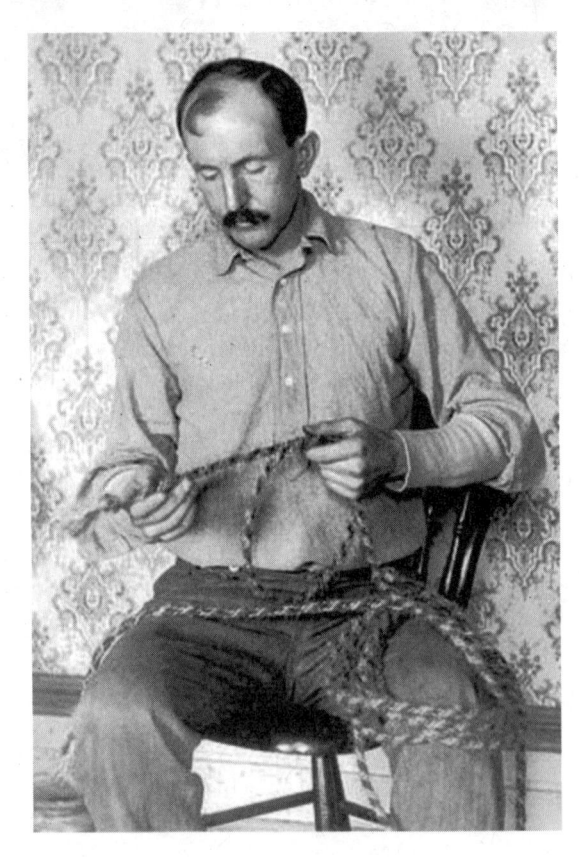

Tom Horn braids rope in the Cheyenne jailhouse.

Posse members approaching Earl Durand's hideout

TARZAN OF THE TETONS

PARK COUNTY, WYOMING • MARCH 16–24, 1939

Quitting school after eighth grade because "it was too much like being in jail," Earl Durand pursued a rugged wilderness existence, spending much of his time in Wyoming's Absaroka mountains. An imposing physical specimen, he was an expert hunter and trapper who once saved himself from starvation (so he claimed) by killing a wildcat and eating it raw. He was a legendary marksman who could toss a baseball into the air and put four rifle bullets into it before it hit the ground. His brawny, wild man looks and outdoors way of life would earn him the nickname "Tarzan of the Tetons."

Scorning such societal rules as hunting regulations, Durand thought nothing of bagging game out of season and, in mid-March 1939, was arrested, tried, and sentenced to six months in jail for poaching two elk. He remained behind bars for less than twenty-four hours. When an undersheriff, Noah Riley, took him his supper at about 5:00 p.m. on Thursday, March 16, Durand snatched the milk bottle from the tray, smashed Riley on the head, grabbed his pistol, and, taking the dazed lawman hostage, forced him to drive to the home of Durand's parents.

An hour later, alerted to the jailbreak, two officers arrived at the farmhouse, where they were shot dead by Durand, who fled into the night. For the next five days, he eluded a posse of one hundred

WYOMING • 277

men with shoot-to-kill orders, at one point showing up at the home of a neighbor and leaving a written message for the sheriff leading the manhunt: "Of course I know that I am done for and when you kill me I suggest you have my head mounted and hang it up in the courthouse for the sake of law and order."

Tracking Durand to a high ridge in the Beartooth Mountains, a much larger posse, equipped with munitions supplied by the governor, tried smoking him out, but Durand's "rocky fortress" proved impregnable. When two members of the posse tried rushing his position, Durand fatally shot them both. Afraid to retrieve the corpses, the posse withdrew to its headquarters at a nearby ranch, allowing Durand to slip away under cover of nightfall.

Making his way to the town of Powell, he entered the First National Bank, lined up the four employees and five customers at gunpoint, helped himself to $3,000 in cash, then began shooting up the place, firing at the windows, walls, and ceiling. Hearing the sounds, armed citizens converged on the bank.

When Durand emerged from the building using three of his hostages as a human shield, the townsmen let loose with a fusillade of shots. One hit twenty-year-old teller Charlie Gawthrop, who fell to the ground, mortally wounded. Another, fired by seventeen-year-old high school student Tipton Cox, struck Durand in the chest.

Crawling back into the bank, the soon-to-be-legendary outlaw stuck the barrel of his revolver under his jaw and pulled the trigger.

A COMEUPPANCE IN CHEYENNE

Cheyenne, Wyoming
November 16, 1982

A criminal investigator for the IRS, Richard Jahnke was a terror to his family, subjecting them to almost daily outbursts of verbal and physical violence. His tyrannized wife, Maria—the "bitch-swine-asshole," as he called her when enraged—suffered regular beatings, as did his "little slut" of a daughter, Deborah, whom he not only smacked around for any minor infraction but sexually molested before she reached puberty. But his most vicious and unrelenting abuse was reserved for his son and namesake.

The corporal punishment began when Richard Jr. was a toddler and escalated throughout the years. Besides the savage thrashings with fists and brass-buckled belts, the boy endured unceasing humiliation from his father, who derided him as a "shit-ass mama's boy." By the time young Richard was big enough to fight back, the two were at open war with each other, at one point engaging in a particularly nasty fistfight that spurred the teenaged boy to file an abuse complaint against his father. The climax of their mutually hate-filled relationship occurred on November 16, 1982.

Before leaving for an anniversary dinner with his wife, Richard Sr. found yet another pretext to manhandle his sixteen-year-old son, called him "a disgusting piece of shit," and promised that he'd find a way "to get rid of him." As soon as his parents left the house, Richard Jr. informed

Richard Jahnke leaves the courthouse accompanied by child abuse worker Sharon Lee Tilley.

his sister that the time had finally come to free themselves of their tormentor. Deborah raised no objections.

Equipping himself with a loaded .12-gauge shotgun—one of several dozen firearms his father kept around the house—Richard Jr. waited inside the garage until his parents returned. When his father pulled into the driveway and stepped out of the car to lift the garage door, Richard Jr. let loose with several blasts from the weapon and killed Richard Sr. Public outrage over the parricide turned to widespread sympathy for Richard Jr. and his sister when details of their father's brutalities emerged in the press.

Both children were then tried and convicted—Richard Jr. of voluntary manslaughter, Deborah of aiding and abetting—but their sentences were commuted by the governor thanks to a flood of appeals for clemency.

PHOTO CREDITS

Alamy: ARCHIVIO GBB p. 135; Glasshouse Images p. 161 (top); PJF Military Collection p. 68; World History Archive p. 178. Alamy: Science History Images p. 153. AP Images: AP Photo pp. 80, 95, 107, p. 203 (bottom); *Atlanta Journal-Constitution* p. 62; John Bartley p. 188; Jim Cole pp. 113, 165 (left); Connecticut Judicial Branch p. 48 (top and bottom); John Harrell p. 165 (right); Rutland Herald p. 253; Gene Herrick p. 132 (left); Patricia McDonnell p. 125; Nashville Police p. 233; POOL, Frank Jacobs III p. 170 (bottom); XAVIER MASCARE-AS/TCPALM p. 58; Atlas Obscura: oddthingsiveseen.com p. 161 (bottom). Courtesy Use: Saundra Adams p. 189; Bristol Bay Heritage Land Trust p. 15; *Chicago Tribune* Historical Photo p. 79; Dennis Historical Society p. 120; Idaho State Historical Society p. 71; Indiana Historical Society p. 85; Institute for Regional Studies, NDSU, Fargo p. 192; Irene Hall Museum Resource Center p. 226; Oklahoma Highway Patrol Collection p. 205; Open Road Media p. 148; *Texas Daily* p. 235; The Bancroft Library University of California Berkeley, CA p. 32; The North Carolina Government & Heritage Library p. 185; *The Providence Journal* p. 218; Windsor Historical Society p. 46; Getty Images: *Anchorage Daily News* p. 16 (bottom); *Denver Post* p. 279; Handout pp. 59, 273; Hulton Archive p. 103; Steve Liss/Life Images Collection p. 123; Dee Liu p. 98; Marny Malin p. 198; George Napolitano p. 63; Frank Scherschel/The LIFE Picture Collection p. 272; Tribune News Service p. 171; Library of Congress: LOC pp. 17, 217; Philadelphia: P.S. Duval & Son Lithography, 1858. p. 211; John Vachon p. 191; Newspapers.com: pp. 28 (top), 52, 67, 74, 78, 81 (top), 86, 111 (bottom), 124, 133, 138, 154 (top and bottom), 168, 182; Public Domain: Fayetteville Arkansas/Flickr p. 27; Alabama Department of Archives and History p. 11 (top); Stacie Berg-Nelson/Find A Grave p. 92; Joyce Drown Brennan p. 151; Carmen P/Find a Grave p. 251 (top); Jerici Cat/Flickr p. 212; *Chicago Daily News* p. 81 (bottom); Chicago Iroquois Theater p. 77; City of Puyallup p. 262 (top); Cleveland County District Attorney's Office p. 204 (bottom); Courier File Photo p. 93; *Courier-Post* p. 169; Crime Feed / FBI p. 41; Cultural Front p. 142; *Detroit Free Press* Photo Archive p. 127; Digital Public Library of America p. 237; FBI pp. 97, 122, 143, 164, 263; Bonnie Fortney/Find a Grave p. 159; FOX 8 p. 186; Frankie/Find a Grave p. 180; B. Helmer/Find a Grave p. 251 (bottom); Bryon Houlgrave/The Register p. 91 (top); IMDb p. 117; James F. Stubbins County and Municipal Building Postcard Collection p. 257 (top); Kalamazoo Public Library p. 252; Carol Kaliff/Danbury *News-Times* p. 47; King County Superior Court p. 265; KOB TV p. 175; Julie Lara/Find a Grave p. 115; Argus Leader p. 229; Live Work Dream p. 39; Maine State Prison p. 111 (top); Malita/Find a Grave p. 215; Kevin T. Mason/Notes on Iowa p. 89; Derek McCulloch, Shepherd Hendrix p. 141; Medium.com p. 102; Medium/*The Oklahoman* p. 203 (top); S G Michael/Find a Grave p. 267; Michigan State Police p. 128; Murder by Gaslight pp. 119, 162, 163, 195; Murderpedia p. 228; *New York Daily News* p. 110; *New York Post* p. 183; Elmer Ogawa, Courtesy Todd Matthews p. 264 (top); Oklahoma Highway Patrol Collection p. 207; *Oklahoman* Archives p. 204 (top); Park County Archive p. 277; R. W./Find a Grave p. 53 (top and bottom); Robert/Find a Grave pp. 244, 262 (bottom); Rogue Columnist p. 23; Fred Seibert/Flickr p. 73 (top); Taos News archival photo p. 173; *Texas Monthly* p. 241; The *American* Magazine of the *New York Journal* (N.Y.) p. 179; The *Billings Gazette* p. 147 (top); *The Detroit News* p. 129; The History Handbook p. 132 (right); *The Mckenzie Banner* p. 232; *The Oregonian* p. 208; *The Salt Lake Tribune* p. 247; University of California p. 34; *Urbana Daily Citizen* p. 196; Washington State Archives— Digital Archives p. 261; Weber State University

p. 246; Western Mining History pp. 157, 231 (top); Sherry Lynn Winters/Find a Grave p. 21; Barry Wong, *Seattle Times* p. 264 (bottom), Nicolas Wysocki/Find A Grave p. 96. TESSA: Digital Collections of the Los Angeles Public Library: John Randolph Haynes and Dora Haynes Foundation p. 36.

Wikimedia: The following images are used under a Creative Commons Attribution CC BY-SA 2.0 License (https://csreativecommons.org/licenses/by-sa/2.0/deed.en) and belongs to the following Wikimedia Commons user: TravelingOtter p. 16 (top); The following images are used under a Creative Commons Attribution CC BY-SA 3.0 License (https://csreativecommons.org/licenses/by-sa/3.0/deed.en) and belongs to the following Wikimedia Commons user: Jfoldmei p. 12; The following images are used under a Creative Commons Attribution CC BY-SA 2.0 License (https://csreativecommons.org/licenses/by-sa/2.0/deed.en) and belongs to the following Wikimedia Commons users: Archery Hall of Fame & Museum p. 11 (bottom); Mattconz p. 147 (bottom); Wellcome Collection Gallery p. 105; Science History Institute p. 28 (bottom); DatBot pp. 29 (left), 45. Public Domain: Bing Crosby Productions p. 24; Dsmurat p. 272 (left); FastilyClone p. 243; FMSky p. 170 (top); History.nebraska.gov p. 155; Huffington Post p. 269; Jengod p. 33; JKBrooks85 p. 18 (bottom); Ktr101 p. 121; Lord G n p. 18; Mashir43 p. 72; Master Strategist p. 275 (right); Oklahoma State Penitentiary p. 202; Arthur Rackham p. 167; SerSem p. 31; South Dakota State Penitentiary p. 227; State Journal Co. p. 152; SteinsplitterBot p. 65; Texas Department of Criminal Justice p. 239; The Night Marauder Project p. 231; TSamuel p. 223; WhisperToMe p. 245.

BOOKS CONSULTED

Please visit hachettebookgroup.com/50StatesOfMurder for a complete list of sources used for this work.

INDEX

Abbott, George, 162–163
Adams, Cherica, 189
Akeman, David, 232–233
Akeman, Estelle, 232–233
Akin, Joseph Dewey, 13
Albright, Charles, 240–241
Albuquerque, New Mexico, 174
Alfonsi, Ferdinand, 213–214
Alfonsi, Stella, 213
Allen, Raymond and Betty Faye, 21
Allen family, 256, 258
Allenstown, New Hampshire, 163–164
Almy, Frank C., 162–163
Anchorage, Alaska, 19
Anderson, David, 265
Anderson, Mary, 28
Anderson, Olin, 92
Anderson, Peter, 152
Anderson, Robert Leroy, 228–229
Anderson, Rozena, 28
Andrews, Franklin R., 46
Andrews, Lowell Lee, 96–97
Andrews, William, 245–246
animal magnetism, 105
Ann Arbor, Michigan, 128
Annan, Albert, 79
Annan, Beulah May, 79–80
Ansley, Michelle, 245–246
Antioch, Tennessee, 233
Archer, James H., 46
Archer-Gilligan, Amy, 46–47
Armistead, Norma Jean, 37
Armstrong, Herbert W., 273
arson, 16, 39, 71, 137, 148, 207, 271. *See also* burning, crimes involving
Ashley, Leslie Douglas, 237–238
Atlanta, Georgia, 61
Auburn, New York, 178
Augusta, Maine, 109–110
Averito, Roberta Ululani, 66
Avery, Ephraim, 217

Bacon, Minor, 154
Baker, Frankie, 142
Ball, Joe, 235
Baltimore, Maryland, 115–116
Baranyi, Alex, 265
Barrett, Eugene, 66–67
Bashara, Bob and Jane, 129
Bath Township, Ohio, 198–199
Beatson, Cindy, 113
Beattie, Henry Clay, Jr., 255–256
Beaudin, Denise, 164
Behaud, Julian, 152
Bell, Larry Gene, 222
Bellevue, Washington, 265
Benedict, Bill, 133
Benoit, Chris, 63
Berg, Alan, 42
Berning, Dolph, 159
Bertucci, Clarence Vincent, 244
Berven, Edna, 92
Berven, Joe, 92
Bethea, Rainey, 103
Bevan, Catherine, 51
Bevan, Henry, 51
Billiot, James, 139
Binford, Beulah, 255, 256
Bingham, Utah, 243–244
Birmingham, Alabama, 13
Biros, Kenneth, 199
Blanchard, Dee Dee, 145
Blanchard, Gypsy-Rose, 145
Blixt, Claus, 131
Blymire, John, 212
Bolber, Morris, 213–214
Bolles, Eunice, 45
Bollinger, Natalie, 43
bombings, 35, 36, 99, 246–247
Bonnie and Clyde, 244
Booker, Betty Jo, 236
Boone, Frank, 201–202
Borthwick, Mamah, 271
Boston, Massachusetts, 119, 122–124
Botkin, Cordelia, 52

Brach, Helen, 81
Bradley, Edgar, 197
Breen, Joseph, 122
Bridgeport, Connecticut, 49
Britt, Allen, 142
Brookfield, Wisconsin, 273
Brookfield Township, Ohio, 199
Brooklyn, New York, 180
Brooks, Birdie, 28
Broomfield, Colorado, 43
Brophy, Daniel, 209
Brophy, Nancy, 209
Brown, John and Marvin, 232–233
Brown, Margaret, 168
Brown, Raymond Eugene, 12–13
Brown, Willa, 28
Bruce, C. C., 155
Brucia, Carlie, 57
Brumley, Tom, 201
Brunswick, Maine, 110–111
Bulette, Julia, 157–158
Bullard, Julie, 113
Bullard, Selby, 113
Bundy, Ted, 19
Bunker, Clara, 225
Bunker, William and Lydia, 225
Burk, Harold "Arkie," 106
Burlingham, New York, 177
Burnett, Crawford and Lavinia, 27
Burnett, John, 27
Burnett, Minerva, 27
burning, crimes involving, 48–49, 62, 113, 117, 137, 152, 168, 175, 177, 207, 211, 212, 233, 237–238, 271. *See also* arson
burning, execution by, 51
Busch, Mary, 33
Butler, Eugene, 191
Butler, Robert, 182

Caldwell, Idaho, 71–72
Calloway, Joseph P., 106

Camden, New Jersey, 168–169
Campbell, Henry Colin, 168
"Candy Man, The," 238
cannibalism, 49, 59, 174, 218
Capote, Truman, 97
Carawan, George W., 185
Carey, Howard, 53
Carey, James, 53
Carey, Lawrence, 53
Carey, May, 53
Carlton, Julian, 271
Carpenter, John Henry, 24
Carroll County, Virginia, 256–258
Carruth, Rae, 189
Carter, Frank, 155
Carter, W. M., 138
Cassidy, Butch, 244
Cataumet, Massachusetts, 121
Cedar Falls, Iowa, 93
Cesnick, Cathy Anne, 116
Charleston, South Carolina, 221
Charlotte, North Carolina, 189
Chatsworth, California, 36
Chavez, Armand, 174
Cheshire, Connecticut, 48–49
Chew, Girly, 174
Cheyenne, Wyoming, 278–279
Chicago, Illinois, 78–81
Childs, Mary, 37
Chisago County, Minnesota, 134–135
Christensen, Brendt, 82
Christensen, Steve, 247
Cincinnati, Ohio, 195, 197
Clark, Sanford, 31
Clayton, Steven, 223
Clayton County, Iowa, 89–90
Clegg, Zenovia, 111
Clover, South Carolina, 223
Club 54, 258
Cody, Buffalo Bill, 243
Collins, John Norman, 128
Columbus, Ohio, 196–197
Connell, Richard, 17
Connelly, Lisa, 56
Cook, Billy, 144

Coolen, Guy, 110
Coolen, Shirley Mae Murray, 110–111
Coors, Adolph, III, 41
copycats, 22
Corbett, John, Jr., 41
Cornell, Sarah, 217
Covina, California, 39
Coweta County, Georgia, 62
Cox, Tipton, 278
Crafts, Helle, 47
Crafts, Richard, 47
Crane, Bob, 24
Crawford County, Pennsylvania, 215
Croll family, 139
Crump, Danny, 99
Crutchley, John Brennan, 55
Cullen, Charles, 171
Culp, Roger, 18
Cunanan, Andrew, 134
Curry, John, 212
Curtiss, Nick, 262–263
Curtiss, Renee, 262–263

Dahmer, Jeffrey, 198–199
Dallas, Claude, 75
Dallas, Texas, 240–241
Damenoff, Peter Duma, 36
Darrow, Clarence, 72, 102
Davis, Alden, 121
Davis, Dora, 231
Davis, Johnny Paul, 233
Davis, Sammy, Jr., 238
Dean, Cora Lucyle, 74
Deer Park, Texas, 238–239
Demery, Larry, 188
Demler, Andy, 226–227
Denton, Jacob, 34
Denver, Colorado, 42
Deschamps, Etienne, 105
Detroit, Michigan, 127
Dewey, Robert, 144
Dickins, Ruth, 139
Dietsh, Juliette, 105
Dingle, Charles, 183
Donaldson, Sam, 175
Dooley, Bill, 142
doomsday cults, 36
Dorsey family, 211
Dover, Arkansas, 29
Dover, Delaware, 51–52

Downs, Diane, 208
Dumansky, Larisa, 228–229
Duncan, Daniel, 221
Dunning, John, 51–52
Dunning, Mary Elizabeth, 51–52
Durand, Earl, 277–278
Duxbury, Vermont, 250–251
Dworecki, Walter, 169
Dworecki, Wanda, 168–169
Dzvirko, Derek, 56

Eappen, Matthew, 125
East Tennessee, 231–232
Eastling, Heather, 193
Eddy, Shelia, 269
Edmond, Oklahoma, 205
Edwards, Lischia, 103
Egner, Andrea, 195
Egner, Frederick, 195
Egner, Julia, 195
Einthoven, Willem, 152–153
electric chair
    first use of, 178
    first use of on woman, 180
    malfunctioning, 107
    only use of in South Dakota, 227–228
    use of in Massachusetts, 121
    woman executed by, 106
Elizabeth, New Jersey, 168
Elizabethtown, Kentucky, 101
Elkins, John and Hattie, 89–90
Elkins, Wesley, 89–90
Elko, Nevada, 159
Elliott, Austin "Aussie," 201
Elmendorf, Texas, 235
Elms, Wilson Conley, 75
Engstrom, Tami, 199
eraser killers, 123
Erickson, Mark, 133
Erickson, Timothy, 133
Estherville, Iowa, 92
Etna, New Hampshire, 165
Eugene, Rudy, 59
Evangelist family, 127
Evans, Bob, 164
Evans, Dale, Jr., 138

Falater, Scott and Yarmila, 25
familicides, 29, 48–49, 92, 109–110, 127, 137, 139, 144, 151–152, 175, 186–187, 192–193, 268–269. *See also* mass murders
Farmer, Lori Lee, 202–203
Favato, Carina, 213–214
Fayetteville, Arkansas, 27
Fayetteville, Georgia, 63
Ferrell, Arch, 12
Fisher, Constance, 111–112
Fitzpatrick, Mrs. Manuel, 102
Floyd, Charles Arthur "Pretty Boy," 143, 201
Folk, Carl J., 21
Foreman, Jason, 218
Francis, Willie, 107
"Frankie and Johnny," 142
French, James Donald, 201–202
Fuller, Albert, 12

Gacy, John Wayne, 121
Gage, Wesley, 201
Gall, Donald, 133
Gallatin County, Montana, 147
Garden City, Idaho, 74
Garrett, Silas, 12
Garrison, Don, 68
Gates, James, 207
Gates, Michele Dee, 207
Gawthrop, Charlie, 278
Gein, Edward, 273
Geller, Max, 182
Gentz, Joe, 129
Gibson, Orville, 252
Gilligan, Michael W., 46
Ging, Kitty, 131
Gingerich, Edward, 215
Glacier National Park, Montana, 149
Gleason, James Marvin, 86
Gleason, Lloyd C., 86
Godejohn, Nicholas, 145
Gollum, George "Bud," 35
Gonzalez, Angel, 49
Goodlettsville, Tennessee, 232–233
Graham, Jordan, 149
Grammer, Dorothy, 115
Grammer, G. Edward, 115
Grand Forks, North Dakota, 193

Green, Daniel, 188
Green Parrot Bar and Grill, 182
Greenlease, Bobby, Jr., 95
Greenlease, Robert Cosgrove, 95
Grega, Christine, 253
Grega, John, 253
Griffith, D. W, 85
Griffith, Richard, 236
Griswold, Sally, 249–250
Grosse Pointe, Michigan, 129
Guse, Michelle Heather, 202–203

Hadley, Blake, 58
Hadley, Mary Jo, 58
Hadley, Tyler, 58
Hall, Carl Austin, 95
Halliday, Lizzie, 177
Halliday, Paul, 177
Hamer, Frank, 244
Hamilton Township, New Jersey, 170
Hammond, Indiana, 85–86
Hampton Roads, Virginia, 259
hanging
  execution by, 27, 31, 33, 45, 51, 53, 66, 74, 77, 103, 115, 161, 162, 163, 167, 221, 251, 271, 275
  murder by, 217
  suicide by, 34
Hanover, New Hampshire, 162–163
Hansen, Kenneth, 81
Hansen, Robert, 16–17
Hanson, Dan, 113
Harlson family, 151–152
Harris, Esther Louis, 211
Harrison, Kenneth, 122
Hart, Alexander, 32
Hart, Brooke, 32
Hart, Gene Leroy, 203
Hartford City, Indiana, 87
Hash, A. L., 103
Hayes, Steven, 48–49
Haywood, Adry, 131
Haywood, Harry, 131
Haywood, William "Big Bill," 72
Hazzard, Linda Burfield, 261
Heady, Bonnie Emily, 95
Heaster, Mary, 268

Heaster, Zona, 267–268
Heaton family, 219
Hennard, George, 239–240
Henning, Linda, 174
Henry, Claude "Cowboy," 106
Hess, Milton, 212
Hickcock, Richard, 97
Hicks, Steven, 198–199
Hill, Anita, 239
Hines, Charles "Teddy," 197
Hirl, Edith Caudill, 197
Hitchens, Robert R., 53
Hivner, Daniel, 199
Hix, Theodora, 196–197
Hofer, Jacob, 192
Hofmann, Mark, 246–247
Hogan, Emily, 82
Hogan, Mary, 272–273
Hollis, Jimmy, 236
Holmes, Jack, 32
Honeychurch, Marlyse, 163–164
Honolulu, Hawai'i, 66–69
Hood, Toni Jo, 106
Horn, Tom, 276
Hossencofft, Diazien, 174
Houston, Texas, 237–238
Hricko, Kimberly and Stephen, 117
Hurkos, Peter, 128
Hyde County, North Carolina, 185

Iron Mountain, Wyoming, 276

Jackson, Elton Manning, 259
Jaeger, Susan, 147
Jahnke, Deborah, 278–279
Jahnke, Richard, 278–279
Jahnke, Richard, Jr., 278–279
James, Robert, 33
Jarbridge, Nevada, 158
Jensen, Gordon Curtis, 164
Johannson, Erik, 227
Johnson, Cody Lee, 149
Johnson, Frank, 65–66
Johnson, Ross W., 155
Johnson County, Kansas, 95
Johnston, Leon, 211
Jones, Frank Fernando, 90
Jones, Louis "Grandpa," 232
Joplin, Missouri, 144
Jordan, James, 188

Jordan, Michael, 188
Judson, Lee, 34–35
Julian, Nebraska, 152–153
Jun, Eusson, 164

Kalstedt, Harry, 79–80
Kanka, Megan, 170
Kansas City, Missouri, 143
Kastner, Roxanne, 67
Kaufman, Derek, 56
Kearney County, Nebraska, 151–152
Keeton, Juanita "Ouida," 138
Kelly, Devin Patrick, 240
Kelly, Lyn George Jacklin, 91
Kelvig, 15
Kemmler, William, 178
Kenosha, Wisconsin, 271
Kent, Bobby, 56
Keyes, Israel, 19
kidnappings, 19, 23, 31, 32, 41, 55, 57, 82–83, 85, 95, 144, 183, 203, 222, 229
Killeen, Texas, 239–240
Kizer, John R., 28
Klenner, Fritz, 187
Klu-tuk, 15
Knapp, George W., 267–268
Knik River, Alaska, 16–17
Knoth family, 159
Koenig, Samantha, 19
Koeninger, 226
Komisarjevsky, Joshua, 48–49
Komiya, Mariko, 67–68
Koons, Greg, 25
Kopf, Charles, 152–153
Kraft, Joseph, 192
Ku Klux Klan (KKK), 85–86
Kuhl, Ben, 158
Kunnecke, William, 226–227

Lacey, Harry, 225
Lafitte, Jean, 105
Lake Charles, Louisiana, 106
Landregan, Bridget, 119
Langmaid, Josie, 161
LaPage, Joseph, 161
Larey, Mary Jeanne, 236
Lassiter, Clement, 185
Latter-Day Saints church, 247
Laurel, Mississippi, 138
Lawson family, 186–187
Layer, Henry C., 192–193

Leetown, Mississippi, 139
Leland, Mark, 207
Leland, Mississippi, 139
LeMonte, Linda, 13
Lester, Seymour, 272
lethal injection, first use of, 199
Lewisburg, West Virginia, 267–268
Lexington County, South Carolina, 222
lie detector tests, early use of, 152–153
Lima, Carolyn, 237–238
Lincoln, Nebraska, 153–154
Lindsay, Bertie, 231
Litzman, 226
Living Church of God, 273
Livingston, New Jersey, 171
Lloyd, C. B., 201
Locust Grove, Oklahoma, 202–203
Logan, Margaret and Arthur, 34–35
Lopez, Joseph Michael, 43
Lopez, Rafael "Red," 243–244
Lorenz, Melvin and Linda, 204
Los Angeles, California, 33, 37
Loveless, Floyd, 159
Lovelien, Joel, 193
Lubelsky, Max and Rose, 221
Lynch, Delores, 187
Lynch, Janie, 187
Lynch, Tom, 187
lynchings, 27, 32, 221, 252, 275
Lyons, Billy, 141

Madson, David, 134
Mahan, Carl, 102
Mailhot, Jeffrey, 219
Mak, Kwan Fai "Willie," 263–264
Malabar, Florida, 55
Manby, Arthur Rochford, 173
Manley Hot Springs, Alaska, 18
Manson, Charles, 36
Mark, Jerry, 93
Mark, Leslie and Jorjean, 93
Martin, Eri, 252
Martin, Kenneth, 122
Martin, Paul, 236

Martinez, Jim, 173
Maskell, Joseph, 116
mass murders, 22, 29, 38, 39, 68–69, 90, 93, 204, 205, 213, 239–240, 263, 271. *See also* familicides
Mauthe, Esther, 155
May, Catherine, 181
Mayo, Keith, 47
Mays, Maurice, 231
McAlester, Oklahoma, 201–202
McCabe, Retta, 179–180
McCaffary, John and Bridget, 271
McCoy, Tim, 233
McCrary, Gregg, 219
McDevitt, William, 155
McFerren, Minnie, 87
McGinnis, Annabelle, 78
McGinnis, Michael, 78
McKenna, Alvin, 137
McKinley, William, 71
McQuillan, Margaret, 177
McQuillan, Sarah Jane, 177
McQuiston, Anne Beatrice, 106
McRae, David, Jr., 258
Meaker, Almon, 250–251
Meaker, Emeline, 250–251
Meaker family, 250
Megan's Law, 170
Meirhofer, David, 147
Merrifield, Charles, 245
Mesa, Arizona, 22
Meyer, Edward, 72
Miami Beach, Florida, 59
Miglin, Lee, 134
Milam, Garland Ray, 233
Millian, John, 158
Milner, Doris Denise, 202–203
mine workers revolt, 71–72
Minneapolis, Minnesota, 131, 134–135
Miranda, Ernesto, 23
Miranda rights, 23
Missoula, Montana, 148
Monroe County, Mississippi, 137
Montgomery, Alabama, 12–13
Moore, Charles, 101
Moore, Lena, 101
Moore, Polly Ann, 236
Moore, Raymond, 201

Moore family, 90–91
Morning, William McClellan, 153–154
Morrison, Colorado, 41
Mosser family, 144
"Most Dangerous Game, The" (Connell), 17
Mowry, Mary, 168
Moyer, Sam, 90
Mozynski, James, 181
Mueller, Paul, 91
Muller, Ralph Smith, 36
Munchausen syndrome by proxy, 145
murder-suicides, 63, 67–68, 214
Murphy, Patrick, 155
Murphy, Peter, 51

Nabokov, Vladimir, 115
Naisbitt, Carol, 245–246
Naisbitt, Cortney, 245–246
Nance, Wayne, 148
Nash, Frank "Jelly," 143
Navajo County, Arizona, 21
Nee, Francis, 78
Neese, Skylar, 269
New Brunswick, New Jersey, 167
New Castle, Delaware, 51
New London, Connecticut, 45
New Orleans, Louisiana, 105
New York, New York, 181–182
Newbury, Vermont, 252
Newport Harbor, California, 35
Newry, Maine, 113
Newsom, Susie, 187
Newton, Connecticut, 47
Newton, Massachusetts, 125
Ng, Keung Ki "Benjamin," 263–264
Ng, Wai Chiu "Tony," 263–264
Niagara, North Dakota, 191
Nickell, Willie, 276
Nielsen, Charles, 113
Nielsen, Christopher, 113
Noakes, Elmo, 214
Noll, Emma, 212
Norfolk, Virginia, 258
Northcott, Gordon Stewart, 31

Nushagak District, Alaska, 15

Oberholtzer, Madge, 85
O'Brien, W. W., 80
O'Bryan, Ronald Clark, 238–239
O'Bryan, Timothy, 238–239
O'Connell, John, 65
Ocuish, Hannah, 45
Ogden, Utah, 245–246
Oklahoma City, Oklahoma, 204
Olalla, Washington, 261
Olathe, Kansas, 99
Omaha, Nebraska, 155
Omar, Delaware, 53
O'Neil, Ruth Anne, 207
Orchard, Harry, 72
Order, The, 42
Osborne, John Eugene, 275
Osborne, Walter, 41
Ottino, Natyah, 207
Overell, Beulah, 35
Overell, Walter, 35
Owen, Louisa, 255–256
Owensboro, Kentucky, 103
Owyhee County, Idaho, 75

Pacific Palisades, California, 34–35
Paintsville, Kentucky, 102
Palmarin, Lucy, 122
Pardo, Bruce, 39
Park County, Wyoming, 277–278
Parker, Clover, 122
Parker, James, 165
Parrott, "Big Nose" George, 275
Patterson, Albert, 11–12
Peete, Louise, 34–35
Peete, Richard, 34
Pembroke, New Hampshire, 161
Pencovic, Francis Herman, 36
Pennington, John B., 51
Perez, Leslie Elaine, 238
Persons, Gordon, 12
Peterson, Robert, 80
Petit family, 48–49
Petrillo, Herman, 213–214
Petrillo, Paul, 213–214
Phenix City, Alabama, 11–12

Philadelphia, Pennsylvania, 213–214
Phillips, Annie, 66
Phoenix, Arizona, 23, 25
Pierce, Winifred, 214
Pierre, Dale Selby, 245
Pine Grove Furnace State Park, Pennsylvania, 214
Pine Grove, Wisconsin, 272–273
Piper, Thomas, 119
Place, Ida, 180
Place, Martha, 180
Place, William W., 180
Ploch, Myna, 78
Poe, Edgar Allan, 167
Poelman, Bernie, 147
Pogue, William, 75
Poison Ring, 213
poisonings, 13, 28, 33, 46, 51–52, 72–73, 117, 121, 185, 213–214, 223, 226, 238–239, 250–251
Poppo, Ronald, 59
Port St. Lucie, Florida, 58
Portland, Oregon, 207, 209
Posey, Cody, 175
Posey, Paul, 175
Posey, Tryone, 175
Post, Diane, 99
Potter, Adelia and Charles, 249–250
Potts, Lamar, 62
Pounds, Donna, 148
Preston, John Alfred, 268
Price, Craig, 219
Price, Robert J., 13
Pryor, Alice, 142
Puccio, Marty, 56
Purrington family, 109–110
Puyallup, Washington, 262–263

Queens, New York, 183

Rabb, Nicole, 49
Randolph County, Arkansas, 28
Raney, Michael, 147
rape, 12–13, 17, 19, 21, 23, 31, 49, 55, 82, 85, 103, 105, 111, 128, 137, 148, 159, 170, 183, 217, 229, 231, 236, 246, 253

Rasmussen, Terry Peder, 163–164
Ratzmann, Terry, 273
Rawlins, Wyoming, 275
Redden, Hazel, 87
Redden, Leonard, 87
Reese, William, 134
Rehmeyer, Nelson, 212
Rein, Clifford, 154
Renner, Clark, 93
Rexroat, Mildred, 77
Richards, Stephen D., 151–152
Richland County, South Carolina, 222
Richmond, Virginia, 255–256
Ridings, David, 137
Ridings family, 137
Riggs, Mrs. Robert, 28
Riley, Noah, 277
Ring, Elizabeth, 181
Robeson County, North Carolina, 188
Robinson, Lizzie, 28
Robinson, Peter, 167
Robson, Harriet, 87
Rodgers, James W., 245
Rohrbecker, Billy, 226–227
Rohrbecker, Charlie, 226
Rolphe, Governor, 32
Rosenberg, Ethel, 95
Roswell, New Mexico, 175
Rufer, George, 195
Russellville, Arkansas, 29

Sacco, Sylvia, 269
Salina, Utah, 244
Salt Lake City, Utah, 246–247
San Diego, California, 38
San Jose, California, 32
San Juan County, Utah, 245
Sapulpa, Oklahoma, 201
Sarasota, Florida, 57
Schade, Charles, 78
Schewchuk, Peter, 169
Schilling, Herman, 195
Schmid, Mary Lee, 175
school shootings, 38, 87
Schussler, Anton, 80
Schussler, John, 80
Scottsdale, Arizona, 24
Searcy, Fred, 158
Searles, Austin, 155
Seattle, Washington, 263–264
Selby, Jonathan, 27

Sellers, Floyd, 201
Semenec, Donald, 56
serial killers, 19, 28, 34, 46–47, 61, 66, 72–73, 119, 121, 128, 131, 137, 148, 151–152, 155, 163–164, 171, 181, 198–199, 219, 231, 233, 235, 236, 259
Seth (enslaved man), 185
Shallenberger, Fuller, 152–153
Sheets, J. Gary and Kathy, 247
Sheffey, William, 231–232
Shelton, Eddie Lee, 202
Shelton, Lee, 141
Sherman, Dale, 218
Sherrill, Patrick, 205
Shoaf, Rachel, 269
Shook family, 148
Shorthouse, Joe, 207
Showers, William, 101
Shue, Erasmus, 267–268
Silka, Michael, 18
Simmons, Ronald Gene, 29
Simmons, Sheila Maria, 29
Sioux Falls, South Dakota, 225, 228–229
Sitts, George, 227–228
Skarupa, Paul, 77
Smallegan, Sandra, 147
Smith, Andrew D., 259
Smith, Joseph, 57, 247
Smith, Perry, 97
Smith, Robert Benjamin, 22
Smith, Shari Faye, 222
Smith, Susan, 123
Smith, Tyree, 49
Smoke, Sheila, 13
Snook, James, 196–197
Snow, Edwin Ray, 120–121
Snowden, Raymond, 74
Soles, Michael Ray, 98
Soller, Mary, 159
South Kingston, Rhode Island, 218
Sowley, Noel, 181
Spearfish, South Dakota, 227–228
Speck, Richard, 22
Spencer, Brenda, 38
Spencer, Henry, 77
Spencer, Rebecca, 219
Spring Green, Wisconsin, 271

Springfield, Missouri, 145
Springfield, Oregon, 208
St. Cloud, Minnesota, 133
St. Louis, Missouri, 141–142
St. Martinville, Louisiana, 107
St. Michaels, Maryland, 117
St. Paul, Minnesota, 131–132
stabbings, 12–13, 23, 25, 56, 61, 66, 74, 105, 127, 128, 132, 139, 145, 147, 148, 199, 218, 219, 265, 269
Stackolee, 141
Stafford, Harold, 204
Stafford, Roger Dale, 204
Stafford, Verna, 204
Stanley County, South Dakota, 226–227
Star City, West Virginia, 269
Starks, Virgil, 236
starvation, 261
Stay, Travis, 193
Stephenson, D. C., 85
Steunenberg, Frank, 71–72
Stillinger, Lena and Ina, 90
Storm, Mark, 268–269
Storm family, 268–269
Strange, Willis, 201
Streyle, Piper and Vance, 229
Stuart, Carol, 123–124
Stuart, Charles, 123–124
Stuart, Matthew, 123–124
suicides, 19, 34–35, 36, 63, 67–68, 86, 105, 112, 122, 214, 217, 240, 258, 271
Sullivan, Nancy, 63
Surratt, Mary, 95
Suydam, Abraham, 167
Swales, Heather, 56
Swinney, Youell, 236

Taliesin, 271
Taos, New Mexico, 173
Tarricone, Joseph, 262–263
Tecchio, Umberto, 127
"Tell-Tale Heart, The" (Poe), 167
Terry, Charles E., 110–111
tetrahydrozoline, 223
Texarkana, Arkansas, 236
Texarkana, Texas, 236
Thomas, Andrew, 107
Thomas, Clarence, 239

Thompson, Carol, 131–132
Thompson, Florence, 103
Thompson, Idella, 139
Thompson, T. Eugene, 131–132
Thornman, Lillian, 211, 181
Thurman, Harold, 32
Timmerdequas, Jesse, 170
Tiverton, Rhode Island, 217
Tones, Fred A., 238
Toppan, Jane, 121
Trail, Jeff, 134
Trice, Rosa, 61
Troy, New York, 179–180
Trueblood, Lyda, 72–73
Tulloch, Robert, 165
Turner, Wilson, 62
Turtle Lake, North Dakota, 192–193
Twin Falls, Idaho, 72–73
Tyner, Mary, 119

Urbana-Champaign, Illinois, 82–83
Utica, Illinois, 81–82
Uyesugi, Bryan Koji, 68–69

Valdez, Juan, 243
Van Gilder, Roy, 90–91
Van Hoose, Cecil, 102
Vanner, Larry, 164
Venta, Krishna, 36
Verona, Roxana, 165
Versace, Gianni, 134
Villisca, Iowa, 90–91
Viramontes, Kathryn, 37

Virginia City, Nevada, 157–158

Wah Mee Club, 263
Waialua, Hawai'i, 65–66
Walker, Mary "Belle," 61
Walker, Orren, 245–246
Walker, Stanley, 245
Wallace, John, 62
Wallick, Malinda, 153–154
Wallick, Wallace, 153–154
Walsh, Lana Sue, 223
Ward, John, 250
Warden, Andrew, 162
Warden, Christie, 162–163
Warwick, Rhode Island, 219
Waterville, Maine, 111–112
Watkins, Van Brett, 189
Wayne, Illinois, 77
Weger, Chester, 81–82
Wells, Kris and Doug, 148
Wells, Luther, 232
West Dover, Vermont, 253
Western Federation of Miners, 71–72
Weston, Florida, 56
Wharton, Henry and wife, 65–66
Wharton, Simeon, 66
Wheeling, West Virginia, 268–269
white supremacists, 42, 85–86
Whitehurst, James, 113
Whitman, Charles, 22
Whittemore, Jimmy, 120–121

Wichita, Kansas, 98
Wilbur, Thomas, 217
Williamson, Claire and Dora, 261
Willis, Ali, 56
Williston, Vermont, 249–250
Wilson, Eldon, 201
Windsor, Connecticut, 46–47
Wineville, California, 31
Winston-Salem, North Carolina, 186–187
Wolcott, Kansas, 96–97
Wolf family, 192–193
Woodmansee, Michael, 218
Woodward, Louise, 125
Woonsocket, Rhode Island, 219
Worden, Bernice, 272
Worldwide Church of God (WCG), 273
Wright, Frank Lloyd, 271
wrongful convictions, 253
wrongful executions, 231

Yarmouth, Massachusetts, 120–121
York, Pennsylvania, 211–212
Yorktown, Indiana, 86
Young, Mabel, 119
Ypsilanti, Michigan, 128

Zantop, Half and Susanne, 165
Zhang, Yingying, 82–83
Ziegler, Tillie, 178